THE PHILOSOPHY
AND PRACTICE OF
WILDLIFE
MANAGEMENT

THE PHILOSOPHY AND PRACTICE OF WILDLIFE MANAGEMENT

SECOND EDITION

by

Frederick F. Gilbert, Ph.D.
Professor of Natural Resource Sciences
Washington State University

and

Donald G. Dodds, Ph.D.
Cervid Consulting
Nova Scotia

KRIEGER PUBLISHING COMPANY
MALABAR, FLORIDA
1992

Second Edition 1992

Printed and Published by
KRIEGER PUBLISHING COMPANY
KRIEGER DRIVE
MALABAR, FLORIDA 32950

Library of Congress Cataloging-in-Publication Data

Gilbert, Frederick F., 1941-
    The philosophy and practice of wildlife management/by Frederick
F. Gilbert and Donald G. Dodds.—2nd ed.
      p. cm.
    Includes bibliographical references and index.
    ISBN 0-89464-438-6 (alk. paper)
    1. Wildlife management. I. Dodds, Donald G. II. Title.
SK355.G45 1991
639.9—dc20   90-45215
                                      CIP

10 9 8 7 6 5 4 3 2

Contents

The Philosophy and Practice of Wildlife Management

Preface

This book is not meant to be exhaustive in any one area but endeavors to expose the preprofessional and professional wildlife biologist to concepts necessary for effective wildlife management. It is meant to be thought provoking rather than to provide a rigid model. We assume that students who read this book have already been adequately exposed to such subject areas as animal physiology, ecology, wildlife nutrition, and wildlife biology. We are attempting to fill the existing void in literature suggesting how to apply this basic knowledge to management of wildlife species. The constraints, be they social, economic, political, or biological, need to be addressed in individual cases. An effective manager balances objectives and communicates them to different interest groups. Where compromise is possible, it should be employed. Where special interests must be met, (e.g., endangered species), the manager must eloquently explain why other interests cannot be accommodated. A wildlife manager is a spokesman for wildlife, a custodian of a variety of public interests, and a key element in the decision-making process regarding land use. To meet effectively this demanding role requires basic knowledge of wildlife species and their biological requirements and a consummate skill in people management.

We hope this book provides sufficient insight into the appropriate mechanisms for achieving these aims. Both of us share a background of public, private, and institutional involvement. We have worked for state, provincial, and federal agencies, have consulted for private developers, park services, and foreign governments, and have been heavily involved in the academic milieu. We hope this experiential background, coupled with our knowledge of wildlife, has allowed us to impart some useful tips to aspiring and practical wildlife managers.

These were the comments we made at the beginning of the first edition of this book, and they are still valid. It is exciting to have the opportunity to fine-tune our work and update it in a second edition. It is always nice to have a second chance. What is almost overwhelming is the bulk of new material which our profession has generated in the past 5 years and the magnitude of environmental issues. It is difficult to remain optimistic about the fate of our planet and the species *Homo sapiens* when reviewed through the myriad problems we face, most of which we have created. We hope that other wildlife managers may find some succor, some commiseration, and perhaps even some enlightenment from our words. If so, the task of rewriting the book will have been worth the efforts.

The book has chapters leading the reader from the historical bases of wildlife management and the evolution of wildlife legislation and administration in North America through some of the more controversial management problems of the 1990's. Chapter 1 explores the special relationships which have existed between the human species and wild creatures from prehistoric to modern times. Although the emphasis is on North American culture and the various user societies which have existed there, parallels can be found in other geographical areas of the planet. Chapter 2 details the development of wildlife management as a special discipline, showing the relationship to other environmental concerns and the underlying legislative and administrative structures in Canada and the United States. Chapter 3 examines the necessary biological understanding which underpins effective wildlife management. It highlights rather than details the intricate and comprehensive knowledge which must ultimately be made available at the species and community levels. Chapter 4 concentrates on tools of management, regulation and computer modeling in particular. Chapter 5 reviews habitat management primarily from an assessment perspective for integration into the land-use planning process. Several species examples and specialized areas of management are highlighted in Chapters 6 and 7. The somewhat emotional area of endangered species management is reviewed in Chapter 8, and Chapter 9 looks at environmental impact assessment as it impinges on the professional wildlife manager. Chapter 10 is an attempt to expose the reader to the international arena and the socioeconomic realities of wildlife management in the underdeveloped countries of Africa, as well as some of the sophisticated management approaches in Europe. Finally, Chapter 11 is our attempt to predict the future role of the wildlife manager and the changes to which he will be exposed or will help bring about.

We have enjoyed the collaborative experience of writing this book and the sharing of ideas garnered during our separate professional careers, which have had many surprising parallels and have touched each other academically and professionally several times in the past three decades. Our experience has included interactions with so many other professionals throughout North America and the rest of the world that we are really products of these reciprocal influences, our past and present management responsibilities, and our attempts to transmit this information to students in a university environment.

People to whom we want to extend particular thanks and who contributed directly to the book are: Ulysses S. Seal, chairman of the Captive Breeding Specialist Group IUCN/SSC, T. J. Foose and N. Flesness, also of the IUCN Specialist Group, who reviewed Chapter 8; William Couch, director, FEARO, who reviewed Chapter 9; and Diana Gilbert, who contributed the illustrations made from slides taken by the authors. Many others have made important contributions to this book in many ways, from providing pertinent references, to allowing us to quote them, to the physical task of typing drafts of the manuscript. To attempt to name them all would run the risk of omitting someone. Let us simply say we are grateful to all these people, and without them this project would never have come to fruition.

Two final comments are necessary. The masculine gender has been used throughout the text merely as a convention of the English language, with no pejorative connotation intended. Citations have been minimized to increase readability, and the reader is directed to the bibliographies within each chapter for all the literature used as reference material.

Finally, there is something to be said for coauthoring a book. With all the other demands on our time, it is unlikely that either of us, alone, would have been able to complete the task. The sense of obligation hung heavy at times, and the end result benefitted immensely from the constant critical review of two writers. We each lost some of our sensitivity to protecting our "sacred prose" and also discovered unknown idiosyncrasies in our writing styles. We hope that you, the reader, will find our second effort to have been worthwhile.

I THEN AND NOW—Wildlife Management, Jurisdictional Responsibilities, Legislation and Administration

Perspectives From History

When Noah released the animals from the ark he was in fact reintroducing birds and mammals. According to Genesis 8:19: "All the animals and birds went out of the boat in groups of their own kind." Since Noah had been told to protect "two pairs of each kind of ritually clean animal, but only one pair of each kind of unclean animal" (Genesis 7:12), we can also assume that wild animals had been recognized by species, and used according to religious law for some time previously. Thus, regulatory harvesting was the first manipulation of wildlife that can be inferred from the Biblical record. Regulatory management reappears in Leviticus 11:4–6, and again in Deuteronomy 14:4–20. These verses indicate that specific animals were designated fit for human consumption, including deer, wild sheep, and wild goats. Others, including the rabbit and rock badger (probably the hyrax), were declared unfit. Then in Deuteronomy 22:67, the management becomes somewhat more sophisticated when Moses includes a recognition of the need to keep the breeding females alive: " . . . If you happen to find a bird's nest in a tree or on the ground with the mother bird sitting either on the eggs or with her young, you are not to take the mother bird. You may take the young birds, but you must let the mother bird go. . . . "

Probably some kind of harvest selection has occurred since our Neanderthal ancestors hunted, although the taking of one species, sex, or age rather than another may well have been more a function of evolved animal behavioral patterns than a design established by predatory man. With the arrival of Cro-Magnon man about 35,000 B.C., harvest selection was modified as a component of ritual as cultures evolved and replaced one another. Similar ritual-oriented selection continues today among many primitive cultures.

The written historical record of wildlife management beginnings was reviewed by Aldo Leopold in the first chapter of his classic work, *Game Man-*

1

agement (Table 1.1). These were the beginnings of purposeful human intervention into the lives of wild creatures, but as we will note, they were seldom invoked to benefit the animals alone. Chronological examples for the United States until 1900 are presented in Table 1.2, and a similar chronological list for Canada appears in Table 1.3. A literature survey turns up many management happenings such as the ones we have chosen to list. Alison (1978), for example, traced Egyptian hunting records to the sixth dynasty (2625–2475 B.C.) and notes records left by Greeks, Etruscans, Persians, and Aztecs. In Egypt an office of government was established to deal exclusively with waterfowl hunters and the marshes, implying management.

With the exception of Kublai Kahn, who engaged in both regulatory and habitat management; Henry VIII, who established reserves; and James I, who propagated and stocked mallards, the management activities between 1200 and 1800 were primarily regulatory in nature. Often the attempts to restrict harvest or prevent trespass were implemented for the benefit of the privileged classes rather than to enhance the populations or habitats of animals. So it was the general rule in Europe that regulatory measures were initiated by kings or others in high authority. Bubenik (1976) noted that to the end of the Middle Ages, the right to reduce game to possession was the "privilege of the sovereign" who entrusted the right to "the highest aristocracy, clergy, and later on to free towns."

In the United States the early history is almost solely regulatory in nature, and severe penalties were handed out to offenders. For example, the Act for the Preservation of Deer, passed at the first convening of the Vermont legislature in February 1779, protected bucks, does, and fawns from 10 January to 10 June, and it was noted that anyone convicted of violating the act "shall forfeit and pay for every such offence, the sum of fifteen pounds." Half of the fine went to the prosecutor and half to the town treasury. If the offender was unable to pay, he was "assigned in service" to the complainer or another person for a "sufficient term." Royal Provincial Law enacted in 1741 in New Hampshire protected deer from 31 December until 31 August and provided for a fine of ten pounds or forty days work for the local government. For a second offense the penalty was increased to fifty days work! Each town in New Hampshire chose two officers know as deer reeves or deer keepers to enforce the law and to prosecute violators. They were also given authority to search premises without warrant.

To control wolves and panthers in 1779, Vermont offered a bounty of "eight pounds paid out of the public treasury; and half so much for every wolf's whelp that sucks, which he shall kill and destroy" (Slade 1823). To prevent fraud the heads were brought to selectmen or constables who cut off the ears. Stealing from another's pit or trap brought a penalty of whipping

Table 1.1 Some Wildlife Management Beginnings[1]

Source	Approximate Dates	Original Concern	Type of Action	Category of Management
Solon	About 600 BC	People	Forbade people to hunt	Regulatory
Marco Polo	Late 13th century	Animals	Restricted hunting and planted grain	Regulatory and habitat
Edward, Duke of York	14th century; recorded 1406–1413	Animals and privileged people	Controlled methods, seasons, sex & ages taken	Regulatory
Henry VII	1485–1509	People	Trespass protection	Regulatory
Henry VIII	1536±	Animals and privileged people	Closed seasons and areas	Regulatory and reservation of land
James I	1603–1625	Animals and privileged people	Trespass protection and closed areas	Regulatory and reservation of land
	1631	Animals	Artificial propagation	Stocking
William and Mary	1694	Animals	Prohibited burning of cover	Regulatory and habitat
Mulmesbury	1799	People	Cover control for efficiency of harvesting	Regulatory

[1]In part from Leopold, 1933. Game Management. Scribners, N. Y.

Table 1.2 Early Legislation Dates Reflecting the Beginnings of Wildlife Management in the United States to 1900[1]

Source	Date	Concern	Area	Management
Trippensee, 1948	1623	People	Plymouth Colony	Free hunting and fishing—no mgmt.
	1646	Deer	Portsmouth, R.I.	Regulatory (closed season)
Dasmann, 1981[1]	1677	Exports	Connecticut	Regulatory
	1699	Deer	Virginia	Regulatory
Leopold, 1933	1718	Deer	Massachusetts	Regulatory
Dasman, 1981	1730	Deer	Maryland	Regulatory
	1738	Deer	Virginia	Regulatory ("firelight" prohibited)
McClintock, 1888	1741	Deer	New Hampshire	Regulatory (with wardens)
Slade, 1823	1779	Deer	Vermont	Regulatory
	1779	Wolves-panthers	Vermont	Regulatory
Phillips, 1928	1789	Exotics	New Jersey	Stocking (ring-necked pheasant)
Leopold, 1933	1790	Exotics	New Jersey	Stocking (Hungarian partridge)
	1850	Game	Massachusetts	Regulatory (protection)
			New Hampshire	Regulatory (warden system)
	1850	Nongame	New Jersey	Regulatory (license required)
	1864	Game	New York	Regulatory (license required)
Dasmann, 1981	1872	Wildlife	Wyoming	Preserve—National Park (Yellowstone)
Leopold, 1933	1875	Game and nongame	Arkansas	Regulatory (market hunting prohibited)
	1878	Game	Iowa	Regulatory (bag limits)
Dasmann, 1981	1878	Game	California	State game agencies
			New Hampshire	State game agencies
Trefethen, 1961	1885	Animals	United States	Bureau of Biological Survey
Severinghaus, 1974	1887	Deer	New York	Parks for propagation
Dasmann, 1981	1900	Game	United States	Regulatory (Lacey Act, prevented interstate trade of game taken illegally)[2]

[1] In part, from Graham, E. H. 1947. The Land and Wildlife. Oxford. N.Y.

[2] One of the most important pieces of legislation for wildlife in the United States. It elevated the Bureau of Biological Survey to be a strong base for the Fish & Wildlife Service and prevented importation of foreign species. This act also curtailed market hunting.

Table 1.3 Early Legislation Dates Reflecting the Beginning of Wildlife Management in Canada to 1900

Source	Date	Concern	Area	Management
Dagg, 1974	1793	Wolves	Ontario-Upper Canada	Predator control (bounty)
Clarke, 1976	1821	Deer	Ontario-Upper Canada	Regulatory
Dagg, 1974	1821	Game	Ontario-Upper Canada	Regulatory
Dodds, 1982	1839	Wolf	Newfoundland	Predator control (bounty)
Benson and Dodds, 1980	1843	Moose	Nova Scotia	Regulatory (methods of harvest)
Dagg, 1974	1856	Game	Ontario-Upper Canada	Regulatory
Benson and Dodds, 1980	1862	Caribou	Nova Scotia	Regulatory
Dodds, 1960	1864	Snowshoe hare	Newfoundland	Stocking (introduction)
Dagg, 1974	1865	Exotic	Quebec-Lower Canada	Stocking (house sparrow)
Dagg, 1974	1867	Resources (wildlife)	Canada	Provincial jurisdiction
Benson and Dodds, 1980	1874	Deer	Nova Scotia	Regulatory (closed season)
Pimlott, 1953	1878	Moose	Newfoundland	Stocking (introduction)
Nova Scotia (Statutes of)	1884	Game species	Nova Scotia	Regulatory (license required)
Benson and Dodds, 1980	1894	Deer	Nova Scotia	Stocking (reintroduction)
Dagg, 1974	1895	Fox squirrel	Ontario (Pelee)	Stocking
Dagg, 1974	1895	Game	Ontario	Regulatory-Game and Fisheries Act
Nova Scotia (Statutes of)	1896	Game	Nova Scotia	Regulatory-Game and Fisheries Act
Piers, 1898	1897	Exotic	Nova Scotia	Stocking (ring-necked pheasants, introduction)
Piers, 1898	1898	Starp-tailed grouse	Nova Scotia	Stocking (introduction)

"on the naked back,—not exceeding ten stripes." Fines of about twenty-five dollars (ten pounds) amounted to several weeks' salary for the working man in 1779. Forty day's work was an approximate equivalent of the fine.

A bounty on wolves was established in Ontario in 1793. Even though the animal was becoming increasingly scarce in 1839, at that time a bounty was placed on wolves in the Colony of Newfoundland. Deer were first protected, from 10 January to 1 July, in Ontario in 1821, and regulatory management was extended to the whole of Upper Canada in 1856. Penalties were also severe in Lower Canada, and late in the nineteenth century the Consolidated Statutes of Nova Scotia, passed on the nineteenth day of April, 1884, provided for a fine of five dollars minimum and ten dollars maximum for taking a single grouse, partridge, woodcock, snipe, or teal out of season. The loss of one or two weeks' pay for killing one bird might have been cause for concern except that precious few people were apprehended. Doubtless the harsh penalties in both Canada and the United States in years past attest to the importance placed upon wildlife resources by a people who prior to emigration had been forced to poach animals to which they were denied title. In North America the settlers were originally zealous in their desire to guarantee free access to wildlife, but as stocks declined, the sportsman and naturalist became equally zealous in protecting their precious wildlife resource from abuse by the greedy and selfish.

The Evolution of Modern Wildlife Management-United States

The records show that wildlife management is an ancient practice, but they also tell us something of a peoples' relationship to animals, as well as something about the upper classes of society that protected what was for many years a private access to wild animals. North American patterns of management developed first from earlier experiences in Europe and later from the very different North American experience and reaction against European traditions. After settlement of the New World, the public's role in wildlife management was gradually defined and expressed over a long period. For almost two hundred years the freedom to hunt, including commercial hunting, combined with devastating effects of settlement such as destruction of vast areas of the continent's eastern hardwood forests. These practices spelled disaster for much of the New World's wildlife. As the nineteenth century drew to a close,

the black cloud of extermination hung low over the game ranges of North America. The great herds of bison, that a scant generation earlier, had offered the most thrilling spectacle in nature had vanished from the plains. The dainty pronghorn persisted in dwindling numbers in secluded prairies that were taken up by ranchers and settlers as rapidly as they could be located (Trefethen 1961).

According to Leopold, the dominant preoccupation in the minds of those dealing with wildlife in America until about 1905 was to perpetuate hunting. Managers generally believed that restriction could "string out the remnants of the virgin supply." Leopold also noted that game laws reflecting this feeling were "essentially a device for dividing up a dwindling treasure which nature, rather than man, had produced." Game protection failed to halt the accelerating decline of many species, however, and necessary changes in approach came about ever so slowly over a period of many years. There was no single action that appeared to alter government thinking or public policy, but a reasonable starting point for us to begin is Theodore Roosevelt's melding of forest and wildlife and the evolution of his doctrine of conservation. In 1893, Roosevelt noted that "the preservation of forest and game go hand in hand. He who works for either works for both" (Trefethen 1961). Whether precisely accurate or not, we have in that statement the beginning of a systems approach that grew and began to flower in Roosevelt's presidency. Leopold notes that with men such as Roosevelt and Gifford Pinchot leading, "conservation" became the label of a national issue overnight. In Roosevelt's mind conservation was indelibly tied to "wise use," and he thought that the renewable organic resources of wildlife, forests, ranges, and waterpower "might last forever if they were harvested scientifically, and not faster than they reproduced" (Leopold, 1933). Roosevelt's doctrine is divided into four parts, still relevant today:

1. A recognition of outdoor resources as integral systems.
2. A recognition of conservation through wise use as a public responsibility.
3. The recognition of private resource ownership as a public trust.
4. A recognition of science as a means of discharging the responsibility of resource management.

And so the ground work was accomplished for conservation in the United States. In the area of preservation, the first bird sanctuary (Pelican Island, Florida) was established in 1903, and by 1905 three more such sanctuaries were proclaimed. Other wildlife and big game refuges followed in the U.S. in 1905 and 1908. The first thirty years of this century were still incubation years. The ideas that wildlife was a product of the land and that its use could be perpetuated, although present, were not as yet specifically addressed by conservation leaders. Increased protective legislation, the establishment of more refuges, and the development of natural history studies[1] in schools continued. In 1930 the realization of the marriage of land and wildlife was finally articulated in a national platform at the seventeenth American Game Conference. The American Game Policy was produced by a committee of fourteen, chaired by Aldo Leopold. It clearly stated the basic requirements of wildlife and its management by recognizing:

a. protection, food, and cover requirements
b. inducements for landowners
c. a classification of game into farm, forest and range, and wilderness
d. the need for facts, skills, funding, and public-sportsman cooperation

The program included the extensions of public ownership and management, the recognition of the landowner as the custodian of public game, the need to experiment, the need to find facts, the need to recognize the non-shooting protectionist and scientist, and the need to train managers. In addition to recognition, the policy detailed these needs and spelled out both public education programs and funding requirements. Here indeed was a major breakthrough, or at least it should have been. Perhaps if governments and sportsmen alike had followed the direction their American Game Policy established sixty years ago, today's massive social and land-use conflicts regarding wildlife in the United States might have been partly avoided. But a policy does little by itself. There were certainly men of good will in 1930, it's true, but with an economic depression spreading throughout North America there was little money to implement policy. The United States and most of the rest of the industrialized world were in the trough of the most catastrophic economic decline of the century. Then in 1932 Franklin Delano Roosevelt, the second "conservation president" with the Roosevelt name, intervened. By 1933, money had been promised to support the conservation (including wildlife) work programs of Roosevelt's massive National Recovery Administration. With strong leadership from men like Leopold, J. N. "Ding" Darling, and Dr. Ira Gabrielson, the thirties became the great decade of positive change for wildlife in the United States. The Migratory Bird Treaty had been signed between the United States and Canada in 1916, and the Fur Seal Treaty with Canada, Japan, and USSR in 1911, but the thirties saw the passage of the Federal Aid in Wildlife Restoration Act (1937), a federal-state cooperative approach to wildlife research funded from taxes on arms and ammunition. Known generally as the Pittman-Robertson or PR Act, this bill gave impetus to wildlife research and management which has never been equalled anywhere in the world.

In February 1936 the first North American Wildlife Conference, replacing the American Game Conference, was called by Franklin Roosevelt. This gathering brought representatives of competing land-use agencies together more effectively than ever before and provided forums for each group to air its views and discuss programs. The National Wildlife Federation constitution was also drafted at that conference through the efforts of Darling; and although not a formal part of the proceedings, The Wildlife Society was also born at the 1936 conference. Arthur A. Allen, one of North America's great ornithologists; R. T. (Terry) King, a forest-wildlife expert at the University of Minnesota and later Syracuse; W. L. McAtee of the United States Bureau of Biological Survey; and Miles Pirnie of the Kellogg Bird Sanctuary in Michigan were primarily responsible for getting The Wildlife Society started. This joining of professionals was an important step in the growth of wildlife management. There were four objectives noted at the time of the Society's formation. Two of them have been responsible, to a considerable degree, for elevating the wildlife profession in North America to a level of scientific competence recognized the world over. The four objectives were

1. to develop wildlife management on a biological basis
2. to establish a medium for publication
3. to maintain professional standards
4. to protect the interest of its members

It is the first two that have been so successful not only in producing an excellent body of North American wildlife research and management literature, but at the same time, helping to establish biologically oriented wildlife management practices throughout much of the continent.

The 1930's produced more for wildlife. The Wildlife Management Institute (1946), which had its origins in 1912 as the American Game Protection and Game Propagation Association, got its start as an important lobbying and educational body with the 1936 conference. At that time it was named the American Wildlife Institute, after a 1930 change in title from the American Protective Association. The Institute flourished from the start. Whereas The Wildlife Society would obtain its funding from membership dues and the National Wildlife Federation depended on both private funding and dues, the Institute would always lean heavily on the sporting goods manufacturing industry for its financing. The objectives of the Institute were to support research, educate the public and professionals, and act as a lobbying organization to influence the public's political conscience. Through its research input at the Delta Waterfowl Research Station in Manitoba, and for a time at the University of New Brunswick in Canada, and through its support role in the development of cooperative wildlife research units at land grant institutions throughout the United States, the Institute has had a marked effect on both professional research and education. In addition it has funded research directly, in Canada as well as in the United States. The Institute provided support for moose research in Newfoundland soon after that colony confederated in 1949. It also assisted Canada's newest province in laying the groundwork for both its Wildlife Act and its original wildlife policy. The Institute has published a number of important books, but its educational efforts have been used best in its constant positive influence for wildlife on elected political representatives at the federal level. Its Washington policy statements and newsletter, which are concerned with important conservation issues, reach thousands of conservation-minded citizens each month.

None of the wildlife organizations that came to life in the thirties would have been successful without leadership. It was people like Ding Darling, the magnificent cartoonist-administrator, who originally piloted the National Wildlife Federation. It was Dr. Ira N. Gabrielson who guided the Bureau of Biological Survey and later the Wildlife Management Institute for many years; and it was the first Wildlife Society presidents (Rudolph Bennet, Arthur A. Allen, and Aldo Leopold), who were responsible for an eruption of wildlife interests that has carried through to the present.

The Society of American Foresters (1900) was organized thirty-six years ahead of The Wildlife Society, but corresponding federal agencies for "trees and animals" began at about the same time. Gifford Pinchot became chief of the Division of Forestry in 1898, and the division became the U.S. Forest Service in 1905. The Biological Survey (1885) in the Department of Agriculture became the Bureau of Biological Survey in 1905, and in 1940 it became the U.S. Fish and Wildlife Service. Later the USFWS became the Bureau of Sport Fisheries and Wildlife, but in 1974 an act of Congress renamed the bureau and it became the U.S. Fish and Wildlife Service once again. Other advances in the great wildlife decade included the establishment of the Soil Conservation Service in 1935, which provided a mechanism to counter wetland drainage and elimination of natural cover, and the Migratory Bird Hunting Permit (Duck Stamp) Act of 1934 which, following the Migratory Bird Conservation (Refuge) Act of 1929, provided a steady source of funding for refuge acquisition. It was the final federal touch required to provide for effective migratory bird management.

The great conservation movement began around the turn of the century and by the thirties was moving ahead full steam. It was not only driven by government legislation, agencies, and conferences but also by sportsmen's organizations, sporting magazines, and by the results of education and training. There were many hunting, fishing, and naturalists' groups, local and national, but the most prestigious, influential, and wealthy organization until about 1940 was the Boone and Crockett Club founded on the initiative of Theodore Roosevelt in 1888. The club had the distinction that all of its members were wealthy and therefore influential. The club's influence in wildlife policy matters at federal and state levels, its movements in support of game refuges, and its early support in other areas of wildlife management were detailed in 1961 by James B. Trefethen in his *Crusade for Wildlife*.

Perhaps three people stand out in Trefethen's history; Theodore Roosevelt, Major Charles Sheldon, and George Bird Grinnell. Charles Sheldon was a conservation crusader, naturalist, hunter, and author leading the fight for big game wilderness preservation. Grinnell was the editor of *Forest and Stream Weekly* which later became *Forest and Stream* and merged with *Rod and Gun*. He was also primarily responsible for the founding of the National Association of Audubon Societies in 1902. Along with many other great professional zoologists, curators, and naturalists such as Clinton Hart Merriam, Carl Akeley, and Edmund Heller, he also served on the governing board of *Forest and Stream* until the early twenties. T. Gilbert Pearson, another Audubon Society leader, and Ernest Thompson Seton, the great naturalist-author, later served on the magazine's advisory board. Needless to say, the quality of the material in the magazine was high in the formative years of United States wildlife management.

For wildlife education and training, the years 1919, 1929, and 1932 were landmarks. The Cornell School of Game Farming and Roosevelt Wildlife Experiment Station of the New York State College of Forestry at Syracuse began in 1919. Aldo Leopold began lecturing on wildlife management at the University of Wisconsin in 1929, and in 1932 Ding Darling was responsible for the first cooperative wildlife program between Iowa State College and the Iowa Fish and Game Commission. We should also make note of the year 1933, for that was the year Leopold's masterful book *Game Management* first appeared.

The Evolution of Modern Wildlife Management-Canada

Traditional use of wild animals for food and shelter is as old in Canada as it is elsewhere in North America, but it has steadfastly remained a practice in much of northern Canada, more than in the U.S. Beaver helped open the western lands to settlement as trappers sought them in what seem to us now, almost inaccessible areas. Because of the beaver's fur value in Europe, it was gradually reduced from the east to the west coast, and by the early nineteenth century was almost gone from most of what is now Canada. But the species came back; first with the inadvertent help of man as land-use practices changed from pure exploitation to human settlement, agriculture, and forestry, and later with the purposeful intervention of man through management. In Newfoundland, closed seasons were initiated in 1923, and transplantations from small remaining populations began in 1935. Protection and reintroduction from remnant populations occurred in most provinces until beaver were once again found throughout acceptable range.

The saga of the buffalo in Canada is not as pleasant a story, however. Between the 1820's and the 1860's the Metis of the Canadian prairies killed some 200,000 buffalo a year, and others were taken by white American (U.S.) and Indian hide hunters. Indians who had once depended upon buffalo were starving for lack of meat as early as 1850, and by 1889 only 256 buffalo were known to exist in Canada. So the same "black cloud of extinction" that hung over much of the United States also covered a part of Canada by the turn of the century. Ernest Swift, writing about the United States in 1958, spoke for all of North America when he said:

> there would have been no conquest of (North) America if there had been no wildlife. There would have been no Indians to meet the Spanish, or John Smith, or Champlain, if the Continent had not been well stocked with game. There would have been no fabulous journeys of exploration, no Radisson, no Hudson's Bay Company, no Lewis and Clark. . . . Game was elemental to survival, a basic part of the ecology; it still has a mystic and profound grip on the lives and emotions of millions of (North) Americans. The killing off of the wildlife and its general disappearance through other causes, has probably aroused more national attention and produced more concerted effort to the general tenets of conservation than any other issue.

At the federal level, wildlife management began in Canada with the Commission of Conservation, which was constituted by Sir Wilfred Laurier under the Conservation Act (an act of Parliament) in 1909 (amended in 1910 and 1913). Following the lead of Teddy Roosevelt and the eighth principle emanating from his 1908 Conservation Conference of Governors, which called for such commissions, Laurier and his government constituted the Canadian commission with federal membership from the Ministries of Interior, Agriculture, and Mines. Provincial members, ex officio, were drawn from each natural resource agency, while the governor-general-in-council appointed twenty university members and the chairman. The chairman, from the commission's inception in 1909 until its demise, was Sir Clifford Sifton, a one time minister of interior, great parliamentarian, and avid conservationist.

In 1916, an interdepartmental Advisory Board on Wildlife Protection, also with members appointed by the governor-general-in-council, was established to work closely with the commission. With C. Gordon Hewitt serving as secretary, the advisory board drafted legislation under the Migratory Bird Treaty and revised the Northwest Game Act of 1906, both in 1917. It cohosted several national conferences with the commission, including the National Conference on Game and Wildlife Conservation of February 1919, when Hewitt gave a stirring plea for a "nationwide effort in wildlife con-

servation.'' Following changes in responsibility for administering new legislation, and no doubt missing the influence of Hewitt, who died in 1920,
the commission was dissolved in 1922.

Gordon Hewitt is the conservation giant who stands out as Canada's great
wildlife crusader during conservation's formative years from 1909 until his
untimely death in 1920. He was the one primarily responsible for securing
the Migratory Bird Treaty, drafting the Migratory Bird Convention Act Regulations, and preparing the (revised) Northwest Game Act. He was an en-
tomologist by profession and today is recognized annually by the Canadian
Society of Zoologists, but perhaps his greatest accomplishments were in the
area of wildlife policy. He served as consulting zoologist to the government
and the Commission of Conservation, as well as secretary to the Advisory
Board on Wildlife Protection. Hewitt also guided the Entomological Service
as it evolved into an important branch of the Department of Agriculture. His
book, the *Conservation of Wildlife in Canada*, and his representation on behalf
of Canada at major international wildlife conferences, where he served so
ably, were the contributions that helped launch Canada's wildlife management movement.

Beginning with the ratification of the Migratory Bird Treaty in 1917 and
continuing until 1947, the national wildlife legislation in Canada was administered by the Parks Branch of the Department of Interior. In 1918 Hoyes
Lloyd, a chemist and amateur ornithologist, was hired by the branch as an
ornithologist with a mandate to administer the Migratory Bird Regulations.
Lloyd was soon named supervisor of wildlife protection and given full authority to administer the Northwest Game Act. After his retirement Lloyd
served as chairman of the International Commission for Bird Preservation,
Pan-American Section.

Since 1932 the Royal Canadian Mounted Police have maintained a primary
responsibility for enforcement of the Migratory Bird Convention Act, although provincial officials are also empowered to enforce these federal regulations. The more senior Canadian federal and provincial wildlife authorities
meet annually to enhance federal-provincial wildlife cooperation. This annual
meeting is known today as the Federal-Provincial Wildlife Conference, which
began under a different heading back in 1922. Finally, the Canadian Wildlife
Service, the country's primary wildlife agency, was formed in 1947 as a
division of the National Parks Branch and is now, like Parks Canada a separate
entity in the Canada Department of Environment (Environment Canada).

Jurisdictional Responsibility in the United States and Canada

In the United States the federal government maintains five general areas
of responsibility over wildlife resources. The government is fully responsible

for the resource on all federal lands including refuges, national parks, and about 191 million acres of national forests. Federal jurisdictional responsibility is also present relative to the government's tax levying authority (e.g. the duck stamp) and its power to make treaties. Offshore, the federal government is primarily responsible for marine mammals and fish although areas of conflict may exist with some coastal states. Finally, federal authority extends to the control of the interstate transport of wildlife. More specifically, the federal government exercises primary authority over migratory birds, marine animal resources, interstate and international traffic in wildlife, and all animals on federal land. State jurisdictional responsibility is maintained over all sedentary or resident animals, both "game" and "nongame," over reptiles, fishes, and amphibians. The states also exercise tax levying authority through the issuing of various licenses and permits.

In Canada, federal jurisdiction extends to migratory birds, all animals on federal lands including refuges and national parks, and mammals migrating across provincial-territorial boundaries when in the territories. Federal wildlife responsibility also exists in the Yukon and Northwest Territories, although the roles of the federal and territorial governments tend to be somewhat more fluid than the federal-provincial roles, and indeed are in the process of change. All jurisdictional responsibilities are likely to be reviewed in Canada in the next few years, because Canada's Constitution was patriated in April 1982, and the British North America Act of 1867 no longer serves as the sole basis on which to determine jurisdictional authority. Of course, the federal government of Canada also has tax levying power (e.g., migratory bird permit) and treaty power, as is the case in the United States. Marine mammals have also been considered a federal responsibility in the past and remain so today. The provinces have jurisdiction over resident game birds and mammals and over migratory mammals when inside provincial boundaries.

Responsibility for fish is confusing at present. The federal government has primary responsibility for anadromous and fresh water fish in all coastal provinces except Quebec. Nevertheless, provincial acts relating to water, pollution, or environmental matters may affect this specific responsibility through the control of fish habitat. Inland provinces presently exhibit considerable authority over both their fish and fish habitat, even though the original responsibility was federal under Section 91 of the British North America Act.

Of the many federal agencies involved in wildlife management in the United States, the U.S. Fish and Wildlife Service is probably the best known. The predecessors of this agency originated in the Department of Agriculture, with economic concerns and predator or depredator control problems as early justification for their existence. Today the Fish and Wildlife Service is in the

Department of the Interior under the assistant secretary for fish and wildlife. This agency has promoted national and international wildlife legislation and is the federal body that sees to the administration and enforcement of most federal wildlife acts and their regulations. The service is also concerned with the research and management of migratory birds and maintains three major research centers. One at Patuxent, Maryland, is involved primarily but not solely with migratory birds and serves as the North American bird banding data center; another, the Northern Prairie Wildlife Research Center at Jamestown, North Dakota, is involved with waterfowl studies; the third in Denver, Colorado, was heavily involved in wildlife disease research and control studies, although the latter were recently transferred to the USDA-Animal and Plant Health Inspection Service. The USFWS has a major wildlife disease laboratory in Madison, Wisconsin. Some 467 federal refuges encompassing over 90 million acres also come under the aegis of the Fish and Wildlife Service, and it is this agency that is most closely involved in international wildlife cooperation. The service administers federal aid such as Pittman-Robertson funding to state governments and also controls the cooperative wildlife and fisheries research unit program.

The Soil Conservation Service of the Department of Agriculture is somewhat different from most of the United States federal agencies in its approach to wildlife management, in that its biologists may work directly with landowners. Biologists are involved in habitat management programs on land areas managed within a soil conservation district for multiple use. Subsidy programs can allow landowners, as individuals or groups, to take advantage of the knowledge and skills of SCS biologists to enhance field and forest edges, or to establish marshes, ponds, hedgerows, or windbreaks to benefit wildlife populations from songbirds to rabbits.

The Forest Service is also in the Department of Agriculture, and its biologists conduct research as well as experimental and applied management in both forest-wildlife complexes and forest-grazing-wildlife complexes. The National Park Service is in the Department of the Interior. Its wildlife biologists work only in the parks within the framework of National Park policy. Other agencies in the federal government involved in wildlife work are the Tennessee Valley Authority in the southeastern U.S., and the U.S. Army Corps of Engineers, where development mitigation efforts are of considerable importance.

There are many agencies whose land-use practices and policies affect wildlife in addition to the ones mentioned. The Bureau of Land Management, which administers about 271 million acres of public land, the Reclamation Service, and the Bureau of Indian Affairs are three such agencies. Other agencies may be involved somewhat indirectly such as the Treasury Department through its Coast Guard, which may enforce portions of the Lacey Act relating to the importation of exotics, and the Customs Service, which may be involved with the importation of exotics and endangered species.

In Canada, the Canadian Wildlife Service is most closely involved with wildlife matters on a national level. Its branches and their personnel are involved in enforcement (migratory birds), research on migratory birds, socioeconomic evaluations, public relations, land-unit surveys, and land classification and purchase. The CWS is responsible for the administration and management of eighty-two sanctuaries and thirty-nine wildlife areas and has been involved with both interpretation[2] and education. Its biologists also conduct research within provinces on both sedentary and migratory species by virtue of the Canada Wildlife Act of 1973; however, present policy does not encourage research on sedentary species. The only other federal agency specifically involved in wildlife management is Parks Canada, which has recently established permanent positions for resource advisors and wildlife planners. The CWS cooperates with Parks in both research and management within Canada's National Parks and Historic Sites.

All states and provinces have designated branches of government to administer wildlife legislation within their respective jurisdictions, to cooperate with other agencies at state, provincial, and federal levels, to conduct research and management, and to carry out interpretive educational and/or public relations endeavors.

Legislation: the United States and Canada

Federal wildlife acts in the United States have allowed for the development of wildlife regulatory management, wildlife research, and habitat management (Table 1.4) where federal responsibility exists. Beginning in 1900 with the Lacey Act, federal legislation complemented the various state acts and their regulations to provide a substantial body of law for the protection and management of all species. In Canada, federal wildlife legislation includes the Territorial Ordinances[3], The Game Export Act[4], the Migratory Bird Convention Act of 1917[5], the Migratory Bird Hunting Permit of 1966, and the Canada Wildlife Act of 1973. Federal legislation also complements specific provincial acts or portions of acts to provide a basic body of statute law for wildlife protection and management in Canada.[6]

In addition to the Migratory Bird Treaty, both Canada and the United States have been principals in other international legislation of importance. (Great Britain signed for Canada prior to World War II.) The Fur Seal Treaty of 1911, which included the USSR and Japan as participants, is credited with saving the seals from extinction and perpetuating a healthy and economically

Table 1.4   Some Important Federal Wildlife Legislation—the United States[1]

Title	Date	Intent
Lacey Act	1900	Regulated market hunting, controlled import of exotics, controlled interstate transport of illegally taken game, controlled trespass on refuges
Migratory Bird Treaty Act	1918	Protection of migratory birds, either complete or through regulation
Migratory Bird Conservation Act	1929	Provided for establishment of refuges
Migratory Bird Hunting Stamp Act (the Duck Stamp Act)	1934	Provided for a federal migratory bird license; proceeds to finance acquisition of refuges and production areas
Fish and Wildlife Coordination Act	1934	Authorized conservation measures in federal water projects and required consulation with USFWS and states concerning any water project
Convention. USA and Mexico for the protection of migratory birds and game mammals	1936	Protection of certain migratory birds; cooperation and control concerning both mammals and birds along the border
Pittman-Robertson Federal Aid in Wildlife Restoration Act	1937	Provided for an excise tax on sporting arms and ammunition to finance research on federal-state cooperative basis
Convention. USA and Mexico, for the protection of migratory birds and game mammals	1940	Committed U.S. to protection and husbandry including refuges; implementation in 1973 (Endangered Species Act)
Fish and Wildlife Act	1956	National wildlife policy and general considerations
Endangered Species Conservation Act	1973	Protected species threatened with extinction or in imminent danger of becoming extinct
Fish and Wildlife Conservation Act	1980	Authorized development of wildlife conservation plans and actions to benefit wildlife, especially non-game types
North American Wetland Conservation Act	1989	Authorized founding for wetland restoration and conservation linked to supporting the North American Waterfowl Management Plan

[1]See Appendix 1 for a more complete listing

viable population. The first whaling treaty in 1937 included Norway and Germany and was an important initial step in whale preservation and resource management. The whaling and fur seal treaties have been revised and continue in operation today. Canada and the United States are participants in the 1975 Convention on International Trade in Endangered Species, which seeks to protect threatened species of wildlife from extinction wherever they may exist. We examine the endangered species issue later in Chapter 8.

The United States and Canada have legislation specifically designed to protect rare and endangered species such as bald eagle and musk ox. Some legislation is general (such as the Endangered Species Preservation Act of 1966, 1969, 1973, U.S.), while other specific state and provincial regulations are in effect to protect regionally threatened wildlife.

The Land and Wildlife: Ownership, Rights, and Restrictions[7]

One of the most important areas of concern affecting wildlife management in North America is the question of public wildlife ownership and land tenure. It was William the Conqueror who imposed the feudal land system in 1066. Because he personally owned all the real property in England, he was able to establish a pyramidal system of control with himself at the top. At each descending level in the hierarchy, there was an exchange of a form of service for the privilege to use the land. The service-to-use ratio increased with each step downward in the following hierarchy:

King
Knight of Service
Grand Sergeanty
Petty Sergeanty
Frankalmein
Villenins, hewers and drawers

Total work and allegiance was demanded from those at the bottom in exchange for space to accommodate a bleak and bare existence.

Since the church was also a strong force at the time and ecclesiastics also deigned to maintain certain land-use rights, in 1290 conveyances to the church were forbidden without the king's permission; so politics entered the trespass scene in England. In 1660, "a fixed annual sum" (rent) was required from the land holders (the Statute of Tenures). In Canada today a holdover from the early tenure of 1660 is the "Doctrine of Escheat," confirmed by statute in some jurisdictions; e.g. Escheats Act R.S.N.S. 1957, c.91, which prevents title to land lying in abeyance. This principle also can be seen in one of the cardinal rules of conveyancing: the Rule Against Perpetuities states that "title to land must vest within the lives in being plus twenty-one years." That is, if a person dies intestate, leaving no heirs, the land returns to the Crown after twenty-one years.

Today land is not owned absolutely. The owner has tenure over the land he has registered and described, but there are some restrictions on the use the owner may make of the land, wherever it is located in Canada or the United States. Landowners only have rights to exclusive possession and use not prohibited by statute. In some jurisdictions, for instance, zoning legislation may prevent the land being used for purposes other than those stated. Forest management or agricultural production may be restricted relative to harvest or crop production. Access may be guaranteed to certain classes of persons for specific purposes such as when necessary to reach water areas where fishing is allowed. The extent to which a landowner is controlled in his use of land varies greatly between states and between provinces. In Nova Scotia, for instance, there are some twenty-four provincial acts affecting one's title and sixteen or more which may restrict use.

According to common law, the ownership of domestic animals is absolute, but the ownership of wild animals is more complicated. Prior to the beginning of the concept of land title, man had a kind of property right in wild creatures and there were no restrictions on pursuit. With the right of property (land tenure) pursuit became more difficult. Under Roman law, common ownership was vested in the people subject to the right of the landowner to forbid the killing of game on his property.

At one time in England, the title to all wild animals was considered to be vested in the sovereign, and this right was dealt with by Henry III in 1225 in the Magna Carta and the Charter of the Forest. The position of ownership at common law since 1225 is that ownership of wild animals is in the state in its collective sovereign capacity as a representative of all its citizens. It has also long been the common law of England that landowners have a qualified property in wild animals and that this qualified property becomes absolute upon the death of the animal. There is an inherent conflict between the hunter's right to pursue game which is held in trust for the people and the landowner's right to protect himself and his property from trespassers, particularly those carrying firearms. Another position from which to view the same problem is that wildlife which belongs to all, but to no one person, is found on lands belonging to a few, and those few can prohibit access of all people to the wildlife.

Absolute property is not confined to animals killed by the owner but extends to trespassers as well, for a trespasser may have no property rights in the animal he kills. Thus at common law, the right of killing was annexed to the soil although the landowner did not own the animals while they were living.

Common law did not afford the landowner protection, however, for killing an animal on another's land was not a punishable offense, and the offender could only be sued for nominal damages. This was not a deterrent to trespass (nor is it today). In North America, we reverted to statute law to strengthen the position of both landowners and trespassers. In many jurisdictions, the landowner is protected by legislation and the regulations require no advertising concerning boundaries of ownership. Other legislation may protect the landowner under certain specified conditions of land use rather than ownership, and in some jurisdictions, there may be no protection except by civil suit for common trespass, which is really no protection.

Legal decisions are often based upon precedent, which means that decisions determined in a particular case based upon statute law are a determinant in future cases of a similar nature. Such case law develops over time so that those jurisdictions with the earliest legislation should also be the ones with the richest case law. The United States has accumulated a greater amount of case law based on precedents involving wildlife and other conservation concerns than Canada, and doubtless more than Mexico, but perhaps less than England.

In Canada today, the title to free-living wild animals is vested in the Crown in the right of the province where the animals exist. Similarly, title to wild animals in the United States is held by the public (the people) represented by their respective state governments. In jurisdictions throughout the United States and Canada, the possession of living wild animals and the pursuit or hunting of wild animals are detailed in one or more legislative acts. If possession is allowed at all, permission is usually required to keep wild animals in captivity. Endeavors like fur farming, game farming, and ranching also are controlled by legislation. The hunting, trapping, possessing, and pursuing or harassing of wildlife are usually controlled by regulations under a wildlife act.

Administration and Policy: the United States and Canada

With every new act and the regulations thereunder more decisions must be made and more paperwork is required. This is the stuff of administration: determining manpower schedules, finalizing budgets, approving reports, preparing and submitting reports, developing policy, and handling correspondence. Administering a wildlife agency differs from the administration of another resource agency primarily in its subject matter. It is paper work, telephone work, meetings, and conferences. But a good administrator is also a good manager, and the department or branch head or director must have both skills. The management part of his job has to do with people. The reports he approves are written by people; the budgets he finalizes are drafted by staff; and the manpower schedules he posts determine individuals' daily and yearly work programs. It is necessary to know something about wildlife to aspire to a wildlife administrative post, but it is even more important to get along with others, both senior and junior. The administrator-manager should know the field, but he must also command respect while being understanding and insightful.

It is the wildlife administrator's job to know procedure within his own department (or branch or division) and between his department and others. The administrator must also understand the processes by which legislation is approved and the limits of authority in the public service domain versus the political domain. At the end of the authority lines as well as at the end of the procedure and protocol lines in all North American government agencies, there is an elected representative of the people. These lines of authority are typically represented by flow charts. Five examples are shown (Figures 1.1– 1.5). Each chart has been simplified to show the structure and major headings only.

Usually the amount of paper work and the degree of authority and influence tend to increase as one moves toward the apex of a flow chart. In the provincial example, which does not necessarily typify all provinces, the planning and operations people are separated. There is no direct line from planning biologists to the biologists carrying out the field programs. In such cases, an informal shortcut may be employed with letters or memos of information directed to the senior administrators involved; it often depends upon the size of the organization and understandings that have developed. In the state examples given (Figures 1.2, 1.3) the responsibilities are also noted. These are the kinds of general responsibilities found in equivalent positions elsewhere throughout North America. The fourth example is a regional division of the Canadian Wildlife Service (Figure 1.4) and the fifth is the U.S. Fish and Wildlife Service (Figure 1.5). Each example should help to convey an idea of the complexities of modern bureaucracies, especially if one realizes that the charts are simplified. The Canadian federal diagram, for example, shows one of five regional offices relating to the central Ottawa office, that in turn relates closely to several other agencies in a major department (ministry). Because bureaucracies tend to grow and change, these examples should be understood as structural possibilities previously used by agencies.

In the Canadian parliamentary system of government, the senior civil servant of a general resource agency, including wildlife, is the deputy minister.

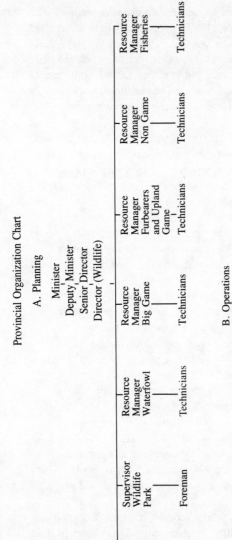

Figure 1.1 Partial organization chart for the province of Nova Scotia's wildlife department

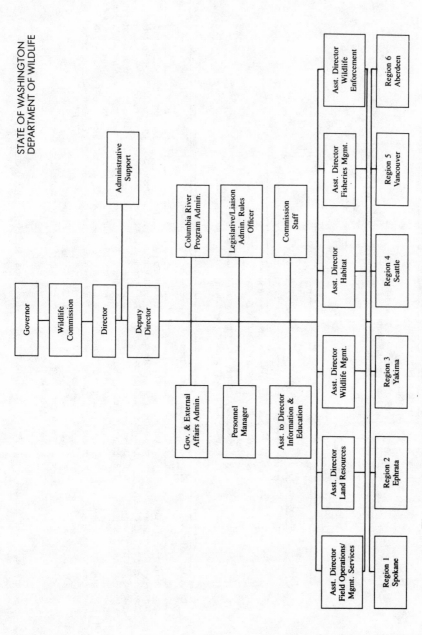

Figure 1.2 Organization chart for the Washington Department of Wildlife

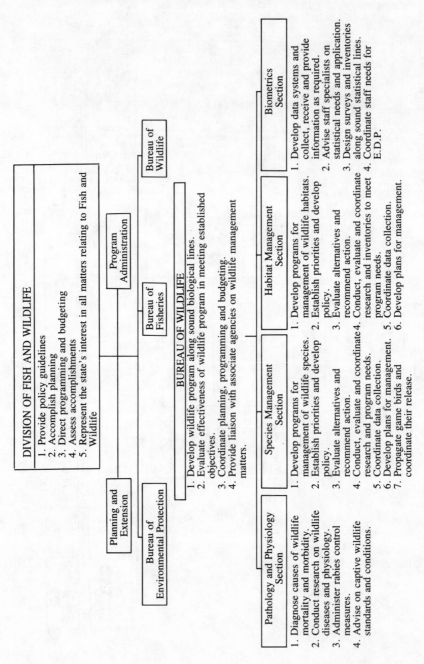

Figure 1.3   Fish and wildlife program divisional structure for an eastern state

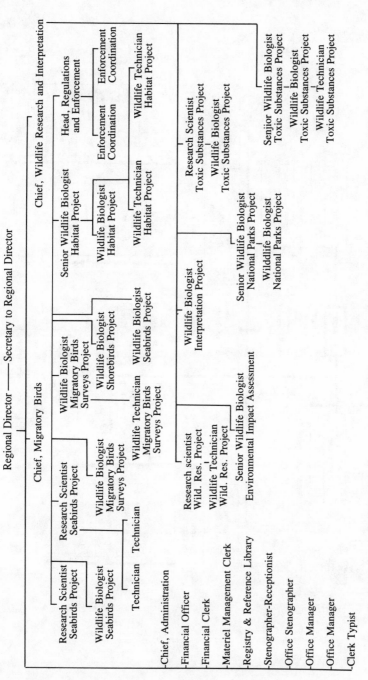

Canadian Wildlife Service
Atlantic Region

Regional Director ——— Secretary to Regional Director

Chief, Migratory Birds

Chief, Wildlife Research and Interpretation

Research Scientist
Seabirds Project

Wildlife Biologist
Seabirds Project

Technician

Technician

Chief, Administration

Financial Officer

Financial Clerk

Materiel Management Clerk

Registry & Reference Library

Stenographer-Receptionist

Office Stenographer

Office Manager

Office Manager

Clerk Typist

Wildlife Biologist
Migratory Birds
Surveys Project

Research Scientist
Seabirds Project

Wildlife Biologist
Migratory Birds
Surveys Project

Wildlife Technician
Migratory Birds
Surveys Project

Wildlife Biologist
Migratory Birds
Surveys Project

Wildlife Biologist
Shorebirds Project

Wildlife Biologist
Seabirds Project

Research scientist
Wild. Res. Project

Wildlife Technician
Wild. Res. Project

Senior Wildlife Biologist
Environmental Impact Assessment

Wildlife Biologist
Interpretation Project

Senior Wildlife Biologist
Habitat Project

Wildlife Biologist
Habitat Project

Wildlife Technician
Habitat Project

Head, Regulations
and Enforcement

Enforcement
Coordination

Enforcement
Coordination

Wildlife Technician
Habitat Project

Research Scientist
Toxic Substances Project

Wildlife Biologist
Toxic Substances Project

Senior Wildlife Biologist
National Parks Project

Wildlife Biologist
National Parks Project

Senior Wildlife Biologist
Toxic Substances Project

Wildlife Biologist
Toxic Substances Project

Wildlife Technician
Toxic Substances Project

Figure 1.4 Organization chart for the Atlantic region of the Canadian Wildlife Service

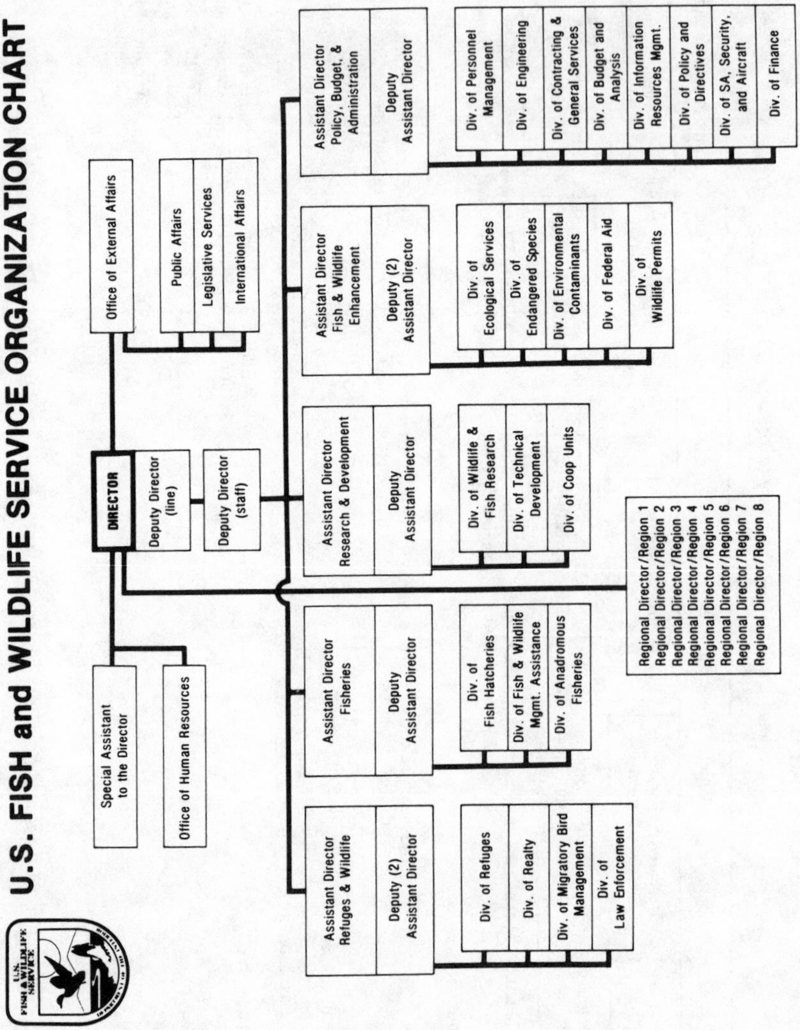

U.S. FISH and WILDLIFE SERVICE ORGANIZATION CHART

Figure 1.5   Organization chart for the U.S. Fish and Wildlife Service

The deputy and the assistant (ADM) give final approval to regulatory changes, revisions of existing statutes, or other policy deemed necessary. The deputy minister recommends revisions to the minister, who is an elected representative appointed to the portfolio by the premier (provincial) or prime minister (federal). Before the revisions are approved by the minister, they receive a thorough legal review by the attorney general's department (provincial) or the solicitor general's department (federal). A bill or regulatory revisions may also be reviewed by one or more legislative committees or even debated by legislative bodies in a provincial situation.

In some cases, regulatory changes may be accomplished by order-in-council (governor-general-in-council or governor-in-council), which means that the minister and cabinet can approve without legislative approval. In the Canadian parliamentary system, the order-in-council route usually means there is less political influence involved, for if a regulatory change must go through the legislative assembly, all elected representatives may have a voice, if they choose to, on second and third readings, and each representative could be influenced by people in his constituency. The elected representative in a Canadian province is known as the M.L.A. or member of the legislative assembly. Federally, the elected member is the M.P. or member of Parliament. Representation is by electoral district and is approximately based on population. A knowledge of provincial and state processes is important for anyone interested in wildlife because most legislation and regulatory changes relating to wildlife take place within the government arenas of provinces and states. National and international legislation is obviously important, but new acts and amendments or changes occur in these areas less frequently. The average working biologist may be less involved with federal legislative alterations than with state or provincial ones.

In a U.S. state, the position equivalent to deputy minister is usually that of secretary of a commission, depending upon whether the state operates with a commission system or with a line system. In a flow chart example provided (Figure 1.3), the senior post is that of commissioner of environmental conservation. The representative equivalent to a minister may be either a commissioner or a commission chairman, appointed by the state governor; or according to the system, there may be several commissioners. In the latter instance, some states have formulae that disallow one governor from appointing more than a certain number of commissioners during his term of office. This procedure is supposed to reduce partisan political influence. The process for a regulatory change is not greatly different in the states from that of the provinces. The people involved may have different titles, but the end result is pretty much the same. Many states and provinces have added advisory boards or councils. In the United States, the advisory groups most often represent the hunting, fishing and non-hunting publics, universities involved in state-supported research (through Pittman-Robertson), federal cooperative agencies, and sometimes, major private landowners or industrial interests. In Canada, advisory groups may reflect various publics concerned with wildlife and/or provincial geographical representation. Such bodies serve as effective screening groups, advising against obviously unsound policy or poor regulatory changes and improving the better recommendations which may emanate either from biologists or interest groups.

Poole (1980) has provided a thorough discussion of the U.S. federal legislative process. A basic difference of some importance between the U.S. and Canadian federal systems should also be understood. In the United States, the senior federal legislative body is the Senate, composed of two elected members from each state regardless of size or population. The House of Representatives is comprised of congressmen elected from states, depending upon their population. One state may have several congressmen but always only two senators. Both houses comprise Congress and each house must pass the federal wildlife legislation in question. In Canada the honorable members of the House of Commons are elected on the basis of population, and it is the important legislative body. Unlike elected-term senators in the United States, the senators in Canada's parliamentary system are appointed for life by the governor-general (actually the prime minister) when vacancies occur. The Senate in the Canadian parliamentary system generally serves to improve, rather than to initiate or determine, legislation.

Over periods of several years Canada and the United States have developed policy statements concerning wildlife. The United States has a "wildlife policy" serving as a guide for its agencies and for the nation. In 1982, Canada completed its "Guidelines for Wildlife Policy in Canada" generally subscribed to by federal and provincial agencies involved with wildlife. In 1990, a final draft of this policy was approved by the Federal government and provinces.

Both countries originally established waterfowl management plans which complement each other on a flyway and a continental basis. Cooperation between the United States and Canada has always been exceptionally good regarding all wildlife resources, and this cooperation extends from policy guidelines at senior levels of government down to regional, technical matters of species management considered by biologists. For example, a North American Waterfowl Management Plan (NAWMP) has recently been approved, and as in many such areas of policy, the International Association of Fish and Wildlife Agencies was very much involved. This organization represents all North American jurisdictions and forms an important base for policy development and implementation with respect to wildlife resources.

In Canada, several joint ventures have been initiated under the NAWMP which address either regional conditions (e.g. Western Joint Venture) or species concerns (e.g. Snow Goose Joint Venture). Overall funding is essentially 50 per cent from the United States and 50 per cent from Canada; however, the formula may vary to 75:25 depending upon the ratio of "in kind" to "cash" support in Canada. A typical joint venture project funding approach would find Canada's portion of a project supported one third federally, one third provincially, and one third by a non-government organization, such as Ducks Unlimited, Canada. Other non-government organizations involved might typically be Wildlife Habitat Canada, the Nature Conservancy, or local sportsmen's associations. Projects submitted within joint venture approaches generally originate with provincial waterfowl biologists, are screened by the Canadian Wildlife Service and then considered by a joint venture committee comprised of senior Canadian government, United States government, and non-government organization representatives. Each project must be approved by all joint venture participants. Depending upon the project, a Funding Administrative Agency or "banker" might be Ducks Unlimited or Wildlife Habitat Canada. Because the Wildlife Habitat Canada mandate is broader than Ducks Unlimited's and encompasses cooperative terrestrial habitat projects as well as wetland programs, Ducks Unlimited, at present, is the more active non-government organization in projects within joint ventures under NAWMP.

Nongovernment Wildlife Organizations in the United States and Canada

We have previously referred to the importance of citizens' organizations, professional and otherwise, in the evolution of wildlife conservation in the United States. There are several which continue to be important. Without them the wildlife cause might soon dwindle and die in the United States. In Canada, nongovernment organizations have also become a strong influence in shaping both provincial and federal wildlife policy.

The Wildlife Management Institute is the watchdog organization in Washington. Its "News Bulletin" carries the latest happenings from congressional committees and from the floors of both houses. As a lobbying organization gaining support before the votes are taken, it serves the wildlife profession and the wildlife resource everywhere. The National Wildlife Federation is also an effective lobbying organization. Its Washington office is on top of the wildlife scene throughout North America, and its influence is also felt through its educational materials and its publication, "National Wildlife." The National Audubon Society, originally concerned primarily with birds, has over the years supported many general wildlife movements, including the national wildlife refuge system. It remains a powerful support force for wildlife conservation, and "Audubon" ranks among the top wildlife publications in the world. Among the other national, regional, state, and local groups which support sound wildlife conservation are the Sierra Club, The Wilderness Society, Ducks Unlimited, Defenders of Wildlife, Wildlife Preservation Trust, The Nature Conservancy, and National Parks Association. The Conservation Foundation and New York Zoological Society are organizations concerned with wildlife problems in North America and other countries. The Wildlife Society and professional bird, mammal, fish, and herpetological societies all lend weight to conservation causes.

Gilbert et al (1980) have noted that the presence of a "larger, better organized, and more vocal public" helped the United States progress more rapidly than Canada in developing a major wildlife presence and movement. This is true, but Canada is catching up. The Canadian Wildlife Federation, which originated with the 1961 Resources for Tomorrow Conference, is a strong voice for conservation causes and boasts the largest membership of all Canadian conservation groups. The Canadian Arctic Resources Committee, Canadian Nature Federation, Canadian Parks and Wilderness Society, Ducks Unlimited Canada and The Nature Conservancy of Canada are playing roles in molding a stronger wildlife conservation movement. Professionally, Canadian wildlife managers have been generally unsuccessful in forming a permanent Canada-wide organization. In 1959, the Canadian Society of Wildlife and Fishery Biologists was organized, and its first general meeting was held in 1960. The name was later changed to the Canadian Society for Environmental Biologists, and non wildlife professionals were welcomed into the organization. The CSEB exists only regionally today, and the Atlantic region has reverted back to the original name. In 1971 the Canadian Society of Zoologists added a wildlife section as a specialty group, but its membership was composed primarily of academics, and in 1990 it was disbanded. Then, the Wildlife Society of Canada was formed in 1981. It, too, has failed to obtain the support needed to provide professionals with a society that would benefit the resource and its professional following. Of course, Canadian wildlife workers should have their own society and wildlife resources in Canada would ultimately benefit from one.

Notes

1. From 1867 until 1908 "nature study" grew and developed in the universities (Cornell) and normal schools (Oswego), filtering down to secondary and elementary schools (Bailey, 1909).
2. The environment minister announced on 13 November, 1984, that interpretation would be offered to the provinces or private sector.

3. The Northwest Game Act of 1917. Presently the Game Ordinance, North-west Territories and Game Ordinance, Yukon Territory.
4. The Game Export Act, chap. 128, Revised Statutes of Canada, 1952.
5. Revised, 1970.
6. See Appendix 1, for a more complete list of both Canadian and U.S. Federal legislation.
7. Excerpted in part from Lutes, R. E., unpublished review. Wolfville, N. S., 1978.

Bibliography
Alison, R. M. 1978. The earliest records of waterfowl hunting. Wildl. Soc. Bull. (4):196—199.
Anon. Deuteronomy 14:4–20.
Anon. Deuteronomy 22:6–7.
Anon. Genesis 7:12.
Anon. Leviticus 11:4–6.
Anon. 1968. Organization, authority and programs of state fish and wildlife agencies. Wildl. Manage, Inst., Washington D.C. 5 pp. plus charts.
Bailey, L. H. 1909. The nature-study idea. The MacMillan Company, New York, NY. 246 pp.
Benson, D. A., and D. G. Dodds. 1977. Deer of Nova Scotia. Department of Lands and Forests, Halifax, N. S. 92 pp.
Bubenik, A. B. 1976. Evolution of wildlife harvesting systems in Europe. Trans. Fed-Prov. Wildl. Conf. 40:97–105.
Clarke, C. H. D. 1976. Evolution of wildlife harvesting systems in Canada. Trans. Fed-Prov. Wildl. Conf. 40:122–139.
Dagg, A. I. 1974. Canadian wildlife and man. McClelland and Stewart Ltd., Toronto, ONT. 192 pp.
Dasmann, R. F. 1981. Wildlife biology. Second ed. John Wiley and Sons, New York, NY. 212 pp.
Dodds, D. G. 1983. Terrestrial mammals. Pp. 509–550, *In* G. R. South, Ed. Biogeography and ecology of the Island of Newfoundland. Junk, The Hague, Holland. 723 pp.
Foster, J. 1978. Working for wildlife. University of Toronto Press, Toronto, ONT. 283 pp.
Gilbert, F. F., E. Bossenmaier, L. Carbyn, D. Hebert, M. Hoefs, J. Huot, G. Mitchell, W. Prescott, A. Simmons, and L. Sudgen. 1980. The Wildlife Society of Canada-A reality in 1981? Wildl. Soc. Bull. 8 (3):179–198.
Gustafson, A. F., C. H. Guise, W. J. Hamilton, Jr., and H. Ries. 1949. Conservation in the United States. Comstock Publishing Co., Ithaca, NY. 534 pp.

Hewitt, C. G. 1919. The need of a nation-wide effort in wildlife conservation. Pp. 8–18, *In* National conference on game and wildlife conservation, Ottawa, 183 pp.

Johnson, M. K. 1979. Review of endangered species: policies and legislation. Wildl. Soc. Bull. 7 (2):79–83.

Leopold, A. 1933. Game management. Charles Scriber's Sons, New York, NY. 481 pp.

Lewis, H. F. 1965. The Canadian Wildlife Service—its functions and scope. Oryx 2 (3):173–178.

Lewis, H. F. 1967. Wildlife conservation through the century. Rod and Gun in Canada, Jan.-Feb. 1967. 3 pp.

McClintock, J. N. 1889. History of New Hampshire. B. B. Russell, Cornhill, Boston, MA. 742 pp.

Munro, D. A. 1961. Legislative and administrative limitations on wildlife management. Pp. 867–880, *In* Resources for tomorrow. Volume 2. The Oueen's Printer, Ottawa.

Nova Scotia. 1884. Consolidated statutes.

Phillips, J. C. 1928. Wild birds introduced or transplanted in North America, U.S. Dept. Agric. Tech. Bull. No. 61, Washington, DC. 64 pp.

Piers, G. 1898. In Annual report, Nova Scotia Game and Inland Fishery Protection Society. Halifax, 1899. 21 pp.

Pimlott, D. H. 1953. Newfoundland moose. Trans. N. Am. Wildl. Conf. 18:563–581.

Poole, D. A. 1980. The legislative process and wildlife. Pp. 489–498. *In* Wildlife management techniques manual. The Wildlife Society, Washington, DC. 686 pp.

Severinghaus, C. W. 1974. Return of the deer. The Conservationist. August-September.

Slade, W., Jr. 1823. Vermont state papers. Being an account of the first and second councils of censors. J. W. Copeland, Middlebury, VT. 567 pp.

Swift, E. 1958. The glory trail. The great American migration and its impact on natural resources. The National Wildlife Federation, Washington, DC. 50 pp.

Tober, J. A. 1981. Who owns the wildlife? The political economy of conservation in nineteenth century America. Greenwood Press, Westport, CT. 330 pp.

Trefethen, J. B. 1961. Crusade for wildlife. The Telegraph Press, Harrisburg, PA. 377 pp.

Trippensee, R. E. 1948. Wildlife management, upland game and general principles. Volume I. McGraw-Hill Book Co. Ltd., New York, NY. 479 pp.

Recommended Readings

Audubon Wildlife Reports. Annual 1985, 1986, 1987 and Biannual 1988/
89, 1989/90. Comprehensive reports considering major U.S. and international wildlife issues, featuring one U.S. wildlife related government agency in each volume. An invaluable reference guide for all
North American wildlife workers.

Foster, J. 1978. Working for wildlife. The beginning of preservation in Canada. Univ. of Toronto Press. Toronto, ONT. 283 pp.

Langenau, E. E., Jr. and C. W. Ostrom. Jr. 1984. Organizational and political
factors affecting state wildlife management. Wildl. Soc. Bull. 12:107–
116.

An interesting hypothetical model of state wildlife administration
developed to examine the relationships between the factors of demand,
resource base, management structure and public benefits.

Sherwood, M. 1981. Big game in Alaska. A history of wildlife and people.
Yale University Press, New Haven, CT. 200 pp.

A generally even presentation of some of the political, social and
jurisdictional complexities in the history of wildlife conservation prior
to Alaskan statehood.

Tober, J. A. 1981. Who owns the wildlife? The political economy of conservation in nineteenth century America. Greenwood Press. Westport,
CT. 330 pp.

An excellent, well-documented study of the evolution of wildlife
conservation and wildlife policy in the United States.

Trefethen, J. B. 1961. Crusade for wildlife. Highlights in conservation progress. The Telegraph Press, Harrisburg, PA. 377 pp.

The history of the Boone and Crockett club but also a good review
of the wildlife conservation movement in continental United States.

II MAN AND WILDLIFE—Culture, Conflicts, and Values

One school of thought among anthropologists is that the American Indian believed himself and the animal he hunted were brothers derived from one Creator; they were of the same species. Whisker (1981) notes that in the Indian manner of thinking, the Creator made man a hunter and all other animals the hunted. Animal mythology was passed from the old to the young, and a deep respect for his animal brothers usually made the Indian a careful killer.

Nature and its animals were supposed to be the standard of goodness for the Amerindian. All human behavior could be measured against nature and the animals in precise measurements. Animals were generally seen to be courteous, kind, loyal, strong, brave, reverent, clean, alert and loving. Before taking an animal in the hunt one had to be prepared to attest to his own purity of heart. He could not kill that which was more moral than himself. This, of course assumed an intimate knowledge for the problems of moral behavior of the animals he hunted.

Subarctic Indians were obsessed with the responsibilities that man and animal had to one another. The injunction against killing too many animals ranked as the first law the Amerindian must obey. That he may be killed by a man who was his moral equal was the first law for animals. Thus the animal, when seeing that his meat, hide and so on was needed by the true hunter, was required to voluntarily surrender itself to the hunter. A hunter or an animal which did not obey the law violated the rules of nature (Whisker).

Man was the animal with the high intelligence and, therefore, greatest responsibility. Man communicated with animals through the hunt. Here was a built-in conservation ethic supported by ritual that guaranteed the continued existence of the wild populations upon which man was partly dependent. According to Martin (1978), this mutually beneficial relationship, which was basic to the Indian religious experience, was quickly broken following the initial European visits to the New World. The Indians misinterpreted the cause of increased sickness and death resulting from European contact, and sought revenge by punishing the animals they thought caused the illness. Whether this "war between the Indians and animals" existed or not, the Indian-animal brother relationship did break down with the advent of trading with the Europeans, and most especially, with the beginnings of the fur trade. Culture changed rapidly when a market economy for wildlife was introduced into North America, for the animals were soon moved from a primary support position and an importance in ritual to a means of obtaining status though material possessions.

The Micmac Indian of the maritime region of Canada was probably among the first to undergo an attitudinal and cultural change relative to wild animals because European contact was earlier in that area of North America than elsewhere. The Micmac's dependence upon hunting and gathering was total; they were not cultivators and used animals daily for food, clothing, and shelter for themselves and food for their dogs. Many species of fish, shellfish, birds, and mammals were also used in ritual feasts like the Tabagie. Because of this dependency upon wild things, the cultural and dietary changes that occurred at the time of European contact were instantaneous and shocking. The Indians' dependency soon moved from mother nature to brother humans (French missionaries and traders in the case of Micmacs). As it turned out, these were changes for the worse. Similar changes apparently occurred across much of North America with differences only in degree, depending upon the diversification of the Indians' natural economies and the relative importance of the fur trade to both Europeans and Indians. With the white man came the means to over exploit populations of wild animals. The primitive weapons of the Indians may have been more responsible for their "conservation ethic" than were their beliefs.

In Africa, the Bisa of the Luangwa Valley of Zambia once ritualized both the hunt and the kill, and the relationships between the hunter, the animal, and the hunter's ancestors were a strong influence on the hunter and his future successes. The ritualistic position of the animal was most important. Certain animals that were both fat and brown in color, such as the buffalo (*Cyncerus cafer*), were particularly sought for food while others, colored black and white, such as the zebra (*Equus* sp.), were seldom taken. This selective killing based upon religious belief with its attending rituals, partly determined population levels and might well be considered a sort of culturally induced species management. Some aspects of ancient Bisa culture, as they affect dealing with animals, are still present, but they were already eroding long ago when the ivory trade first brought an economic dimension into the picture. Now bound by laws imposed upon them by government and restricted in their movements by national park boundaries, the Bisa are gradually moving into a modern era more dependent upon developed society and less dependent upon nature. Their altered environment sometimes reflects considerations for game management which may well be less beneficial for some wild species. In some instances, these management changes have forced "honest" people to become violators.

If we continue to go backward in time to observe the relationship between man and animals, we learn that man has probably always hunted.

With man's capacity for both abstract thought and speech, the meal provided by the hunt offered a truly splendid opportunity to become social. There is every logical reason to assume that man talked about the past hunting successes, grumbled about the hunt's failures, and planned the next day's hunt. As he spun his tale, fanciful elements would have been introduced. (Pretty much like the hunting yarns you and I tell). Primitive man could easily have formed the basis of religion and myths.

The meals would have provided an excellent opportunity to choose leaders and to establish various forms of rank within the group. The great hunter would logically have been honored at such feasts, and the unsuccessful hunter might, with equal logic, be demoted or disgraced. Certainly, the criteria for promotion and demotion would be clear in a society so tied to the hunt as its single supreme necessity.

There is also considerable evidence that primitive man thought of the hunt as the most logical subject of his art. In addition to the probable magic content of the cave paintings and rock drawings that early man fabricated with probable reference to success in the hunt, he also exhibited his purely esthetic powers in the creation of weaponry more beautiful than would ever be needed merely for practical purposes. Some of the many truly beautiful knives and spearheads may have been badges of authority or magical instruments, but they are also quite enviable works of art in themselves (Whisker, 1981).

Regarding Cro-Magnon man about 35,000 B.C., Howell (1971) has written:

There are more than 50 known pictures of strange-looking sorcerers or shamans-human figures clad in the skins of animals, sometimes depicted with animal heads or horns, often appearing to be engaged in some kind of dance. These may have been attempts, by illustrating it in advance, to guarantee successful stalking by hunters disguised as animals. Or they may have been more highly symbolized projections of the hunter's feeling that a ritual dance by a magician or spellbinder would work more potent magic on the game. Or they may even have been attempts to portray a superhuman figure, the spirit of the hunt or the deity of the animals.

We can only speculate about these tantalizing and long-lost rituals, but they have so many parallels in hunting societies of more modern times that there is no doubt at all that Cro-Magnon man was a ritualist too. Any society that lives by hunting spends most of its time thinking about the animals that it hunts, and many elaborate systems of totems and taboos are still known among hunting tribes today, telling them what they must and must not do. These range from propitiating the spirit of the animal, so that it will submit easily and gracefully to being killed, to attempts to disarm its spirit after death so that it will not come back to haunt or harm the killer. The cultures of Eskimos, American Indians and many of the primitive tribes of subarctic Siberia-all of them, like Cro-Magnon man, cold-weather followers of big game-were steeped in rituals of this kind.

Another thing that preoccupies hunting societies is the problem of fluctuations in the game supply. Cro-Magnon man apparently dealt with this in his magic system by emphasizing the fertility of many of the beasts he painted. Pairs of animals were often shown together, sometimes in the act of mating. Horses, does and cows were painted with the swollen bellies of advanced pregnancy. In others, the udders were enlarged, as if to emphasize the rich supply of milk that the mother would be capable of giving to any offspring that might be born. That scarcity of game was periodically a problem with Cro-Magnon man is likely. During the colder episodes of the last glacial period he probably did all right. Mammoths, woolly rhinoceroses, ibex, a cold-adapted shaggy little steppe horse, and particularly reindeer flourished in large numbers in the tundra environment that came with the cold. As it warmed up, from time to time he undoubtedly switched over to the deer, bison, and wild cattle that replaced the cold-loving species. But increasing numbers of men, and the beginnings of a tendency toward a settled life (in winter, at least) hinted at by cave occupancy, may well have led to local depletion of the game in many areas and seriously complicated Cro-Magnon man's ability to make a comfortable living. If so, he must certainly have turned to sympathetic hunting magic to help him out.

Religion, Man, and Wild Animals

It is understandable that archaic, animistic, and early spiritualistic societies would have evolved with animal-human relationships that were beneficial to man. Any other conditions would not only have been unreasonable but could well have slowed man's development or even threatened his existence. The major modern religions, however, usually recognize animals as responsibilities of man, either as hunted prey or as domesticated creatures. Ritualization is still present in the Jewish tradition. In the past, the initial slaughter by designated people was not only symbolic but also a means of guaranteeing that proper care was taken in the handling of animal food to be eaten. Thus ritual killing logically followed the designation of "clean" or "unclean" as a matter of health and discipline. The people who obeyed the religious laws remained healthy and were reminded of the law each time they ate meat.

Mosaic law also forbade man to eat animals which had died a natural death, as well as those killed by other predators. Presumably the health of the people was also a concern here. Orthodox Jews do not kill today, and ritualized slaughter continues. Neither do Orthodox Jews hunt, for hunting could result in killing, although the Old Testament nowhere forbids hunting. On the contrary, there are many references to eating wild meat and hunting. Another reason to restrict the number of people having contact with the act of taking an animal's life (done only by the Jewish priests) might have related to a desire to maintain a peaceful, nonaggressive nature among the masses. After all, killing is a violent act. A casual view of history and today's newspapers suggests that either those responsible for the law were wrong in their belief that preventing men from killing animals would necessarily create a more peaceful people; or perhaps this reduction of violence had nothing whatever to do with ritualized rabbinical killing. Kertzen (1955) had this to say concerning the sanctioned or ''kosher'' laws:

> The Old Testament (Leviticus) sets down certain definite dietary restrictions: 1. It is forbidden to eat the meat of certain animals (such as the pig and horse) and certain sea foods (shrimp, lobster, crab, oyster). 2. Meats must be slaughtered according to ritual and must meet specific health standards. 3. Meat products and dairy products may not be eaten together. (The Bible says that meat must not be boiled in milk. This was a pre-Biblical, pagan custom).
>
> Maimonides, a distinguished physician as well as philosopher, said that ''kosher'' food restrictions were health measures—particularly in the case of pork, which deteriorates rapidly in warm climates. He also saw important moral values in applying restraint to eating habits—for if we practice discrimination in satisfying our appetite, we may be more self-controlled with the other temptations of life. Many of the laws concerning kosher food deal with the *method* of slaughtering the animal: it must be done without pain to the beast, with the greatest possible speed, and by a God-fearing man. Incidentally, Jews are forbidden to hunt.
>
> Jews who follow the dietary laws do not feel a sense of deprivation. They regard kosher practices as a symbol of their heritage, a daily lesson in self-discipline, and a constant reminder that human beings must feel pity for all living things. How many Jews obey the dietary law today? No one can answer authoritatively. A safe guess is that less than 20 percent of the Jews in America conform strictly to the laws governing kosher food.

It is also possible that the dietary restrictions of the Old Testament were prompted by parasitic diseases which caused many deaths before the taboos were in place. Trichinosis in pork and ''red tide'' in shellfish are but two examples.

Both the New Testament and the Book of Mormon include references to man's use of wild animals as food. The New Testament refers to the eating of fish while the Book of Mormon mentions the eating of wild animals or beasts. The liberal Christian church today proclaims a respect and a concern for all matters environmental. For them, the old-time stewardship, which often dealt only with financial matters, is usually replaced by a "stewardship of life" concept, which refers to God's providential sovereignty over all things and makes man, as the servant of God and Christ, fully responsible for God's work.

The relationship of man to other animals covers a wide spectrum among the eastern religions of the world. Often animals and man are viewed as possessors of nonphysical souls which upon death may be either relocated or reincarnated in another creature, often another species. New born souls, in both children and animals, may have inhabited a human or a nonhuman in a previous existence. Animals other than man are often central to religious belief, and some species have always been particularly important in mythology and legend.

In many eastern societies, the importance of religion and culture continues relatively unchanged from a thousand years ago or more. Tradition still dictates the role wild and domestic animals will play in the lives of humans in these areas. In the developed or industrialized countries, our relationships to animals other than man have become much more complex. Sometimes, the manner in which a group of people treats a species, or a population, becomes a public issue advancing into economic and political arenas and competing in the media for a share of our time, our money, and our emotions.

Conflict: Man versus the Animals

Throughout the world, mammalian herbivores and birds are competing with man for cultivated and wild food. For millions of Africans, the loss of stored grains to small mammals and birds may help keep them close to the edge of starvation. For thousands of commercial farmers in North America and thousands of collectivized cultivators in socialist countries, losses of growing and stored crops can mean a lower standard of living, and for some, less food in the stomachs of their families. In Africa, the marauding elephant or a herd of buffalo on the move can destroy the crops of an entire village in minutes. In North America, deer may eliminate much of the next year's fruit crop through winter browsing. These conditions are well known, and the man-animal conflict for the same food items has certainly been around since the first precultivators tended their wild plants. What man has done to exacerbate the issue is to make conditions easier for the wild animal by growing large acreages of a single crop favored by one or more species of bird or mammal.

He has also created dumps, dirty harbors, and costal airports where birds congregate for food or rest. Man's agricultural activities have been partly responsible for increases in the numbers of some of his most effective competitors such as the red-winged blackbird, while the gulls have responded to the "richness" of city harbors along our coastlines.

Predators also compete with man, and become depredators of sheep and cattle. The African farmer protects his cattle and his dog from the leopard. The North American sheep farmer guards his flock against coyotes. Sometimes man even gives up his life when a lion hunts near an African village or a tiger inhabits a forest area in India. The predators that have most recently been viewed seriously as competitors with man are the marine mammals. Harp seals and other pinnipeds consume thousands of tons of fish that humans might also harvest or which serve as part of an important trophic level in a complex ecosystem; porpoises (family Phocoenidae) and dolphins consume as much more. In Newfoundland, the fisherman competes with whales, particularly pilot whales (*Globicephela melaena*; a Delphinidae), that may destroy both gear and fish. Wherever the conflicts occur, wild animals are destroyed. We will examine depredator and predator management in Chapters 3 and 7, but now we should consider certain areas of human responsibility which may involve questions of animal awareness, animal rights, and how humans perceive the tame and the wild.

Questions of Responsibility

For centuries, there have been a few individuals who have been well-known locally, nationally, and sometimes internationally for their understanding of, and relationship to, certain animals. Recently a number of popular works have considered man's origin, his behavior, and the behavior of certain primates and cetaceans. Man's closeness to chimpanzees, whales, cats, and dogs may be discussed seriously by some who even claim to "talk" through a kind of telepathic wireless to animals they know, both near and far. Their claims to personal relationships with individual animals sometimes surpass the experiences of St. Francis of Assisi, Ernest Thompson Seton, and Grey Owl combined. But the communication cannot be all one way, for to continue a monologue without response would hardly be rewarding. The mammals or birds, must respond of course, and it is the matter of this response that brings us to the question of animal awareness. In a studied review of the question involving both humanists and scientists, Griffin (1976) concludes:

Language has generally been regarded as a unique attribute of human beings, different in kind from animal communication. But on close examination of this view, as it has been expressed by linguists, psychologists, and philosophers, it becomes evident that one of the major criteria on which the distinction has been based is the assumption that animals lack any conscious intent to communicate, whereas men know what they are doing. The available evidence concerning communication behavior in animals suggests that there may be no qualitative dichotomy, but rather a large quantitative difference in complexity of signals and range of intentions that separates animal communication from human language.

Human thinking has generally been held to be closely linked to language, and some philosophers have argued that the two are inseparable or even identical. To the extent that this assertion is accepted, and insofar as animal communication shares basic properties of human language, the employment of versatile communication systems by animals becomes evidence that they have mental experiences and communicate with conscious intent. The contrary view is supported only by negative evidence, which justifies, at the most an agnostic position.

Opening our eyes to the theoretical possibility that animals have significant mental experiences is only a first step toward the more difficult procedure of investigating their actual nature and importance to the animals concerned. Great caution is necessary until adequate methods have been developed to gather independently verifiable data about the properties and significance of any mental experiences animals may prove to have.

It has long been argued that human mental experiences can only be detected and analyzed through the use of language and introspective reports, and that this avenue is totally lacking in other species. Recent discoveries about the versatility of some animal communication systems suggest that this radical dichotomy may also be unsound. It seems possible, at least in principle, to detect and examine any mental experiences or conscious intentions that animals may have through the experimental use of the animal's capabilities for communication. Such communication channels might be learned, as in recent studies of captive chimpanzees, or it might be possible, through the use of models or by other methods, to take advantage of communication behavior which animals already use.

We may then continue to accept a difference in the nature of mental experiences between man and other creatures, but we are not yet able to measure the consciousness levels of other creatures in relation to man, although communications behavior is rapidly increasing our understanding. We must conclude that animals are certainly aware of man, but we do not yet know how aware.

The question of animal rights, too, is basic but quite different. Where the neurophysiologist and behaviorist can measure neurophysiological responses and stimulus-response times in studying consciousness levels, the rights question cannot be held up to scientific testing as easily. Here we are more likely to deal with moral, religious and philosophical parameters. The question of animal rights has been reviewed by Whisker, with the earliest writings dating from about 1723 to the present. Opinions lie roughly in the opposing views that: (a) the animals have rights to remain naturally free and free of pain and maltreatment as clearly as humans have rights, and (b) only humans have rights under God but humans, as stewards, have responsibilities for the welfare of animals. In the case of (a) the questions of domestication, genetic change, animal production and slaughter, as well as of habitat degradation and loss, among others, must often be rationalized. In the case of (b), it is understood that although humans have responsibilities for the welfare of animals, the welfare of humans comes first. This may necessitate the use of animals for medical research, beasts of burden, food, or any other use that may benefit some aspect of man's existence. The differences often boil down to the right of an animal to live versus the right of humans to take an animal's life.

We may clarify these matters slightly or we may muddy them further by turning briefly to the domestic and then back to the wild animal. Are they the same or are they different? One of the most interesting views on domestication we have read does not come from either the scientific or humanistic literature but from a children's story, *The Little Prince*, by Antoine de Saint-Exupery. It occurs when a little boy (the prince) alone in a strange world finds himself confronted by a fox, and a conversation ensues about the word "tame." We readily admit to the anthropomorphism but judge the lesson worth the risks of its use.

"What does that mean—'tame'?"
"It is an act often neglected," said the fox, "It means to establish ties."
"To establish ties'?"
"Just that," said the fox. "To me, you are still nothing more than a little boy who is just like a hundred thousand other little boys. And I have no need for you. And you, on your part, have no need of me. To you, I am nothing more than a fox like a hundred other foxes. But if you tame me, than we shall need each other. To me, you will be unique in all the world. To you, I shall be unique in all the world . . . "

But is this really what domestication is all about in the world today? Sometime it is and sometimes it is not.

The reasons man has tamed animals have never been altruistic. The animal's welfare was not a question of concern. It was man's welfare that was to be improved using formerly wild animals as the means. Man has used domestic and domesticated animals to serve as beasts of burden, to provide milk, to give him hides for shelter, to assure a ready supply of meat, and to increase his pleasure. Cats were probably domesticated in Egypt where they were pampered by those with means. A cat god, Bast, existed and was worshipped in its own city, Bubastis. Dogs from many *Canis* stocks were tamed in several areas around the world. They often served to aid in the hunt. Micmac Indians gave their best hunting dogs to friends as an indication of respect but also ate dogs at feasts. Pigs were tamed in Europe and Asia and became important as food and in religion and ritual. Pig rituals continue today in Borneo, and sacred cattle continue their fascinating but sometimes nearly marginal existence in India. Pet fads are growing in the world today, and a sizable industry exists to provide cat and dog (or other pet) fanciers with food and various, largely unnecessary, paraphernalia. Food is by far the largest industry based upon animals man has tamed, whether it is for pets or animals destined for slaughter, and the tentacles of the animal food industry extend to many areas of most modern economies.

There are two categories of domestic animals: (1) the pet, the watchdog, and the beast of burden, creatures affecting the lives of one or a few humans at most. A unique relationship exists; the animal is totally dependent upon man for its continued existence in that it could not (or would not be allowed to) thrive if it were released or forced to fend for itself. Close ties have been established. (2) animals are raised in meat factories to produce poultry, beef, or pork in a specific manner to meet man's peculiar tastes and desires. Literally millions of genetically altered animals are cared for scientifically for a specific time period, then slaughtered and processed for human consumption. Variations occur within each category throughout the world, but basically we are concerned with either an intimate one-on-one animal-man relationship in which the animal is meant to live as long as possible; or a mass production of 1000 or more animals to one human—a relationship in which the animals are meant to die at the time they provide us with either the choicest food, the most profit, or both.

Clutton-Brock (1981) divides animals in captivity into *exploited captives* where breeding is under the influence of natural selection and *man-made* animals which are essentially controlled by artificial selection. She considers cats and elephants exploited and dogs and domestic livestock man-made. Her book, *Domesticated Animals from Early Times*, is important background reading for any students of wildlife.

Because man first tamed the wild animals and then, through selective breeding, reduced many once-wild creatures to almost complete dependency, our responsibility to these animals should be very great. The domesticated creature usually can not get along without man and the specific conditions in which it has been bred to exist. Dependency is often unilateral, although it is true that domestic animals may fill a definite human, social or psychological need in some instances. The responsibility we have for the domestic animal is often to an individual animal, and whether to individual or group, never extends beyond a confined situation. That is, a population or a species is not a matter of concern here. Management is intensive and it is the individual animal that is most important to us.

Man on the other hand has not reduced wild creatures to a dependency requiring his daily attention although, to be sure, the wild animals' continued existence depends upon him. The individual wild creature is not usually dependent upon one or a few humans. Our responsibility is then not to the individual but to a species, and often to a population of wild animals. As the fox told the Little Prince, this is the difference between the tame and the wild. With tamed or domesticated species, primary responsibility is to the individual or group, and with wild animals, primary responsibility is to the species, or population. The Little Prince would have a specific responsibility to one fox if he tamed that fox. Perhaps, with the Little Prince, we have a collective responsibility to wild populations and to all species. In dealing with the many wild animal-human conflicts such as those between dolphins, seals, and man all preying upon one food supply, the questions of animal awareness, animal rights, and the differences in our responsibilities between the tame and the wild may all come into consideration. The wildlife manager must try to understand as many of the conflicting scientific, humanistic, and historical factors as possible as well as why different people feel as they do.

Attitudes and Values

Few people in our developed societies will fail to express an opinion on an issue involving wild birds or mammals, and many people in underdeveloped countries will also speak out. Sometimes it is obvious that a person's opinions are affected strongly by his degree of dependence on a wild animal population. In other cases, it is obvious that a farmer suffering losses from depredating deer will have opinions on what should be done with the deer! For others, however, the reasons for their emotions about wild animals and issues concerning them are less clear-cut. Wildlife managers should be knowledgeable about attitudes and the elements involved in developing them among the many human population subgroups concerned in any wildlife question. Possibly the only way of gaining this understanding in each instance is to conduct intensive surveys, sampling the various subgroups present. For our purposes, an understanding of how attitudes may differ and what subgroups there are is perhaps most important.

One of the most detailed studies involving attitudes in North American society was completed for the U.S. Fish and Wildlife Service through the

Yale University School of Forestry and Environmental Studies. The attitudes believed to exist among American publics as defined by Kellert are as follows:

Naturalistic: Primary interests and affection for wildlife and the outdoors.

Ecologistic: Primary concern for the environment as a system, for interrelationships between wildlife species and natural habitats.

Humanistic: Primary interest and strong affection for individual animals, principally pets. Regarding wildlife, focus is on large attractive animals with strong anthropomorphic associations.

Moralistic: Primary concern for the right and wrong treatment of animals, with strong opposition to exploitation of and cruelty toward animals.

Scientistic: Primary interest in the physical attributes and biological functioning of animals.

Aesthetic: Primary interest in the artistic and symbolic characteristics of animals.

Utilitarian: Primary concern for the practical and material value of animals.

Dominionistic: Primary satisfaction derived from mastery and control over animals, typically in sporting situations.

Negativistic: Primary orientation on active avoidance of animals due to fear or dislike.

Neutralistic: Primary orientation a passive avoidance of animals due to indifference.

As might be expected, Kellert found that moralistic and utilitarian attitudes conflicted "around the theme of exploitation of animals," while the negativistic and humanistic attitudes tended to conflict "around the theme of affection for animals." A general picture of public attitudes concerning wildlife in the U.S. as derived from the Kellert studies is provided in Table 2.1.

The kinds of factors influencing or forming attitudes in North American society are extremely diverse. Perhaps this is a reflection of the cultural complexity and the rapidly changing concepts affecting developed societies today. Kellert examined regular demographic parameters such as sex, age, marital status, education, income, and profession: he also checked wildlife-related or animal-related interest groups, some occupations, and whether or not individuals attended church (termed "religiousity" in the reports). We might simplify this matter somewhat by looking at attitude formation as reflections of what we do or what we are, and who we are.

Attitudes are not always inclusive; not all wildlife may be viewed as sacred, worthy of preserving, or worthy of killing. Rats, for instance, are viewed quite differently from deer both by those who would preserve deer and those who would hunt them. It depends upon the animal. All lives of wild creatures are not equal in the eyes of man except in a few instances, perhaps, such as with the Jains of India or a certain few individuals who extend a reverence

Table 2.1 Attitude Occurrence in American Society[1]

Attitude	Estimated % of American Population Strongly Oriented Towards the Attitude[1]	Common Behavioral Expressions	Most Related Values/Benefits
Naturalistic	10%	Outdoor wildlife related recreation—backcountry use, nature birding and nature hunting.	Outdoor recreation
Ecologistic	7%	Conservation support, activism and membership, ecological study.	Ecological
Humanistic	35%	Pets, wildlife tourism, casual zoo visitation	Consumptive, utilitarian
Moralistic	20%	Animal welfare support/membership, kindness to animals	Ethical, existence
Scientistic	1%	Scientific study/hobbies, collecting	Scientific
Aesthetic	15%	Nature appreciation, art, wildlife tourism	Aesthetic
Utilitarian	20%	Consumption of furs, raising meat, bounties, meat hunting	Consumptive, utilitarian
Dominionistic	3%	Animal spectator sports, trophy hunting	Sporting
Negativistic	2%	Cruelty, overt fear behavior	Little or negative
Neutralistic	35%	Avoidance of animal behavior	Little or negative

[1]From Kellert, 1980, in Shaw and Zube Eds., 1980.

for life to animals, as Schweitzer appeared to have done for a part of his life. Meadow voles are viewed differently from seals, and starlings differently from warblers. Such variability can lead to an overemphasis on a narrow segment of wildlife, as noted by Kellert, and "overlook more basic considerations of ecological relationships between wildlife and their natural habitats."

In addition to this selectivity of human attitudes toward wildlife, views are often a partial reflection of what people do. This is particularly true of those who obtain their living from the land as farmers, woodsmen, and trappers. In each instance their own economic resource is of primary importance, as might be expected. Farmers and agriculturalists in ancillary services and industrial areas may view the crop as paramount. If a wildlife species is a pest requiring control, their view of the species is likely to be negative. If a farmer is also a naturalist, a hunter, or both, his views may sometimes be ambivalent. Or if no wildlife species affects the individual detrimentally and that person has a naturalist's or hunter's interest, his view may be positive. On balance, the general view from agriculture is likely to be negative, as are many of the agricultural land-use practices which reduce type diversity or eliminate wetland areas. Of course, some agricultural practices have also benefitted many wildlife species.

Foresters, too, will normally have a negative view of any species that may damage reforested areas or restrict natural regeneration and stocking rates. In many instances where single species tree management is encouraged on natural mixed forest sites, wildlife species will suffer because of the decline in plant diversity. Harvesting practices can be either detrimental or beneficial to certain species of wildlife, but since economic considerations will generally determine what these practices are, they will often end up being harmful. As in the case of agriculturalists, and indeed with people in any profession, anywhere, there are some who view wildlife ambivalently and some who are sympathetic to it.

Trappers tend to see wildlife as an economic entity to be managed to provide maximum numbers of animals for harvest and optimum numbers for habitats. They usually have a positive view, wanting to retain species and maintain populations as high as the habitat will allow. They may also be naturalists and invariably are more familiar with their prey's habits than either the average hunter or the average preservationist. Successful trappers must be knowledgeable, and their view is neither more nor less selfish than that of preservationists or farmers. It is in regard to trapping that the humaneness issue has become most important in affecting the management of wildlife. Nowhere has the humane movement been more effective, for better or for worse as far as species are concerned, than in North America and most especially in Canada. The Federal-Provincial Committee for Humane Trapping Report (1981) is a striking example of people's concern with the individual wild animal rather than the population or the species. It has resulted in changes in trapping regulations in most Canadian jurisdictions. Follow-up work of a similar nature by the Fur Institute of Canada also has affected regulations.

Apart from the primary land-based occupations and professions there are few generalities worth considering. It is obvious perhaps, that if there is an economic dimension involved, a person's view will tend to favor whatever is seen to benefit the species in order to continue benefitting the pocketbook. Job or profession related familiarity with wildlife may also help formulate a person's view. Usually the less direct contact someone has had with the land and its ecosystems, including wildlife, the more likely he is to have protective feelings of all animals, especially if his first experiences in natural settings began later in life. But there are many exceptions that may reflect what or who we are or where we live.

Another area which may influence people's views about animals is related to what they are: their sex, age, income, education, and whether they own land or not. Where they live may also be important and whether they are first or second generation residents of the city, country, or certain geographic regions (as Kellert studied in relation to Alaska, the South, and the Rocky Mountain states). Sometimes what or who we are may be the most important element in determining our views on wildlife. Immigrants from a culture with a utilitarian concept of animals may well have different attitudes from a fourth generation American or Canadian whose ancestors came from England. Our ethnic origins may affect our opinion, and sometimes so may our personal theology.

Understanding the bases of attitudes among the various publics he deals with can be helpful to the wildlife manager who faces a great challenge in coping with the conflicting views expressed, and politicized, concerning wildlife issues today. As Kellert has noted:

> While the frequency of positive feeling and concern for animal welfare in America today is somewhat pleasing to note, the emotional rather than intellectual basis for this interest, and its greater focus on pets and limited wildlife species, poses some potential problems.

And further that:

> It will require much patience, empathy and tolerance, and a willingness to be involved with many different kinds of people. The challenge is great, but so are the stakes, and the future well-being of our wildlife resources may depend on the outcome.

The attitudes expressed by Americans in the studies referred to here may be different only in degree from those in other developed countries. In 1981, the European Common Market voted to restrict the sale of manufactured seal commodities in Europe, and this decision was a reflection of the seal hunt controversy in Canada. Perhaps then, attitudes are not greatly different among the industrialized societies, at least concerning issues such as seals and whales. We know that attitudes may be very different between populations of underdeveloped countries and those of industrialized nations; it is important for us to understand this. The utilitarian attitudes of those underdeveloped countries are considered in Chapter 10.

Some human attitudes are closely tied to economic interests, but wildlife values include both conventional economic categories and the less tangible categories in which the measurement of a wildlife experience is more difficult. Wildlife values include a number of categories that either do not enter a market (or national) economy, or cannot readily be estimated in comparative market terms, or both. In recent years economists, sociologists, psychologists, and wildlife managers have all attempted to develop means of measuring wildlife values. Giles (1978) provides a list of twenty-five ways to measure them, and Steinhoff reviews several conceptual systems used for this purpose (Table 2.2). The classification or typology used by a wildlife manager will often depend upon the type of evaluation, survey, or report involved. We consider the King (1947) classification to be easily understood and applied, and this conclusion is also reached by Steinhoff. According to King, all wildlife values and services may be included under six general headings as follows.

1. Commercial values: income derived from sales of wild animals or their products or from direst and controlled use of wild animals and their progeny.
2. Recreational values: monies expended in the pursuit of wildlife in connection with sports and hobbies.
3. Biological values: the worth of the services rendered man by wild animals.
4. Social values: values accruing to communities from the use of wildlife and values associated with organizations that exist because of a common interest in wildlife.
5. Aesthetic values: the values of objects and places possessing beauty, affording inspiration and opportunities for communion, contributing to the arts, etc.
6. Scientific values: values realized through the use of wildlife as a means

Table 2.2 Classification Systems Proposed for Wildlife Values or Related Values.[1]

Author of System	Basis of System	All[2] Values	All[3] Uses	Exclusive[4]	Categories of Value	
King (1947)	The Experience	Yes	Yes	Yes	Recreational Aesthetic Educational	Biological Social Commercial
Hendee (1969)	The Experience	No	No	Yes	Appreciative Consumptive Passive Free-Play	Sociable Learning Active-Expressive
Hendee (1974)	The Experience	No	No	Yes	Back-Country Hunt General Season Party Hunt Meat Hunt Special Skills Hunt Fly Only	Cast-drifting Boat-drifting Plunking etc. (example)
Shaw (1974)	The Experience	No	No	Yes	Utility or Nuisance Consumptive Recreational Aesthetic or Existence	
Hendee (1974)	Elements of Experience	No	No	Yes	Solitude Companionship Escapism Nature Appreciation	Outdoor Skill Trophy Exercise
Nobe & Steinhoff (1973)	Economic Interest	Yes?	No	No	Direct Users Primary Beneficiaries Secondary Beneficiaries Alternative Resource User	Vicarious User Altruist Environmentalist Option Holder

Swartzman & Van Dyne (1975)	Quality of Life	Yes	No	Yes	I. Economic
					  1. Income per capita
					  2. Employment stability
					  3. Net regional product change
					  4. Income distribution
					II. Ecological
					  5. Ecological degradation
					  6. Environmental quality index
					  7. Percentage use of renewable resources
					  8. Annual percent usage of non-renewable resources
					  9. Man-initiated energy consumption
					III. Sociocultural
					  10. Population size
					  11. Social differentiation
					  12. Cultural heterogenity
					  13. Sociopsychological
					  14. Information advantage
					IV. Political
					  15. Scope of governmental services
					  16. Uses of government services
					  17. Political participation
					  18. Property tax base
					  19. Political power advantage
					  20. Dollar investment

Kellert (1978)	Attitude	Yes	No	No	Utilitarian Naturalistic Dominionistic Humanistic Ecologistic Moralistic Negativistic Knowledge of Animals Scientistic Aesthetic
More (1973)	Attitude	No	No	Yes	Display Esthetic Affiliation Pioneering Kill Exploration Challenge

		Includes all wildlife values?[2]	Applicable to all uses?[3]	Mutually exclusive categories?[4]	

Langford & Cocheba (1978)	Sources of Activities	No	No	Yes	I. Current Period Values
					  A. Sensory Perception Values
					    1. Recreational hunting activity
					    2. Non-hunting recreational activity
					      a. Wildlife-based activities
					      b. Wildlife-related activities
					      c. Endemic-wildlife activities
					      d. Recording-based wildlife activities
					  B. Existence Values
					    1. Contemplative wildlife activities
					II. Future Period Values
					  A. Option Values
					    1. Option demand activities

Rolston (1979)	Philosophical Criteria	Yes	Yes	Yes	Economic Life-support Recreational Scientific Aesthetic Life-intelligibility Plurality-unity Stability-freedom Dialectical-environmental Sacramental
Raths et al. (1966)	Educational Criteria	No	No	No	Money Friendship Love and sex Religion and morals Leisure Work Family Maturity Character traits Politics and social origin

[1] Steinhoff, H. W. 1980. Analysis of major conceptual systems for understanding and measuring wildlife values. In W. W. Shaw and E. H. Zube, eds. Wildlife values. USDA Forest Service.

[2] Includes all wildlife values?
[3] Applicable to all uses?
[4] Mutually exclusive categories?

of investigating certain fundamental and widespread natural phenomena.

All of these value categories can be subdivided, and some values can be considered to be both social and scientific (the use of animals in cancer research can create medical and social benefits); or biological and social (use of predators to control pest species is a biological value that translates into commercial and/or social benefits). Other groupings may be apparent to you as well; however, there are often problems of precise definition in dealing with any value classification. Some people feel for instance that the term *consumptive* for a resource entity removed from its habitat and *nonconsumptive* for those entities used and enjoyed but not removed from their natural settings are not definitive. The argument here is that human impact on certain nonconsumptive natural areas so alters the setting that the original condition no longer exists for enjoyment. It is effectively removed.

Obviously, it is necessary to have some means of evaluating wildlife in order to measure elements of the resource and compare the measurements with those of other resources. It is also important in many instances to combine all values: the economic (or commercial, including recreational in King's classification), the socio-cultural (including aesthetic), ecological (including biological), and the scientific in order to provide the kinds of measurements and demand data needed to develop the required management activities, which when supported by adequate budgets provide for effective wildlife programs. In other instances, competitive agencies or interest groups may be involved in planning for the same land unit. Then not only the total wildlife resource must be measured, including the vegetation, fishes, and invertebrates, but also the land itself relative to is productive capacity for both wildlife and competitive resources.

Besides consideration of the wildlife itself, the evaluation process has other significant aspects. Appraisal of relevant wildlife activities and programs is important in maintaining budgets and personnel and effecting changes in research and management policy. In Canada, the federal government has a built-in evaluation methodology within the annual budget process for each wildlife branch and program. In addition, regular in-depth evaluations are made every few years. Similar annual assessments requiring rationalization and budget defense are also commonplace in most other North American jurisdictions.

The many questions of attitudes, ethics, cultures, and socio-economic values relative to wildlife encompass far too broad an area for all wildlife managers to keep fully abreast. Perhaps the best most of us can do is to be aware of the literature, the professions, and the interest groups in the complex process. We can thereby tap the resources and expertise required each time we are faced with human social problems we may not be adequately trained or equipped to handle.

Many issues wildlife managers face today deal with areas of conflict among people or between animals and people. They may not be whale-fish-human conflicts or utilization versus preservation issues, but often will involve justification of management activity. This is usually required for senior people in a wildlife branch and at other levels of government, but it may also be necessary to communicate with several publics that benefit from, or are interested in, the resource you are working with; these publics may be diametrically opposed relative to a philosophy of use. As a wildlife manager, you may have to defend your activities to various groups of nonhunters and different types of sportsmen at the same time. Your task will not be easy even though you may have the help of an effective education and information unit. The manager's role will be increasingly difficult as attitudes become more widely expressed and politicized.

Wildlife managers must prepare themselves on a broader front than they have done in the past. Today, in addition to the scientific, biological, or ecological data bases they normally obtain for their management project they must also:

a. Possess an understanding of their responsibility to the species and the wild population in question.
b. Try to obtain as complete an understanding as possible of the various views of all interested groups of people, including those benefitting directly and those not benefitting directly but who might influence policies through expression of a moralistic, humanistic or other attitude.
c. Have an understanding of the total value of the resource and how that resource and its management fit into the total management program.

Culture, Conflicts, and Values: Examples

Although we usually do not have to search to find conflict in relation to management of wildlife, there are some areas of our globe where the cultural and economic bases of conflict are exemplified better than in others. One such area is Trinidad and Tobago, two islands close to the coast of Venezuela, that obtained independence from Great Britain in 1962.

When last assessed in 1983,there were about 400 species of birds, 100 mammals (including 58 bats), 600 butterflies and some 70 reptiles present on the islands. Trinidad was once a part of the South American mainland and reflects a continental flora and fauna rather than a Caribbean.

Few changes have occurred in the Game Ordinance of 1958. There is a six-month open season on legally hunted animals, no bag limit, and either sex may be killed. Wild meat is legally sold commercially during the open season and often illegally during the closed season. Trap guns, deadly devices ostensibly set for game, are "hunting" 365 days of the year and often kill dogs and maim humans. Birds are frequently trapped and sold inside the country and sometimes smuggled into the United States. The ordinance places all bats on the vermin list to be killed anytime by any means. Many reptiles, birds, and other mammals are also declared vermin. The legal game are cayman (alligator), all lizards, the agouti, the paca, the deer (*Mazama* sp.), the armadillo, and the peccary. Among the legal birds are scarlet ibis (a national emblem), plovers, ducks, herons, cormorants, rails, sandpipers, and many more. Some species of cage birds are extinct and others are endangered; some mammals such as the ocelot and tayra are threatened.

There are four levels of interest clearly identified in the society. One is that of the naturalist and scientist. This is an elite group of about 500 people who publish regularly and share a common desire to conserve animals. A second is the legal hunter (7,000–10,000), but this group is heterogeneous in that perhaps 10–20 percent are conservationists and the remainder are not. A third group is the professional or commercial hunter who obtains his living, or a part of his living, from hunting, and a fourth group is comprised of the consumers of wild meat. This latter group apparently includes businessmen, some professional people, and some senior people in government. There is a constant and ready local market for wild meat which, with the increasing scarcity of game, may bring $40 a kilo in local currency. A single deer or paca can bring in excess of $400!

Policies since independence often have encouraged farm land abandonment, illegal squatting in the forests, quarrying of hillsides, and deforestation of state lands. Policies have not usually provided work incentives nor encouraged either personal or social discipline. There is essentially no game law enforcement.

Although Oriental, Spanish, French, and English elements are present in the population, the two major groups of people are those of African origin and those from India. Racism is a problem and may thwart cooperative endeavors in the civil service. In wildlife matters, much time is spent in controversy. As in many former British colonies, the East Indian has assumed primacy over the business area of the economy and the economic infrastructure. Because those of African origin hold the numerical and voting edge, they have controlled government since independence.

People of both African and Indian origin are involved in trying to enforce game regulations but are subjected to considerable danger if they work in an area where people of an opposing culture live. If they are employed in a region settled by people of their own origin, however, they are subject to bribery, and the temptation is great. The following portions from an anonymous letter written by a Trinidad game warden help place their role in perspective:

Firearm owners lend their guns for other hunters to shoot wildlife. Today there is a rapid increase of unlicensed and trap guns in the forest. Yet as a Forest Officer or Game Warden you've no authority to request the person's Firearm User's License. This is a very dangerous situation.

It is the Game Wardens and Forest Rangers who are exposed to all the dangers of traps, hunter's menacing threats and yet we are not armed. Many officers are often abused and insulted, they know of a lot of illegal activities practiced out there but fear and frustration keep them quiet. As an officer you have authority to charge people for committing an offense. Yet, I believe it is very tough for an unarmed officer to even try to talk to four men carrying unlicensed guns. You see, in the law of nature, self preservation is first. Morale in staff is very low. There is no spirit of brotherhood among the senior personnel of Wildlife Staff and that gap seems to be growing wider daily. Certain young officers also believe that they are superior to men with fifteen to twenty years service by virtue of their E.C.I.A.F. training. I have been threatened, a man tried to chop me and I was not armed. I had to run to save my life. Obviously this has me very depressed and sad.

Too many people are granted permission to hunt. This should be controlled and all hunters should be members of a bona-fida Association. There should be complete ban on the sale of wild meat at the present time. However, if there are projects such as Wildlife farming, then the sale of wild meat from the farms should be approved. All of the protected species such as porcupines, red howler monkeys and mataperro (anteater) are shot ruthlessly and sold to unsuspecting consumers as the more popular species.

Rapid exploitation of the forest such as squatting for short term crops, marijuana cultivation, quarrying and felling of Forest fruit trees have also affected Wildlife populations tremendously.

Providing that hunting continues at the present rate for two decades, our wildlife will become very negligible. Despite all the appeals by the few interested Naturalists and a bunch of frustrated officers, very few hunters hear the voices "crying in the wilderness." Their sole intention is to kill and eat. They shoot pregnant deer, agoutis and lappes. I have heard reports of an extremely greedy hunter killing thirty pregnant agoutis during the closed season.

Parents allow their children to trap robins, use laglee to trap birds. I know of mothers who are so greedy for wild meat that they allow their sons to hunt for hours during the night for manicous (opossum), deer, tatoo (armadillo) and lappe (paca). They usually serve visitors with the wild meat favors.

It is time administration make a positive decision or allow the Wildlife to become extinct by greedy hunters out there.

How should such a state of affairs be approached? Is it logical to try to ban the sale of wild meat if monied people provide the demand? Why should the country become a party to international conventions when the voting populace profits from the sale of rare live birds? How can government be expected to support disciplinary action over such measures as wildlife when the citizens' votes are coveted?

Although some progress in conservation has been made since these conditions were described in 1984, it may be that only the extinction of several species will make all the interest groups realize that their profit and their enjoyment will not continue in the absence of the resource.

A North American Example

Perhaps one of the most complex "culture-conflict-value" problems facing wildlifers today is right here at home. This is the native rights to wildlife issue. While the wildlife issues involved are only part of a larger political milieu, they are important primarily because of the potential effects on wildlife populations and the many use conflicts they bring about between native peoples and other vested wildlife interests. There are three data bases which must be studied if we are to begin to understand such issues. One is the anthropological base relative to the various native groups and tribes, their original degree of agrarian development, their use of wild plants and animals, their degree of nomadism, their seasonal food cycles, their governments, aspects of slavery, warfare between tribes, and effects of European contact on their manner of living. A second is the historical data base regarding all European - Indian conflicts related to European settlement, for a period of over 250 years and the many agreements, treaties, and proclamations that resulted from them. The third is the growing volume of judicial decisions and case law pertaining to aspects of self government, land claims, rights on and off native lands and, most particularly, the decisions involving "rights" to wildlife which usually are based upon early treaties. All of these information sets only tell us something of the complexity of the issues. They do not provide answers for us.

Rather than try to consider such problems as a whole, let us look at some examples which illustrate the kinds of wildlife issues that will be facing us with increasing frequency over the next several years.

In September, 1980, James Matthew Simon, a registered Indian under the "Indian Act" and an adult member of the Shubenacadie Band in Nova Scotia, was driving on a public road adjacent to the Shubenacadie Indian Brook Reserve. Mr. Simon was stopped by the RCMP and searched. He was found, during a closed season, to be in possession of a shotgun and shells of a type not permitted by the Provincial Lands and Forests Act. Mr. Simon was charged with offenses under the Lands and Forests Act. He pleaded in his defence the applicability of the Treaty of 1752.

Mr. Simon was convicted by the Nova Scotia Provincial Court. His appeal from that conviction was dismissed by the Nova Scotia Supreme Court, Appeal Division. Ultimately, he was granted leave to appeal to the Supreme Court of Canada. The decision of the Supreme Court was rendered 21 November, 1985.

What James Matthew Simon v. The Queen, (1985) 2 S.C.R. 387 decided is the subject of debate and interpretation, but includes the following:

1. The Treaty of 1752 was a binding and enforceable agreement between the British and the Mi'kmaq people. "Both the Governor and the Micmacs entered into the Treaty with the intention of creating mutually binding obligations which would be solemnly respected."
2. The Treaty contained a positive recognition of the existing and continuing Indian right to hunt and constituted a source of protection against infringement of these hunting rights.
3. The courts would interpret the Treaty provisions in a liberal and flexible manner which would accord with modern day practice. For example, hunting would not be restricted to the use of spears and handmade knives, as argued by the Attorney General of Nova Scotia. The interpretation of the hunting right would also not be restricted to hunting only for noncommercial purposes.
4. The Supreme Court of Canada held that there was no evidence to indicate that the Treaty of 1752 had been terminated by hostilities, and that the burden of proving any such termination would be upon the Attorney General of Nova Scotia.
5. The Court held that, at a minimum, the Treaty was still available to protect hunting on reserve lands and, as a result, Mr. Simon would have the free right to transport guns and munitions in a safe manner to these areas to carry on hunting activities. Consequently, his possession of the firearms was not contrary to the Lands and Forests Act.
6. The Court ruled that if it is legally possible to extinguish treaty rights

to certain lands by non-Indian occupation, the onus is on the Crown to prove it.

7. The court would not require proof of descendancy of any present day Indian to any particular person in 1752, provided the person concerned could establish a significant connection with those included in the original treaty.

Since the Treaty of 1752 was a valid and enforceable treaty available to Mr. Simon, it overrode the provisions of the Provincial Lands and Forests Act. Mr. Simon was acquitted as a result.

Regardless of what questions may be posed, the most important aspect to the wildlife manager is the challenge to incorporate whatever manner of legal harvesting may result from such decisions into a system which will allow for population management at the level that may be required. This is a concern not dealt with by the courts, and it seems clear both from recent court decisions in Canada and from an excellent review of trapping by aboriginal people by Peter Hutchins (1987), that the fate of wild populations and perhaps even species will not normally be considered in such judgements. This may well mean that the wildlife manager will have to take it upon himself to provide wildlife population and habitat data to all involved and to convince native populations that wildlife should not become a pawn in what are serious political issues. People will come first, most certainly, both native people and other user groups, but sacrificing good wildlife management in power struggles for political gain makes little sense either for the people who stand to gain or the wildlife that stands to lose.

In a recent decision, The Queen v. Thomas Chevrier, an Ontario District Court granted an appeal of Chevrier's conviction for hunting moose out of season. Chevrier, a non-status Metis, had his conviction quashed and was acquitted. The bases of the appeal decisions were:

1. The accused inherited the right to hunt granted to his ancestors by the Crown in exercise of its jurisdiction over Indians. The province has no jurisdiction to take away that right even though the present holder may not be an Indian.
2. Even though the province cannot negate treaty rights, the federal government may still retain the power to regulate their exercise.
3. The Provincial Court Judge erred in holding that the accused's right was a community right which could only be upheld by representative action.

The District Court Judge added the following comments concerning wildlife and rights to wildlife:

"To those who are concerned that this decision may lead to the destruction of our wildlife resources I can only say:

1. This decision will not lead to unrestricted hunting by everyone claiming to have an Indian ancestor because relatively few, other than status Indians, will be able to prove their descent from a signatory tribe.
2. The whites who rely upon these resources must do so recognizing that these resources have come to them subject to prior claims.
3. Although provincial law cannot negate these treaty rights the federal government may still retain the power to regulate the exercise of these rights for the good of everyone.
4. In the final analysis, everyone with a legitimate interest in the continuation of our wildlife resources must agree upon the proper management of these resources. If this is not done we may see animals such as the moose melt from our forests as has the woodland caribou."

Meanwhile, native people in Nova Scotia recently have been awarded a right to "any surplus" in relation to salmon and both the Crown and the native people are considering the addition of wildlife under provincial jurisdiction (Denny, Paul and Sylliboy vs the Queen, March 5, 1990).

In addition to the question of subsistence and religious rights, there has been friction in the U.S. between state wildlife agencies and tribes over who had the authority to regulate non-Indians on reservations. In 1983, the Supreme Court ruled on a case between New Mexico and the Mescalero Apaches. The tribe filed suit because the state was attempting to enforce the state hunting and fishing regulations on non-members of the tribe when they were hunting or fishing on the reservation. Many of the tribal regulations were more liberal than the state's. The ruling stated that the Mescaleros had with federal (BIA, BLM) assistance established a comprehensive scheme for managing the fish and wildlife resources on the reservation. New Mexico's laws on the reservation were pre-empted by federal law.

At the time of the decision, a number of tribes were locked in battle with state agencies over regulation of non-tribal members on reservation lands. The Mescalero decision paved the way for compromise and probably more effective wildlife management on reservations. Cooperation became imperative if the states were to retain any ability to regulate or even monitor hunting activities on tribal lands.

Perhaps the most controversial decision to date in the United States related to resource allocation to native peoples was that of Judge Boldt (United States vs. Washington) in 1974. Although the "Boldt Decision" concerned the rights of a number of northwestern Indian tribes to fish in the Puget Sound and Olympic Peninsula watersheds and adjacent off shore waters, in reality it placed a serious limitation to the state faunal ownership theory. The judge interpreted the treaty language "in common with" to mean sharing equally the opportunity to take fish at traditional fishing areas. The tribes were given the chance to harvest 50 percent of the fish that would be available at the traditional sites above the population necessary for minimum conservation purposes. A few months later, Judge Belloni, in Oregon, made a decision to apply the same 50 percent apportionment to the treaty Indians fishing in the Columbia River system (included in both Oregon and Washington states).

Wildlife managers have not overlooked the possibility that a similar decision could be handed down in the future for any wildlife resource. Consider the implication of a decision that might allocate 25 percent of the elk "surplus" to native Americans in the western states.

Throughout North America, federal, state and provincial jurisdictions will be struggling to effect cooperative management in the 1990's. This is a struggle that will result in amendments to legislation and new structures for experimental management; with good will on the part of negotiating parties, the results will be continued healthy wildlife populations for everyone.

Bibliography

Anon. Enos 1:3.

Anon. Genesis 10:8–9.

Anon. John 21.

Anon. Leviticus 17:15.

Anon. Luke 5 and 24:41–43.

Anon. Mark 6:38–44.

Burley, D. V. 1981. Rapid culture change and the fur trade: A case for the Micmacs of Northeastern New Brunswick. Parks Canada, Winnipeg. (mimeo) 29 pp.

Clutton-Brock, J. 1981. Domesticated animals from early times. University of Texas Press, Austin, TX. 208 pp.

Dodds, D. G. 1976. Evolution of wildlife harvesting systems in Africa. Trans. Fed.-Prov. Wildl. Conf. 40:106–113.

Dodds, D. G. 1982. Micmac food resources at European contact. Presented to Canadian Ethnology Society, Vancouver, B. C. (mimeo) 22 pp.

Federal-Provincial Wildlife Conference. Undated (1981). Report of the Federal Provincial Committee for Humane Trapping. 4 parts.

Filion, F. L., S. Parker, and E. DuWors. 1988. The importance of wildlife to Canadians. Can. Wildl. Serv., Ottawa. 29 pp.

Giles, R. H., Jr. 1978. Wildlife management. W. H. Freeman, San Francisco, CA. 416 pp.

Griffin, D. R. 1976. The question of animal awareness. The Rockefeller University Press, New York, NY. 153 pp.

Howell, F. C. 1971. Early man. Time-Life Books, New York, NY. 200 pp.

Hutchins, P. W. 1987. The law applying to the trapping of furbearers by aboriginal peoples in Canada: a case of double jeopardy. Pp. 31–48; *In* wild furbearer management and conservation in North America. Novak, M., J. A. Baker, M. E. Obbard, and B. Malloch, Eds. Out. Min. Nat. Resour., Toronto, Canada.

Kellert, S. R. 1979. Public attitudes toward critical wildlife and natural habitat issues. U.S. Fish and Wildlife Service, Washington. Rep. by N.T.I.S., U.S. Dept. Commerce, Springfield, VA. 138 pp.

Kellert, S. R. 1980a. Contemporary values of wildlife in American society. Pp. 31–60, *In* Wildlife values. W. Shaw and E. Zube, Eds. Institutional Series Report No. 1, Center for Assessment of Non-commodity Material Resource Values. Rocky Mt. For. Range Exp. Sta., U.S. Dept. Agric. For. Serv.

Kellert, S. R. 1980b. Activities of the American public relating to animals. U.S. Fish and Wildlife Service, Washington. Rep. by N.T.I.S., U.S. Dept. Commerce, Springfield, VA. 178 pp.

Kellert, S. R. and J. K. Berry. 1980. Knowledge, affection and basic attitudes toward animals in American society. U.S. Fish and Wildlife Service, Washington. Rep. by N.T.I.S., U.S. Dept. Commerce, Springfield, VA. 162 pp.

Kertzer, M. N. 1955. What is a Jew? Pp. 65–72, *In* A guide to the religions of America. Simon and Schuster, New York, NY.

King, R. T. 1947. The future of wildlife in forest land use. Trans. N. Am. Wildl. Conf. 12:454–467.

Martin, C. 1978a. The war between the Indians and the animals. Nat. Hist. 87:92–96.

Saint-Exupery, A. de. 1943. The little prince. Harcourt, Brace and World, Inc., New York, NY. 91 pp.

Steinhoff, H. W. 1980. Analysis of major conceptual systems for understanding and measuring wildlife values. Pp. 11–21, *In* Wildlife values. W. Shaw and E. Zube, Eds. Institutional series report No. 1 Center for Assessment of Non-Commodity Natural Resource Values. Rocky Mt. For. Range Exp. Stat., U.S. Dept. Agric. For. Serv.

Whisker, J. B. 1981. The right to hunt. North River Press, Croton-on-Hudson, NY. 173 pp.

Willett, L. T. 1982. Making tabagie: a Micmac parallel to the potlatch? Presented to Canadian Ethnology Society, Vancouver, B.C. (mimeo). 13 pp.

Recommended Readings

Clutton-Brock. J. 1981. Domesticated animals from early times. University of Texas Press, Austin TX. 208 pp.

A well documented account of how animals came to be used by man; when and where it first happened.

Griffin, D. R. 1976. The question of animal awareness. The Rockefeller University Press, New York, NY. 135 pp.

An eminent scientist considers animal awareness from a balanced, unemotional viewpoint.

Herscovici, A. 1985. Second nature. CBC Enterprises, Toronto, ON. 254 pp.

An examination of the animal-rights controversy as exemplified by sealing and trapping issues in Canada.

Martin, C. 1978. Keepers of the game. Indian-animal relations and the fur trade. University of California Press, Berkeley, CA. 226 pp.

An anthropologist's detailed interpretation of Amerindian-animal relationships.

Whisker, J. B. 1981. The right to hunt. North River Press, Croton-on-Hudson, NY. 173 pp.

The first unabashed defense of hunting written by a non-wildlifer includes an unusual review of the literature.

III

The BIOLOGICAL BASES for MANAGEMENT

What are the biological data that need to be known for effective management? Chapter 3 includes considerations such as numerical changes in populations, birth and death rates, and sex and age composition. Equally important to the manager is a knowledge of the factors, such as habitat quality, social interactions, and genetics, effecting these population changes. The more sophisticated models being developed to aid in management decision-making incorporate most of these parameters.

Nutrition and Energetics

Animal species have nutritional requirements that vary with physiological and physical condition, age, sex, and social status. A certain amount of energy needs to be ingested to sustain the metabolic requirements of the individual. A true measure of environmental carrying capacity thus becomes the energy and nutritional elements available to a species within a given area. While social constraints may provide additional limitations to population size, it is the available energy that determines the maximum number of individuals of given age and sex categories that can be accommodated at any particular time of year.

As Moen (1973) stated, "There is an obvious need—for knowledge of the requirements of an animal for maintenance and productive purposes before a meaningful biological appraisal of carrying capacity can be made." Fortunately, there is a growing body of information on the biological energy requirements of wild animals. Although ruminants, especially deer, lead the list (Baker et al., 1979; Fancy and White 1987; Luick and White 1986; Robbins et al., 1979; Kautz et al., 1982; Regelin et al. 1985; Renecker and Hudson 1986), considerable work has been done on other herbivores including rabbit (Rose, 1973, 1974), and on omnivores and carnivores: polar bear (Hurst et al., 1982), coyote (Litvaitis and Mautz 1980; Shield 1972), bald eagle (Stalmaster and Gessaman 1982), wild turkey (Gray and Prince 1988), and raccoon (Teubner and Barrett 1982).

Basic questions that need answering include: what foods are eaten by the animal, what energy is contained therein, and how much of this energy is utilized by the animal? For example, Schitoskey and Woodmansee (1979) determined the monthly diets of California ground squirrels (*Spermophilus beecheyi fisheri*) and the availability of forage on the range land they use. Knowing the average energy requirement per animal per month and the assimilation efficiencies for foliage eaten, they calculated the support capacity of the range per month and the percent of available forage utilized by the existing population as follows (after Harris 1970):

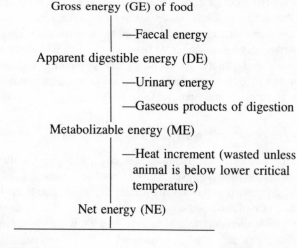

Gross energy (GE) of food

—Faecal energy

Apparent digestible energy (DE)

—Urinary energy

—Gaseous products of digestion

Metabolizable energy (ME)

—Heat increment (wasted unless animal is below lower critical temperature)

Net energy (NE)

Maintenance (NE $_m$)
1. basal metabolism
2. homeothermy costs
3. voluntary activity

Production (NE $_p$)
e.g., 1. growth, milk production, hair, semen, etc.
2. work

In addition to determining carrying capacity, Schitoskey and Woodmansee were attempting to determine if the ground squirrels they were studying were depleting the range for domestic cattle. Based on the squirrels' energetic measurements and the known population size and food habits, they were able to show conclusively that the squirrels' maximum utilization of net aboveground plant production for any month was only six percent. This type of analysis can assist the manager in deciding whether competition is a factor which requires action.

Such an energy analysis is actually a very simple expression of carrying capacity because it does not incorporate other important components such as water and protective cover. Although the authors considered costs of pregnancy and lactation, they were unable to construct complete energy budgets for free-ranging animals, as their estimates of energy requirements were derived by respirometry in a laboratory setting.

Although we have considerable data for many species, these data are limited for the most part to basal metabolic measurements or to behaviors and activities restricted by a laboratory environment. The actual energy costs to the animal of food seeking, social interaction, and homeothermy maintenance in a natural setting have yet to be determined for virtually all wildlife species. What is required is a method for indirect measure of energy metabolism that does not constrain the animal and allows a complete and normal behavioral repertoire. Alternatively, complete time budgets for behavior in the wild need to be collected and the energy costs for each behavior then determined in the laboratory. While time budgets can be constructed for some vertebrates which are highly visible and have restricted home ranges, such studies generally require a high manpower input for a relatively limited data return. For example, Potvin and Huot (1983) devised a working model to estimate the carrying capacity of a white-tailed deer wintering area in Quebec, based on measurements of surface area used by deer, forest cover types, browse accessibility, and nutritive requirements of deer expressed in energetic terms. Rather than measuring the time spent in various behaviors, the model predicted what should be the most energetically advantageous physiological response and how energy might be partitioned as a result of different snow covers. The model's primary weakness is the impreciseness of the data used to construct it. The biological data base is still too weak to allow refinement of such costs as locomotion in snow (recent research by Parker et al., (1984) will be of assistance here) and measurement of the relative energy available to an animal selecting food within a given environment. Hanley and Rogers (1989) estimated carrying capacity of black-tailed deer in four hypothetical forest habitats in Alaska during summer and winter using the quantity and quality of available food and the species' nutritional requirements. Three sets of snow conditions and two levels of metabolic requirements for digestible energy and digestible protein were used. One of the limitations of the model was the persistence of the snow condition for the entire winter season; another limitation was that all available forage, within the constraints established, was eaten. Their algorithm nicely illustrated the fundamental importance of habitat, season, and nutritional status if carrying capacity is to be determined.

An alternative technique using isotope injection offers a method for measuring energy expenditure in free ranging animals. A slightly higher daily energy expenditure estimate is given than that based on activity budget analysis because the energy expended in food processing is included. The water isotopes (doubly labeled deuterium and oxygen 18) are injected into an animal. After they have equilibrated, the animal is released. Several days later, the animal is recaptured and a blood sample taken. The difference in the decay rate in body water and CO_2 gives a measure of energy expenditure. But it is a measure of total expenditure over the period of time between samples without regard to habitat use or the animal's behavioral patterns. Nonetheless, with recapture collars now available for many mammals this technique will have increasing value.

Heart rate is one indirect measure of energy metabolism showing considerable promise. It seems to work for white-tailed deer, mule deer, caribou, marten, prairie dogs, green winged teal, black duck, and red squirrel among other species. Until such a method has been confirmed totally and is available for use with free-ranging wildlife, minimum habitat requirements and land-use allocations for wildlife species will continue to be determined on the basis of less definitive data. With a shrinking wildlife habitat base, more precision is required to ensure that critical mistakes are not made when stating habitat needs for any particular species.

Nutrient deficiencies can also cause problems in populations, and managers should be aware of potential difficulties. Selenium deficiency is a particular problem in the Pacific Northwest where grazing ungulates may not be meeting their minimum requirements. This is one suggested reason why such species were never abundant in the intermountain Columbia Basin area of the Pacific Northwest. Acid precipitation can further reduce selenium availability by forming sulphur-selenium complexes.

It is important to know the mineral availabilities in local soils and vegetation and to compensate, if necessary, for problems that may develop at the population level as a result of deficiencies or over-abundances. For instance, pheasants have never become established south of the 39th parallel in eastern North America. Jones et al. (1968) and Anderson and Stewart (1969) presented evidence that pheasant density was related to the inorganic chemistry of the environment. It has been suggested that pheasants have high calcium requirements and their distribution in eastern North America is primarily limited to calcium rich till soils associated with recent glaciation. Anderson and Stewart (1973) found a potential excess of barium in unsorted grit from an area of low pheasant numbers. As calcium concentration in the environment and trace element absorption are inversely related, calcium poor soils would exacerbate any such trace mineral excesses. We might expect an impact on survival, particularly during fall and winter months when pheasants feed heavily on corn and other grains low in calcium and concurrently consume relatively small amounts of calcitic grit. Such a seasonal response of high fall-to-spring mortality on calcium poor soils may illustrate a toxic response to increased barium concentration in body tissues.

Fraser et al. (1980) have shown that sodium appears to be the major mineral sought by wildlife using mineral licks. Many herbivorous terrestrial mammals cannot meet their physiological needs for certain minerals from the vegetation normally available to them. In addition to mineral licks, some mammals, like moose, can utilize sodium rich plants (aquatic vegetation) and perhaps store the sodium for later mobilization. Another possible mechanism used to conserve sodium is potassium substitution in salivary-rumen fluids when sodium is deficient. Thus we see apparent adaptation to deficiencies (or excesses) of certain minerals in the natural environment.

Human activities can rapidly alter the availability of certain elements, disrupting the physiology of exposed animals, e.g., increased heavy metal (mercury) levels in granitic lakes, fish, and fish-eating wildlife due to acid precipitation and leaching from soils. Similar processes also occur in soils and wildlife due to pesticides, seed dressings, automobile emissions, or aerial fallout from smelters. Even the application of chloride salts to highways can affect wildlife, if only indirectly, by altering vegetation or by attracting wildlife to roadsides where they may be hit by vehicles.

It is important to remember that many nutrient deficiencies occur naturally. For example, vegetation quality measured by crude protein content, calcium, and phosphorus (and the calcium:phosphorus ratio) was below that required for maintenance of white-tailed deer during winter in some Maine yarding areas. With nitrogen and phosphorus deficiencies, these animals are susceptible to winter mortality. The differential mortality observed in Maine deer wintering areas with similar vegetative composition, structure, snow and temperature conditions was likely a function of vegetational quality. Hobbs and Swift (1985), in developing a model to predict carrying capacity of burned and unburned mountain shrub habitat for mule deer and mountain sheep, emphasized that forage quality must be considered along with forage quantity as an integrated feature of habitat. Using their algorithm, a species stocking rate can be predicted based on the selected nutritional quality.

Nutrient deficiencies may become increasingly important as factors for wildlife managers to consider as more whole-tree harvesting and cutting of forests on erosion susceptible soils takes place. Such practices result in nutrient depletion, and without fertilization by forest managers the soils can be expected to produce poor forest crops and unthrifty wildlife populations, at least of herbivores. Switzer and Nelson (1972) showed considerable retention of nutrients in the woody, aerial portions of trees. White (1974) demonstrated that relatively large amounts of phosphorus and potassium were removed from a site when cottonwood (*Populus deltoides*) was whole-tree harvested. In such harvesting all portions of the tree are utilized and no "waste"—branches, leaves, or stumps—is left behind. Whole-tree harvesting of pulpwood species has implications for wildlife management. Either artificial nutrient supplements will have to be provided, which may attract wildlife and potentially increase regenerating tree damage, as sometimes has occurred in Christmas tree plantations; or, if no fertilization occurs, wildlife populations will drop with the decline in quality of the vegetation.

Wildlife species have functioned as sentinels of environmental degradation, forewarning the consequences of contamination by such chemicals as DDT, mercury, PCB's and dieldrin. This has prompted development of a wildlife model using the raccoon in Florida to provide information on environmental quality. The raccoon lives up to 8 years and has omnivorous food habits. Its diet includes aquatic organisms which biomagnify waterborne diseases, toxins, and pollutants. Because of the habitat it uses, it is exposed to blood-sucking vectors of arboviral, rickettsial, and parasitic diseases. Raccoon serum can be used to detect St. Louis and Venezuelan equine encephalitis. Leptospirosis, tularemia, and some enteric bacteria and viruses can also be found in the raccoon. Pesticide residues in the omentum fat can be used to monitor industrial pollution. Radionuclide contamination will show up in whole body counts. Raccoon hair can be used as biopsy material to detect mercury contamination. This species is thus well-suited for use as a wildlife surveillance system. Any such system must include at least: (1) a rather common species that is sufficiently sensitive to indicate the diseases and environmental contaminants to be monitored, (2) sufficient data returns without adversely affecting the population status of the species, (3) adequate base line information to show the current situation with respect to physiological measures, reproductive processes, susceptibility to disease, parasite burdens, pesticide and other pollutant concentrations in body tissues so that any changes can be detected, and (4) capability to integrate with data derived from other surveillance systems. Nutrient deficiencies prompted by environmental alteration should also be detectable with such a system.

Behavior

Social interactions within and between populations place additional constraints on the potential carrying capacity of an area. Many species exhibit density-dependent effects on population size. Intraspecific competition for increasingly limited resources results in physiological and behavioral responses mediated by increased social contact between individuals in the population. The ensuing endocrine gland and hormone production changes can result in lowered reproduction, changes in sex ratio of offspring, increased mortality, or a state of physiological stress—all of which can affect population density.

Territoriality serves to space individuals or family groups within any given environment. The energy costs of territory delineation become greater as population density increases and/or territory size shrinks, although territory size may also shrink as a result of improved environmental conditions such as increased food supply. This means the territorial animal in a high density situation must spend more of its time and energy interacting with other individuals in a threat or defense posture. Thus less energy in a time-energy budget is available for reproduction, foraging, or other activities.

Behavior of the sexes may vary within species at different times of the year. This is particularly important to a wildlife manager attempting to obtain population data for such things as a life-table analysis. It means that erroneous values can be derived from surveys if spatial and temporal patterns of movement are different due to differing behavioral responses of the sexes. Trapping or visual observation of individuals in a population may well produce data that are useless unless the behavior of the sexes and age groups is known.

The behavior of ungulates and how it relates to management was the subject of an international symposium published as part of the IUCN series. In all, fifty-six papers were presented which introduce the reader to the importance of wild ungulate behavior to the process of making management decisions. The summary paper by Cowan (1974) should be required reading for all wildlife managers.

If we search for North American examples of how behavior affects populations of wild animals, perhaps one of the most overlooked is that of the plains bison, which was probably doomed by the advent of the railroad. The wanton destruction so often alluded to as causing the demise of the species was in part a result of their behavior. Thousands were shot from trains because they simply refused to cross the tracks, milled along side them, and were easy targets.

Knowing the behavioral responses of wildlife to human disturbance is important in making correct management decisions. Bald eagles tend to be sensitive to disturbance during the nesting season, and a buffer zone should be provided during that time of year. Elk and grizzly bears are disturbed by vehicular traffic and will abandon preferred habitat in roaded areas unless provision is made to close roads or control traffic. Road development for resource extraction which provides long-term access to areas could disrupt elk and grizzly bear. Caribou have been shown to avoid crossing sections of the trans-Alaska oil pipeline, and what was originally one population is becoming two separate populations with reduced management flexibility. Musk-oxen, caribou, and other arctic species react to low flying aircraft, and minimum flying levels have had to be introduced for oil and mining exploration work in the arctic and subarctic regions of Canada and Alaska to protect the resident wildlife from energy depleting harassment or disturbance. Currently there is considerable controversy over NATO low level exercises in the Canadian arctic and their impact on caribou. The development of a town site (Churchill, Manitoba) in the seasonal migration path of the polar bear has caused considerable human-bear interaction and conflict. Female mule deer have been shown to have reduced reproductive performance following experimental harassment with an all-terrain vehicle.

Other behavioral responses in wildlife may be more subtle. For example, cow moose apparently respond to antler size and configuration in the bull. Such mate selection by the female has ensured that the species maintains a genetic structure reflective of the most vigorous and strongest members of the male sex. Yet man in his dubious wisdom has instituted bulls-only seasons in many areas of moose range. This supposedly protects the productive segment of the population, the female; but in reality it may also lead to social and genetic disruption. Bubenik (1972, 1977) strongly advocates hunting seasons for moose that will protect the "primes" of the population and put pressure on the senile and juvenile segments. This means a selective hunt with each license being issued for a particular age and sex category. Although common to many European countries, such selective and restrictive hunting requirements are rare in North America, but in the long run may well be in the best interests of the game populations and hunting public if adopted here. Ontario has initiated such selectivity by making revisions to its moose regulations.

Other behavioral characteristics important to managers include seasonal migration in many species from summer to winter range and back. The pattern of migration and the types of seasonal ranges required as well as the necessary connecting links between the seasonal ranges will dictate how land acquisition patterns should take place; will delineate critical seasonal habitats such as deer wintering areas; should help indicate where potential barriers such as pipelines or roads might be located to avoid conflict with species like caribou and elk.

These examples again illustrate how critical it is for the manager to have a full and thorough understanding of the basic biological responses of the species to be managed. Without such understanding and knowledge of the limitations and requirements of individual animals within wild populations, a manager is operating with a severe handicap. We can ill afford the luxury of inappropriate action in these times of generally dwindling habitats and stressed populations. Attempting to manage wild populations without first acquiring an adequate knowledge of the environmental constraints, ecological interactions, and zoological realities of the situation can often cause more harm than good. Although the immediacy of response required at times may necessitate action based on limited data, it is contingent on the manager to point out the deficiencies in the data base and strive to fill them as soon as possible so that potentially more appropriate actions can be taken in the future. We should know *why* an animal does what it does, and yet too often we do not even know *what* it does in given situations.

What are the biological limitations of the environment that often dictate behavioral responses? Most are energetically based and reflected in basal metabolic rates, upper and lower critical temperatures, and the ability to extract energy from the environment. Animals move to shaded or generally cooler micro-climates when continued solar exposure would cause them to exceed their upper critical temperature; other adaptations allow them to avoid using energy to maintain homeothermy. Conversely, if the lower critical temperature is exceeded, an animal must improve its insulation, as grouse do by using snow burrows; or moderate the micro-climate as deer may do by huddling and having their respiration (which condenses overhead) reduce radiative heat loss; or as gray partridge do by maintaining coveys and roosting together. Otherwise they must use energy to maintain homeothermy.

One convenient way of expressing the relationship between organism and environment is by the use of climate-space diagrams. In this way the biologist is able to determine if the organism can remain homeothermic in a particular microhabitat at a particular time of day or season. Not only is the energetic relationship between the animal and its environment revealed, but by superimposing the climate-space diagrams of other species, (e.g., predators), the probability and timing of interaction can be predicted, as can the degree of niche separation.

In essence, a climate-space diagram predicts when an animal must thermoregulate by behavioral means. Let us imagine a ruffed grouse in the winter having a choice of three forest stands (hemlock, white pine, and hard maple) or an open field. It should choose the environment which would minimize its exposure to heat sinks and where the net radiant energy exchange is positive. Looking at these four particular environments at T_A ranging between − 10 and + 10° C under clear skies and using an abbreviated Gates's equation

$$M + Q_{abs} = \epsilon A_i \, \sigma T^4$$

where

M = basal metabolic rate
Q_{abs} = average radiation absorbed by all surfaces of the animal

A_i = surface areas presented to streams of radiation (assume 1/2 of grouse's body exposed to sky hemisphere and 1/2 to ground)

ϵ = emissivity of animal's surface to long wave radiation

σ = Stefan Boltzmann constant (8.2×10^{-11}/y $°K^{-1}$ min^{-1})

T = surface temperature ($°K$) of animal (feather surface temperature≈ambient)

T_A = ambient temperature

and by plugging in the appropriate values, the energy balance for a medium sized grouse (500–700 gram) is likely to be positive in the two conifer stands and negative in the hardwood stand and open field. It would therefore be disadvantageous for the grouse to roost in the latter situations when night skies are clear and the T_A less than 10° C. We can predict the behavioral response of a species by knowing the energy flow in the available habitat and its climate-space diagram. Needless to say, grouse behavior coincides with the prediction.

Weather plays an important role in mediating energy exchange, and at no time is this more apparent than in winter in the temperate and arctic zones. The average specific gravity of snow ranges from 0.056 for large fluffy flakes to 0.135 for small flakes. After lying on the ground for a time, or due to slow melting, the snow becomes compacted into ice which has a specific gravity of about 0.920. A key physical relationship for an animal is the direct proportionality of the coefficient of the thermal conductivity of snow to the square of specific gravity: if specific gravity = 0.10, the thermal conductivity = 0.004; if specific gravity = 0.20, the thermal conductivity = 0.0162. Snow is important in providing thermal insulation for biological organisms, in determining the availability of food, and in affecting the locomotion of animals both at and below its surface. These characteristics are all dependent on the hardness, granularity, and thickness of the snow cover. Wildlife most highly adapted for movement on snow are lynx, snowshoe hare, ptarmigan, and caribou. Even these species can be handicapped by deep, fluffy snow (lynx) or heavily crusted snow (ptarmigan and caribou). The hindering of movement is not only dependent on the characteristics of the snow cover but also the morphology and track-load values for the appendages of the wildlife.

Subnivean species can suffer extensive mortality if there is little or no snow cover and the ambient temperature is below 10° C. Even with just a moderate snow cover (10 cm+) there can be great thermal advantages. Marchand (1982) demonstrated that temperature stability in subnivean environments could be achieved with a single snowfall of 15–20 cm of low specific gravity.

The advantage of hibernation in deep burrows becomes apparent with the increasing soil temperature at increasing depth. However, the effect of snow cover is usually lost 100 cm below the surface except in extreme winters with no snow cover.

There are energy costs associated with feeding during periods of snow cover. Caribou dig craters in the snow to access ground vegetation. As snow hardness increases, the average daily cost of digging craters increases. An Alaskan study showed that energy costs to an adult caribou for digging craters increased from 46.6 kcal/day in early winter to 148.5 kcal/day in late winter. During this same time period snow hardness increased from 2300 mg/cm^2 to 9000 g/cm^2. This 50 percent increase in energy expense must be met by increased forage intake or use of stored energy reserves.

Ruffed grouse have very small energy reserves. Increased glycogen levels in the liver and pectoral muscles may enhance shivering thermogenesis, so the response to cold temperature is not lipolytic as in many species but glycolytic. Because the fat reserves only provide about two days' energy for a fasting grouse, the birds must reduce energy expenditures to survive extended periods of inclement winter weather. Snow depth and compaction are important determinants of winter survival. The animals have three winter roosting alternatives: (1) snow burrows, (2) snow bowls, (3) tree roosts. If sufficient soft snow is available (minimum 20–25 cm uncrusted snow), they prefer to burrow. With temperatures rarely falling below $-2°$ C under 15 cm of snow, even with an air temperature of $-20°$ C, the birds are capitalizing on the insulation provided by the snow. The birds use thermogenesis to warm the air spaces in their plumage after burrowing into the snow to further restrict heat loss.

Wind is another important climatic factor. For mammals, fur conductance (hc) determines the convective and radiative heat flow (H) through the fur and surrounding air for a given set of skin (T_s) and ambient air (T_a) temperatures:

$$H = hc \, (T_s - T_a)$$

Fur conductance is also a function of wind speed. For example, caribou calves one to three days old have

$$h = 3.49 + 0.03V^{1-6}$$

where

$$h = \text{conductance (W/m}^2 \cdot °\text{C)}$$
$$V = \text{wind speed (m/sec)}$$

When wind chill (combination of V and T_a) values exceed 1100 kg · cal/m^2 per hour or metabolic rate approaches 25 cal/hour/kg for calves, exposure of long duration usually means death.

As T_A passes out of the thermoneutral zone of a homeothermic animal, the individual will increase its insulation, i.e., decrease conductance by reducing evaporative heat loss. This can be accomplished by increasing tissue insulation by peripheral vaso-constriction, increasing fur or feather insulation by pilo-erection, and reducing the heat dissipating surface by curling up or otherwise attempting to attain spherical form. The effect of wind increases the rate of heat flow from an animal and raises the effective lower critical ambient temperature by reducing the depth of the thermal boundary layer. One of the offsetting environmental factors to wind chill is solar radiation, and in addition to seeking solar exposed locations, animals select bedding sites or habitats which effectively reduce or eliminate the effects of wind.

Deer in some areas of Michigan and Ontario use cedar swamps during the winter. By so doing they reduce the effective wind chill and energy loss due to radiation and convection. Moose will use isolated trees or brushy cover in cut-over areas to minimize the effects of wind when bedding. In western North America, altitudinal migration occurs for the same reason. Deer and elk will move from higher altitudes to more forested lower elevations for the thermal advantages afforded there during the winter months.

An area not so thoroughly explored for wildlife species is that of heat stress. Behavioral adjustments are used here also: seeking shade, nocturnal versus diurnal activity, limiting movements to areas with an adequate water supply, and water baths. These behavioral adjustments often complement physiological and morphological adaptations that are evolutionary factors developed to cope with a predictably xeric and/or hot climate. These include (1) radiative appendages such as the ears of desert jackrabbit or the long legs of coyote (2) an ability to maintain a higher body temperature, such as antelopes' protective heat exchangers to maintain a cooler brain temperature, and (3) conservation of water.

Animals have evolved these adaptive mechanisms as a result of countless millennia of exposure to relatively predictable environmental conditions. Unfortunately, many current environmental changes are outside the adaptive capabilities of most wildlife species. The effects of toxic chemicals on organisms were graphically displayed by the rapid decline of predatory birds and the encouraging population response upon cessation of use of chemicals such as DDT. Yet we continue to contaminate the environment with chemicals which will have biological effects generations hence. Acid precipitation now poses a considerable threat to entire ecosystems in northeastern North America, and species such as otter, which are dependent on aquatic organisms for food, are consequently threatened. If the predictions related to global warning come to pass, vegetation will be drastically impacted as will the dependent faunal communities. What we have to reap from our insults to the environment unfortunately still remains to be seen. Not the least of the currently visible effects are modifications in behavior which can indirectly increase mortality. For example, dieldrin has been shown to reduce vigilance behavior in sheep, operant behavior in bobwhite quail, and a number of behaviors in second and third generation pheasants. Parathion reduced incubation time in laughing gulls, and a number of other chemicals including methylmercury, toxaphene, and endrin have caused other behavioral alterations in wildlife species. Such subtle factors are likely to be overlooked by the manager.

Populations

The unit most often considered by managers is the population, which is a group of organisms of the same species inhabiting a particular geographic area at a particular time. It is defined in terms of both time and space, a fact sometimes ignored by wildlife managers. To manage populations requires an understanding of their dynamics. It is not within the scope of this book to dwell at length on this subject, but we will examine some examples of populations interacting: predator-prey relationships and resource partitioning by similar sympatric species.

A classic wildlife example of predator-prey interaction is the Isle Royale moose-wolf situation. Originally the short-term data base suggested a dynamic equilibrium situation in which the predator and prey populations were in balance. With continued study it became apparent that the wolf population expanded as the moose population increased beyond the limitation of predator pressure. A moose population decline occurred in the late seventies and early eighties, and the expanded wolf population then exerted heavy predator pressure on the declining prey. Both species since have seen precipitous population declines and recently concern has been expressed about gene fixation in the remaining wolves. The fear is that without an infusion of new genetic material into the population a serious genetic decline will occur. Predator populations may be able to suppress a prey population's growth or hasten a decline when the prey population is at a low point in its cyclical pattern that may have been initiated by other factors such as hunting. Stephenson (1973) suggested such a relationship existed between white-tailed deer and wolves north of Montreal, Quebec, and predicted deer populations would not increase unless either hunting or predators were controlled.

A northern Alberta study showed that one pack of timber wolves annually consumed about 15 percent of the yearling and older moose within their territory. With an estimated annual recruitment of new yearlings of about 19 percent, it meant that wolf predation was closely approximating annual recruitment. The study occurred in an area of proposed industrial development that would have resulted in an increase in human population and thus increased hunting pressure. The obvious management conclusion is that with increased hunting pressure and without control of the wolves the moose population would decline.

Densities of white-tailed deer have `een found to be higher in the areas of overlap between wolf pack territories compared to territory centers. Wolves apparently avoid hunting in the areas of territory overlap until they are unable to catch prey elsewhere. Such refuges are most important in the summer range of the deer when the animals are not concentrated and fawning is taking place. These areas ensure reservoirs for deer repopulation of core wolf areas when wolf populations decline due to reduction in deer populations.

Predator removal studies in Minnesota, Texas, and South Dakota have shown that populations of prey species will increase dramatically under such circumstances. In the case of waterfowl, land-use practices such as mowing up to the edges of potholes have made the prey vulnerable to predators like raccoons that concentrate their efforts in these remnant habitats. Accordingly, the high losses of females and ducklings are mitigated by the reduced predator pressure. There is a potential for increased mortality resulting from density-dependent diseases and parasites if intensive predator control is carried out for several years in succession.

Modern research has repudiated a general philosophy which pervaded wildlife management for many years. While compensatory mortality has some validity for extremely prolific species such as bobwhite quail and muskrat, overhunting and overtrapping of even these species can occur. We must recognize that man, acting either as a predator (hunter) or as an eliminator of habitat, is an additive factor. In reality most mortality in natural populations is indeed additive. Certainly, populations generally produce a surplus annually, but this may be small or even locally nonexistent under natural conditions. Even small additions to mortality may precipitate a decline in numbers of individuals in future generations of species with low productivity.

The presence of buffer species must be accounted for in management decisions. Beaver often serve this function by maintaining high wolf populations even while the primary prey species (moose or deer) may be declining in number. An interesting example of management models for a wolf-ungulate system based on biological simulation is presented by Walters et al. (1981) and is recommended for review.

Resource Partitioning

Food habit studies of herbivores and carnivores have shown considerable overlap in diet between certain species. The Canadian National Park Service conducted an elk reduction program in some of the western parks when there was evidence that elk were causing range deterioration which was affecting deer and moose populations. There has been speculation that closely related wildlife species such as mink and otter and coyotes and timber wolves may be competitors. Though diet overlap occurs between these species, each is adapted to exploit particular prey more efficiently. This means that resource partitioning among species is the norm, and the presence or absence of particular species is what defines the amount of niche separation or overlap among species. Nonetheless, larger species will dominate smaller and sometimes force them out of their territories or foraging areas. As an example, red fox in Maine establish their home ranges outside coyote territories or in the boundary areas between adjacent coyote groups.

This type of discussion rapidly leads into theoretical ecology, and the best operative philosophy for a manager often is to ignore most competition between wildlife species as a factor and only expect possible deleterious interaction when domestic livestock or introduced species occupy the same area as native wildlife. There are relatively few situations where competition among naturally occurring wildlife species is a problem. Instead of initially suspecting competition, it is usually more productive to seek other causative factors except when domestic or exotic species are involved.

Parasites and Disease

Until recently, wildlife managers have tended to discount the impact of disease and parasites on wildlife populations. Emphasis has been on those diseases or parasites with direct human impact like rabies, plague, arboviruses, eastern and western encephalomyelitis, and St. Louis encephalitis, or those diseases such as anthrax and brucellosis which impact man's domestic animals. Increasingly we are discovering that such organisms do exert important influences on wildlife populations.

As wildlife populations with particular habitat requirements become more and more concentrated on smaller ranges, the opportunity for disease/parasite transmission rises. Bighorn sheep and mountain goats have somewhat specialized habitat requirements and tend to concentrate on winter range, which creates ideal conditions for parasite transfer. Previously, lung worm was not an important problem, because sheep had more options for feeding and pressure to shift feeding locations due to larger predator populations. In recent decades, increasing sheep and goat populations have required antihelminthic treatment to prevent losses of entire populations because of lamb and kid mortality, or in some cases, mortality at any age. We should recognize that wildlife management will in the future require more intensive animal husbandry: artificial feeding programs, inoculations against disease organisms, and genetic manipulation should become routine management procedures with many populations.

A classic example of a parasite that exerts control over population levels is *Parelaphostronglyus tenuis*. This nematode occurs in its adult stage in the meninges and vena sinuses of the brain of white-tailed deer in eastern North America. The so-called meningeal worm is usually harmless to its normal definitive host, but experimental and field studies in Maine, Minnesota, Nova Scotia, Ontario, and elsewhere have clearly implicated the parasite in extinction of woodland caribou, wapiti, and moose populations in eastern North America. Of these three species, the moose is the most tolerant, which explains the limited sympatry with white-tailed deer; the size and vigor of the moose populations directly correlates with white-tailed deer population density, parasite prevalence level, and opportunity for spatial separation between the carrier and the vulnerable species. As interspecific transmission requires exposure to the intermediate gastropod hosts, sufficient spatial separation between deer and moose populations will result in a viable moose population that cannot expand out of its "refugium" unless there is a change in the surrounding deer situation. This poses a management conundrum. For example, to sustain moose populations at high enough levels for recreational use, white-tailed deer populations may have to be reduced substantially, or if already depressed, sustained at low levels. Because deer will support more "recreation days" than moose and are more popular with the hunting fraternity, at least in areas of past deer hunting tradition, the political options are more limited than the biological ones. Perhaps the moose will adapt on their own, with vulnerable individuals being removed from the population and more resistant ones surviving. Evidence to support this in Maine, Nova Scotia, and Ontario is the increasing number of moose in which *P. tenuis* is able to complete its life cycle. There is circumstantial evidence to indicate that other sympatric populations using separate habitats (snowshoe hare and cottontail rabbit) may do so because of exposure of a vulnerable species to a pathogen carried by the other.

Elaeophora schneideri is another nematode that has affected cervid populations. Elk are the primary host for this worm, which finds its way into the carotid artery and arterioles and blocks or impairs blood flow. Other species may also be susceptible.

Many organisms such as anthrax, brucellosis, epizootic haemorrhagic disease in large mammals, fowl cholera, botulism, enteritis, and leucocyto-zoonosis in waterfowl appear to have a density-dependent relationship. Transmission and the opportunity for epidemics are enhanced in many cases by management practices which concentrate wildlife populations. The waterfowl refuge system now fights a continual and apparently losing battle against diseases such as avian cholera in overwintering duck and goose populations. With 90 percent of the waterfowl populations of the Pacific flyway concentrated in California refuges, it is not difficult to envision the potential for massive die-offs if a disease becomes established. Efforts to disperse the birds premigration are ineffective as the animals simply have nowhere else to go. Contrary to current biogeographic theory, the advantage lies with many small refuges instead of a few large ones, because of the specialized habitat requirements of overwintering waterfowl.

One promising management technique is the use of helminth counts to establish the condition of wild animals. For example, abomasal worm counts in white-tailed deer have been used to determine the physical condition of the population. This technique was developed by the Southeastern Cooperative Wildlife Disease Study. Three classifications of populations: overpopulated, optimum, and suboptimum were correlated to average worm counts giving high ($\geq$1,000), moderate (500–1000), and low (<500) categories of parasite incidence. The technique appears to have general applicability for the southeastern United States where it provides an evaluation of deer herd health as related to range conditions. In areas of more severe cold there is a winter diapause in the parasites' life cycles which makes the technique useless. Demarais et al. (1983) also cautioned that abomasal counts for Mississippi deer collected in December and January did not consistently indicate either current or future trends in herd health compared to measurements such as body weight and antler beam diameter. They suggested the technique, based on summer parasite counts, may not have validity outside that season even in the southeast.

Bibliography

Abell, D. H., and F. F. Gilbert. 1974. Nutrient content of fertilized deer browse in Maine. J. Wildl. Manage. 38:517–524.

Adamczewski, J. Z., C. C. Gates, B. M. Soutar, and R. J. Hudson. 1988. Limiting effects of snow on seasonal habitat use and diets of caribou (*Rangifer tarandus groenlandicus*) on Coats Island, Northwest Territories, Canada. Can. J. Zool. 66:1986–1996.

Anderson, R. C., M. W. Lankester, and U. R. Strelive. 1966. Further experimental studies of *Pneumostrongylus tenuis* in cervids. Can. J. Zool. 44:851–861.

Anderson, R. C., and U. R. Strelive. 1968. The experimental transmission of *Pneumostrongylus tenuis* to caribou (*Rangifer tarandus terranovae*). Can. J. Zool. 46:503–510.

Anderson, W. L., and P. L. Stewart. 1969. Relationships between inorganic ions and the distribution of pheasants in Illinois. J. Wildl. Manage. 33:254–270.

Anderson, W. L. and P. L. Stewart. 1973. Chemical elements and the distribution of pheasants in Illinois. J. Wildl. Manage. 37:142–153.

Anderson, B. L., R. D. Pieper, and V. W. Howard, Jr. 1974. Growth response and deer utilization of fertilized browse. J. Wildl. Manage. 38:525–530.

Andrews, R. V., R. W. Belkap, J. Southard, M. Lorinez, and S. Hess. 1972. Physiological, demographic and pathological changes in wild Norway rat populations over an annual cycle. Comp. Biochem. Physiol. 41A:149–165.

Anon. 1979. EPA research summary-acid rain. U.S. Envir. Protection Agency, Off. Res. Develop. EPA-600/8-79-028. 23 pp.

Anon. 1983. Canadian Wildlife Service. Annual review 1982–1983. Envir. Can., Can. Wildl. Serv. Ottawa. 25 pp.

Baker, M. R., and R. C. Anderson. 1975. Seasonal changes in abomasal worms (*Ostertagia* sp.) in white tailed deer (*Odocoileus virginianus*) at Long Point, Ontario, Can. J. Zool. 53:87–96.

Baker, D. L., D. E. Johnson, L. H. Carpenter, O. C. Wallmo, and R. B. Gill. 1979. Energy requirements of mule deer fawns in winter. J. Wildl. Manage. 43:162–169.

Balser, D. S., H. H. Dill, and H. K. Nelson. 1968. Effect of predator reduction on waterfowl nesting success. J. Wildl. Manage. 32:669–682.

Beasom, S. L. 1974. Relationships between predator removal and whitetailed deer net productivity. J. Wildl. Manage. 38:854–859.

Behrend, D. F., and J. F. Witter. 1968. *Pneumostronglyus tenuis* in whitetailed deer in Maine. J. Wildl. Manage. 32:963–966.

Belovsky, G. E. R., and P. A. Jordan. 1981. Sodium dynamics and adaptations of a moose population. J. Mammal. 62:613–621.

Bigler, W. J., J. H. Jenkins, P. M. Cumbie, G. L. Hoff, and E. C. Prather. 1975. Wildlife and environmental health: raccoons as indicators of zoonoses and pollutants in Southeastern United States. J. Am Vet. Med. Assoc. 167:592–597.

Brand, C. J. 1984. Avian cholera in the Central and Mississippi flyways during 1979–80. J. Wildl. Manage. 48:399–406.

Brown, J. E. 1983. *Parelaphastrongylus tenuis* (Pryadko and Bove) in the moose and white-tailed deer of Nova Scotia. M. Sc. Thesis. Acadia University, Wolfville, NS. 136 pp.

Bubenik, A. B. 1972. North American moose management in light of European experiences. N. Am. Moose Conf. 8:276–295.

Bubenik, A. B. 1977. Moose and man. Recent studies and their relationship to hunting. Annu. Conv. Ont. Fed. Anglers and Hunters. Toronto. 15 pp. (mimeo).

Bubenik, A. B., O. Williams, and H. R. Timmerman. 1978. Some characteristics of antlerogenesis in moose—a preliminary report. N. Am. Moose Conf. 14:157–177.

Buskirk, S. W., and S. L. Lindstedt. 1989. Sex biases in trapped samples of Mustelidae. J. Mammal. 70:88–97.

Cameron, R. D., K. R. Whillen, W. T. Smith, and D. D. Roby. 1979. Caribou distribution and group composition associated with construction of the trans-Alaska pipeline. Can. Field-Nat. 93:155–162.

Carbyn, L. N. 1982. Coyote population fluctuations and spatial distribution in relation to wolf territories in Riding Mountain National Park, Manitoba. Can. Field-Nat. 96:176–183.

Carpenter, J. W., H. E. Jordan, and B. C. Ward. 1973. Neurologic disease in wapiti naturally infected with meningeal worms. J. Wildl. Dis. 9:148–153.

Christian, J. J. 1963. Endocrine adaptive mechanisms and the physiologic regulation of population growth. Pp. 189–353, *In* M. V. Mayer and R. G. Van Gelder, Eds. Physiological mammalogy. Academic Press, New York.

Christian, J. J. 1971. Fighting, maturity and population density in *Microtus pennsylvanicus*. J. Mammal. 52:556–567.

Christian, J. J. 1978. Neurobehavioral endocrine regulation of small mammal populations. Pp. 143–158, *In* D. P. Snyder, Ed. Populations of small mammals under natural conditions. Pymatuning Lab of Ecology, Univ. Pittsburgh, Spec. Publ. Ser. Vol. 5.

Christian, J. J., V. Flyger, and D. E. Davis. 1960. Factors in the mass mortality of sitka deer. Chesapeake Sci. 1:79–95.

Clark, D. R., Jr. 1979. Lead concentrations: bats vs. terrestrial small mammals collected near a major highway. Environ. Sci. Tech. 13:338–341.

Coggins, V. 1976. Controlled vehicle access during elk season in the Chesuimnus area, Oregon. Pp. 58–61, *In* S. R. Hieb, Ed. Proceedings of the elk-logging-roads symposium. For. Wildl. Range Expt. Stn. Univ. Idaho, Moscow.

Cowan, I. McT. 1974. Management implications of behavior in the large herbivorous mammals. Pp. 921–934 *In* V. Geist and F. Walther, Eds. The behavior of ungulates and its relation to management. Vol. 2. IUCN Publ. New Ser. No. 24. Morges, Switzerland.

Dahlgren, R. B., and R. L. Linder. 1974. Effects of dieldrin in penned pheasants through the third generation. J. Wildl. Manage. 38:320–330.

Dale, F. H. 1954. Influence of calcium on the distribution of the pheasant in North America. Trans. N. Am. Wildl. Conf. 19:316–322.

Dauphine, T. C., Jr. 1975. The disappearance of caribou reintroduced to Cape Breton Highlands National Park. Can. Field-Nat. 89:299–310.

Demarais, S., H. A. Jacobson, and D. C. Buynn. 1983. Abomasal parasites as a health index for white-tailed deer in Mississippi. J. Wildl. Manage. 47:247–252.

Diamond, J. M. 1975. The island dilemma: lessons of modern biogeographic studies for the design of natural reserves. Biol. Conserv. 7:129–146.

Downing, R. L., E. D. Michael, and R. J. Poux, Jr. 1973. Monthly differences in the accuracy of sex and age ratio counts of white-tailed deer. Trans. Northeastern Deer Study Group. 9:37–53.

Duebbert, H. F. and J. T. Lokemoen. 1980. High duck nesting success in a predator-reduced environment. J. Wildl. Manage. 44:428–437.

Dunks, J. H., R. E. Tomlinson, H. M. Reeves, D. D. Dolton, C. E. Braun, and T. P. Zapatka. 1982. Migration, harvest, and population dynamics of mourning doves banded in the central management unit, 1967–77. U.S. Fish Wildl. Serv., Washington, D.C. Spec. Sci. Rep. Wildl. No. 249.

Erlinge, S. 1972. Interspecific relations between otter, *Lutra lutra*, and mink *Mustela vison*, in Sweden. Oikos 23:327–335.

Eve, J. H., and F. E. Kellogg. 1977. Management implications of abomasal parasites in southeastern white-tailed deer. J. Wildl. Manage. 41:169–177.

Fancy, S. G., and R. G. White. 1986. Predicting energy expenditures for activities of caribou from heart rates. Rangifer Special Issue 1:123–130.

Fancy, S. G., and R. G. White. 1987. Energy expenditures for locomotion by barren-ground caribou. Can. J. Zool. 65:122–128.

Fisher, R., F. F. Gilbert, and J. D. Robinette. 1987. Heart rate as an indicator of oxygen consumption in the pine marten (*Martes americana*). Can. J. Zool. 65:2085–2089.

Flook, D. R. 1964. Range relationships of some ungulates native to Banff and Jasper National Parks, Alberta. Pp. 119–128 *In* D. J. Crisp, Ed.

Grazing in terrestrial and marine environments. Symp. Br. Ecol. Soc. No. 4. Blackwell, Oxford.

Frank, R., K. Ishida, and P. Suda. 1976. Metals in agricultural soils of Ontario. Can. J. Soil Sci. 56:181–196.

Fraser, D., E. Reardon, F. Dieken, and B. Loescher. 1980. Sampling problems and interpretation of chemical analysis of mineral springs used by wildlife. J. Wildl. Manage. 44:623–631.

Fraser, D. and E. R. Thomas. 1982. Moose-vehicle accidents in Ontario: relation to highway salt. Wildl. Soc. Bull. 10:261–265.

Freddy, D. J. 1984. Heart rates for activities of mule deer at pasture. J. Wildl. Manage. 48:962–968.

Fritzell, E. K. 1978. Habitat use by prairie raccoons during the waterfowl breeding season. J. Wildl. Manage. 42:118–127.

Fuller, T. K., and L. B. Keith. 1980. Wolf population dynamics and prey relationships in northeastern Alberta. J. Wildl. Manage. 44:583–602.

Geist, V., and F. Walther. 1974. Symposium on the behavior of ungulates and its relation to management. (2 vols.). Int. Union Conserv. Nat. Natur. Resour. Morges, Switzerland. IUCN Publ. New. Ser. No. 24. 940 pp.

Gerrard, J. M., P. Gerrard, W. J. Maher, and D. W. A. Whitfield. 1975. Factors influencing nest site selection of bald eagles in northern Saskatchewan and Manitoba. Blue Jay. 33:169–176.

Gesell, G. G., R. J. Robel, A. D. Dayton, and J. Frieman. 1979. Effects of dieldrin on operant behavior of bobwhites. J. Environ. Sci. Health. B14:153–170.

Gilbert, F. F. 1973. *Parelaphostrongylus tenuis* (Dougherty) in Maine: I-The parasite in white-tailed deer (*Odocoileus virginianus*, Zimmerman). J. Wildl. Dis. 9:136–143.

Gilbert, F. F. 1974. *Parelaphostrongylus tenuis* in Maine: II-Prevalence in moose. J. Wildl. Manage. 38:42–46.

Gjessing, E. T., A. Henriksen, M. Johannessen, and R. F. Wright. 1976. Effects of acid precipitation on fresh water chemistry. Pp. 64–85, *In* F. H. Braekke, Ed. Impact of acid precipitation on forest and fresh water ecosystems in Norway. Sum. Rep. on Res. Results from Phase I (1972–75) of SNSF Proj. Oslo, Norway.

Gordon, A. G., and E. Gorham. 1963. Ecological aspects of air pollution from an iron-sintering plant at Wawa, Ontario, Can. J. Bot. 41:1063–1078.

Gray, B. T. and H. H. Prince. 1988. Basal metabolism and energetic cost of thermoregulation in wild turkeys. J. Wildl. Manage. 52:133–137.

Green, B., J. Anderson, and T. Whateley. 1984. Water and sodium turnover and estimated food consumption in free-living lions (*Panthera leo*) and spotted hyenas (*Crocuta crocuta*). J. Mammal. 65:593–599.

Grenier, P. A. 1974. Orignaux tués sur la route dans le Parc des Laurentides. Quebec, de 1962 a 1972. Nat. Can. 101:737–754.

Halls, L. K. 1978. White-tailed deer. Pp. 43–65, *In* J. L. Schmidt and D. L. Gilbert, Eds. Big game of North America: ecology and management. Stackpole Books, Harrisburg, PA.

Hanley, T. A., and J. J. Rogers. 1989. Estimating carrying capacity with simultaneous nutritional constraints. U.S. Dept. Agric. For. Serv. Res. Note PNW-RN-485. 29 pp.

Harper, J. A. and R. F. Labisky. 1964. The influence of calcium on the distribution of pheasants in Illinois. J. Wildl. Manage. 28:722–731.

Harris, L. E. 1970. Nutrition research techniques for domestic and wild animals. Ext. Agric. Serv., Utah State Univ., Logan, UT.

Harrison, D. J., J. A. Bissonette, and J. A. Sherburne. 1989. Spatial relationships between coyotes and red foxes in eastern Maine. J. Wildl. Manage. 53:181–185.

Heinz, G. H. 1979. Methylmercury: reproductive and behavioral effects on three generations of mallard ducks. J. Wildl. Manage. 43:394–401.

Hibler, C. P., J. L. Adcock, R. W. Davis, and Y. Z. Abdelboki. 1969. Elaeophorosis in deer and elk in the Gila Forest, New Mexico. Bull. Wildl. Dis. Assoc. 5:27–30.

Hibler, C. P., and C. J. Metzger. 1974. Morphology of the larval stages of *Elaeophora schneideri* in the intermediate and definitive hosts with some observations on their pathogenesis in abnormal definitive hosts. J. Wildl. Dis. 10:361–369.

Hobbs, N. T., and D. M. Swift. 1985. Estimates of carrying capacity incorporating explicit nutritional constraints. J. Wildl. Manage. 49:814–822.

Holter, J. B., W. E. Urban, Jr., H. H. Hayes, and H. Silver. 1976. Predicting metabolic rate from telemetred heart rate in white-tailed deer. J. Wildl. Manage. 40:626–629.

Hurst, R. J., M. L. Leonard, P. D. Watts, P. Beckerton, and N. A. Oritsland. 1982. Polar bear locomotion: body temperature and energetic cost. Can. J. Zool. 60:40–44.

Hutchinson, F. E., and B. E. Olson. 1967. The relationship of road salt applications to sodium and chloride ion levels in the soil bordering major highways. Highway Res. Rec. 193:1–7.

Hutchinson, T. C., and L. M. Whitby. 1976. The effects of acid rainfall and heavy metal particulates on a boreal forest ecosystem near the Sudbury smelting region of Canada. Proc. Ist Intl Symp. on Acid Precip. and the For. Ecosys. U.S. Dept. Agric. For. Serv. Gen. Tech. Rep. NE-23. Pp. 745–765.

Jenkins, D. 1956. Chick survival in a partridge population. Anim. Health. 7:6–10.

Jones, R. L., R. F. Labisky, and L. W. Anderson. 1968. Selected minerals in soils, plants and pheasants: an ecosystem approach to understanding pheasant distribution in Illinois. Ill. Nat. Hist. Surv. Biol. Notes 63. 8 pp.

Jordan, P. A., D. B. Botkin, A. S. Dominski, H. S. Lowendorf, and G. E. Belovsky. 1973. Sodium as a critical nutrient for the moose of Isle Royale. Proc. N. Am. Moose Conf. 9:13–42.

Karns, P. D. 1967. *Pneumostrongylus tenuis* in deer in Minnesota and implications for moose. J. Wildl. Manage. 31:229–303.

Kautz, M. A., G. M. VanDyne, L. H. Carpenter, and W. W. Mautz. 1982. Energy cost for activities of mule deer fawns. J. Wildl. Manage. 46:704–710.

Kelsall, J. P. 1968. The migratory barren-ground caribou of Canada. Can. Wildl. Serv. Monogr. 3. 340 pp.

Kelsall, J. P., and W. Prescott. 1971. Moose and deer behavior in snow. Can. Wildl. Serv. Rep. Ser. No. 15. 27 pp.

Krefting, L. W., A. B. Erickson, and V. E. Gunvalson. 1955. Results of controlled deer hunts on the Tamarac National Wildlife Refuge. J. Wildl. Manage. 19:346–352.

Kreitzer, J. F. 1980. Effects of toxaphene and endrin at very low dietary concentrations on discriminatory acquisition and reversal in bobwhite quail, *Colinus virginianus*. Environ. Pollut. A23:217–230.

Labisky, R. F., J. A. Harper, and F. Greeley. 1964. Influence of land use, calcium, and weather on the distribution and abundance of pheasants in Illinois. Ill. Nat. Hist. Surv. Biol. Notes 51. 19 pp.

Leopold, A. 1931. Report on a game survey of the North Central states. Sporting Arms and Ammunition Manufacturers' Institute. Madison, Wisconsin. 299 pp.

Litvaitis, J. A., and W. M. Mautz. 1980. Food and energy use by captive coyotes. J. Wildl. Manage. 44:56–61.

Loveless, C. M. 1964. Some relationships between wintering mule deer and the physical environment. Trans. N. Am. Wildl. Nat. Resour. Conf. 29:415–431.

Loveless, C. M. 1967. Ecological characteristics of a mule deer winter range. Colorado Game, Fish and Parks Dept. Tech. Publ. No. 20. 124 pp.

Luck, B. R. and R. G. White. 1986. Oxygen consumption for locomotion by caribou calves. J. Wildl. Manage. 50:148–152.

Lund, G. F., and G. E. Folk, Jr. 1976. Simultaneous measurements of heart rate and oxygen consumption in black-tailed prairie dogs (*Cynomys ludovicianus*). Comp. Biochem. Physiol. 55A:201–206.

Lyon, J. L. 1979. Influences of logging and weather on elk distribution in western Montana. U.S.Dept. Agric. For. Serv. Res. Paper INT-236. 11 pp.

Lyon, J. L. 1980. Coordinating forestry and elk management. Trans. N. Am. Wildl. Nat. Resour. Conf. 45:278–281.

Mack, R. N., and J. N. Thompson. 1982. Evolution in steppe with few large hooved animals. Am. Nat. 119:757–773.

Marchand, P. J. 1982. An index for evaluating the temperature stability of a subnivean environment. J. Wildl. Manage. 46:518–520.

Mautz, W. W., and J. Fair. 1980. Energy expenditure and heart rate for activities of white-tailed deer. J. Wildl. Manage. 44:333–342.

McLellan, B. N. and D. M. Shackleton. 1988. Grizzly bears and resource extraction industries: effects of roads on behavior, habitat use and demography. J. Appl. Ecol. 25:451–460.

McNicol, J. G. and F. F. Gilbert. 1978. Late winter bedding practices of moose in mixed upland cutovers. Can. Field-Nat. 92:189–192.

Mierau, G. W., and B. E. Favara. 1975. Lead poisoning in roadside populations of deer mice. Environ. Pollut. 8:55–64.

Miller, F. L., and A. Gunn. 1979. Responses of Peary caribou and muskoxen to helicopter harassment. Can. Wildl. Serv. Occ. Paper No. 40. 90 pp.

Miller, F. L., F. W. Anderka, C. Vithayasai, and R. L. McClure. 1974. Distribution, movements and socialization of barren-ground caribou radio-tracked on their calving and post-calving areas. Proc. Intl. Reindeer/caribou Symp. 1:423–435.

Moen, A. N. 1973. Wildlife ecology. W. H. Freeman Co., San Francisco. CA. 458 pp.

Newsome, A. E. 1971. The ecology of house-mice in cereal haystacks. J. Anim. Ecol. 40.1–15.

Olsen, A., and A. Woolf. 1978. The development of clinical signs and the population significance of neurologic disease in a captive wapiti herd. J. Wildl. Dis. 14:263–268.

Owen, R. B., Jr. 1969. Heart rate, a measure of metabolism in blue-winged teal. Comp. Biochem. Physiol. 31:431–436.

Owen, R. B., Jr. 1970. The bioenergetics of captive blue-winged teal under controlled and outdoor conditions. Condor. 72:153–163.

Ozoga, J. J., and L. W. Gysel. 1972. Response of white-tailed deer to winter weather. J. Wildl. Manage. 36:892–896.

Parker, G. R. 1966. Moose disease in Nova Scotia: gastropod-nematode relationship. M. S. Thesis, Acadia University, Wolfville. 77 pp.

Parker, K. A., C. T. Robbins, and T. A. Hanley. 1984. Energy expenditures for locomotion by mule deer and elk. J. Wildl. Manage. 48:474–488.

Pauls, R. W. 1980. Heart rate as an index of energy expenditure in red squirrels (*Tamiasciurus hudsonicus*). Comp. Biochem. Physiol. 67A:409–418.

Pimlott, D. H., J. A. Shannon, and G. B. Kolenosky. 1969. The ecology of the timber wolf in Algonquin Provincial Park. Ont. Dept. Lands For. Toronto. 92 pp. plus maps.

Porter, W. P., and D. M. Gates. 1969. Thermodynamic equilibria of animals with environment. Ecol. Monogr. 39:227–244.

Potvin, F., and J. Huot. 1983. Estimating carrying capacity of a white-tailed deer wintering area in Quebec. J. Wildl. Manage. 47:463–475.

Rasmussen, G., and R. Branden. 1973. Standard metabolic rate and lower critical temperature for the ruffed grouse. Wilson Bull. 85:223–229.

Rautenstrauch, K. R., and P. R. Krausman. 1989. Influence of water availability and rainfall on movements of desert mule deer. J. Mammal. 70:197–201.

Regelin, W. L., C. C. Schwartz, and A. W. Franzmann. 1985. Seasonal energy metabolism of adult moose. J. Wildl. Manage. 49:388–393.

Renecker, L. A., and R. J. Hudson. 1986. Seasonal energy expenditures and thermoregulatory responses of moose. Can. J. Zool. 64:322–327.

Robbins, C. T., Y. Cohen, and B. B. Davitt. 1979. Energy expenditure by elk calves. J. Wildl. Manage. 43:445–453.

Rogers, L. L., L. D. Mech, D. K. Dawson, J. M. Peek, and M. Korb. 1980. Deer distribution in relation to wolf pack territory. J. Wildl. Manage. 44:253–258.

Rose, G. B. 1973. Energy metabolism of adult cottontail rabbits, *Sylvilagus floridanus* in simulated field conditions. Am. Midl. Nat. 89:473–478.

Rose, G. B. 1974. Energy dynamics of immature cottontail rabbits. Am. Midl. Nat. 91:473–477.

Rose, G. A., and C. H. Parker. 1982. Metal content of body tissues, diet items and dung of ruffed grouse near the copper nickel smelters at Sudbury, Ont. Can. J. Zool. 61:505–511.

Sandler, B. E., G. A. VanGelder, D. D. Elsberry, G. G. Karas, and W. B. Buck. 1969. Dieldrin exposure and vigilance behavior in sheep. Psychol. Sci. 15:261–262.

Saunders, B. P. 1973. Meningeal worm in white tailed deer in northwestern Ontario and moose population densities. J. Wildl. Manage. 37:327–330.

Schitoskey, F., Jr., and S. R. Woodmansee. 1978. Energy requirements and diet of the California ground squirrel. J. Wildl. Manage. 42:373–382.

Schmidt, R. L., C. P. Hibler, T. R. Spraker, and W. H. Rutherford. 1979. An evaluation of drug treatment for lungworm in bighorn sheep. J. Wildl. Manage. 43:461–467.

Schroeder, H. A. 1965. The biological trace elements or peripatetics through the periodic table. J. Chronic Dis. 18:217–228.

Sheffy, T. B., and J. R. St. Amant. 1982. Mercury burdens in furbearers in Wisconsin, J. Wildl. Manage. 46:1117–1120.

Shield, J. 1972. Acclimation and energy metabolism of the dingo, *Canis dingo* and the coyote, *Canis latrans*. J. Zool. (Lond.) 168:483–501.

Singer, F. J. 1979. Habitat partitioning and wildfire relationships of cervids in Glacier National Park, Montana. J. Wildl. Manage. 43:437–444.

Stalmaster, M. V., and J. A. Gessaman. 1982. Food consumption and energy requirements of captive bald eagles. J. Wildl. Manage. 46:646–654.

Stephenson, B. 1973. Deer management in the North Montreal region, Que. Min. Tourism Fish and Game, Min. Agric. and Colonization. mimeo. 126 pp.

Stokes, A. W. 1954. Population studies of the ring-necked pheasants on Pelee Island, Ontario. Ont. Dept. Lands For., Tech. Bull. Wildl. Ser. No. 4. 154 pp.

Stokes, A. W., and D. F. Balph. 1965. The relation of animal behavior to wildlife management. Trans. N. Am. Wildl. Nat. Resour. Conf. 13:401–410.

Switzer, G. L., and L. E. Nelson. 1972. Nutrient accumulation and cycling in loblolly pine (*Pinus taeda* L.) plantation ecosystems: The first twenty years. Soil Sci. Soc. Am. Proc. 36:143–147.

Teubner, V. A., and G. W. Barrett. 1982. Bioenergetics of captive raccoons. J. Wildl. Manage. 47:272–274.

Thiessen, D. D. 1966. Role of physical injury in the physiological effects of population density in mice. J. Comp. Physiol. Psychol. 62:322–324.

Thing, H. 1977. Behavior, mechanics and energetics associated with winter cratering by caribou in northwestern Alaska. Biol. Pop. Univ. Alaska No. 18. 41 pp.

Thomas, V. G., H. G. Lumsden, and D. H. Price. 1975. Aspects of the winter metabolism of ruffed grouse (*Bonasa umbellus*) with special reference to energy reserves. Can. J. Zool. 53:434–440.

Udevitz, M. S., C. A. Howard, R. J. Robel and B. Curnutte. 1980. Lead contamination in insects and birds near an interstate highway. Kansas. Environ. Entom. 9:35–36.

Verme, L. J. 1973. Movements of white-tailed deer in upper Michigan. J. Wildl. Manage. 37:545–552.

Wagner, F. H., and L. C. Stoddart. 1972. Influence of coyote predation on black-tailed jackrabbit populations in Utah. J. Wildl. Manage. 36:329–342.

Walters, C. J., M. Stocker and G. C. Haber. 1981. Simulation and optimization models for a wolf-ungulate system. Pp. 317–337 *In* C. W. Fowler and T. D. Smith, Eds. Dynamics of large mammal populations. John Wiley Sons, New York, NY.

Westermark, T., T. Odsjo and A. G. Johnels. 1975. Mercury content of bird feathers before and after Swedish ban on alkyll mercury in agriculture. Ambio 4:87–92.

White, D. H., C. A. Mitchell, and E. F. Hill. 1983. Parathion alters incubation behavior of laughing gulls. Bull. Environ. Contam. Toxicol. 31:93–97.

White, E. H. 1974. Whole-tree harvesting depletes soil nutrients. Can. J. For. Res. 4:530–535.

Wooley, J. B., Jr., and R. B. Owen, Jr. 1978. Energy costs of activity and daily energy expenditure in the black duck. J. Wildl. Manage. 42:739–745.

Wren, C. MacCrimmon, R. Frank, and P. Suda. 1980. Total and methyl mercury levels in wild mammals from the Pre-Cambrian Shield area of south central Ontario, Canada. Bull. Environ. Contam. Toxicol. 25:100–105.

Yarmolov, C. M., Bayer, and V. Geist. 1988. Behavior responses and reproduction of mule deer (*Odocoileus hemionus*) does following experimental harassment with an all-terrain vehicle. Can. Field-Nat. 102:425–429.

Zwickel, F. C. and J. F. Bendell. 1972. Blue grouse, habitat and populations. Proc. Intl. Ornith. Congr. 15:150–169.

Additional Readings
Carbyn, L. N. 1983. Wolves in Canada and Alaska. Can. Wildl. Serv. Rep. Ser. No. 45. 135 pp.

    This is a collection of papers by wolf researchers and managers given at an IUCN/Species Survival Commission meeting on wolves in Edmontoñ, Canada.

Geist and Walther, (eds). 1974. Symposium on the behavior of ungulates and its relation to management. (2 vols) Int Union Conserv. Nat. Natur. Resour. Morges, Switzerland IUCN Publ. New Ser. No. 24 940 pp.

This is an excellent collection of papers on ungulate behavior as it relates to management.

Fowler, C. W., and T. D. Smith. 1981. Dynamics of large mammal populations. John Wiley Sons, New York, NY. 477 pp.

Population biology of large mammals is examined from a dynamic aspect. Many fine simulation models are explained.

Hudson, R. J., and R. G. White (eds). 1985. Bioenergetics of wild herbivores. CRC Press Boca Raton, FL. 328 pp.

The contributions in this book cover such topics as energy and nutrient supplies, energy expenditures, foraging behavior and thermoregulation of wild herbivores.

IV MANAGEMENT SYSTEMS

As it was believed that wildlife stocks originally dwindled in North America because of overexploitation, the first government response was to protect the resource. Protection inevitably took the form of restricting use or harvest. We find legislation designed primarily to perpetuate hunting opportunity for all by reducing the influence of market hunting and "game hogs" on the overall supply of game, or alternatively, to protect completely species whose stocks had been severely depleted. By the time of the American Revolution, twelve of the thirteen colonies had enacted closed seasons on some species, several had prohibited certain destructive equipment and methods such as the infamous duck or punt guns, and some had prohibited the export and sale of deerskins. Upper Canada enacted its first protective legislation for game species in 1829 and its first full-fledged game law in 1839. The pro-liferation of laws really curtailed only the honest citizen. The need for game law enforcement officers resulted in Massachusetts and New Hampshire developing the first warden (or conservation officer) systems in North America in 1850.

The increase in protective legislation and the attendant development of an enforcement system failed to stem the decline in wildlife populations. Human populations continued to grow, wildlife habitat continued to disappear, and attention turned to the large predators and their control. These animals were competing directly with man for an increasingly limited resource, and mechanisms such as government trapping and bounties were employed to reduce their numbers. These programs were only partially successful. Predator numbers in reality were lowered by the decline in prey species' numbers and the concerted efforts of the agricultural community to remove bears, wolves, and mountain lions that occasionally harassed livestock and seemed threatening to homesteaders. The prime factor leading to predator decline was habitat change associated with agricultural activities. Extensive clearing of forested land created conditions they could not tolerate.

Most of the modern game laws were pretty much in place in the U.S. by 1880. All states had game laws by that time, and such key regulatory components as licensing of hunters (New York and New Jersey in 1864) and the differentiation between resident and nonresident hunter (New Jersey in 1864), the rest (or closed) day during the week (Maryland in 1872), the banning of market hunting (Maryland in 1872), and the bag limit (Iowa imposed a limit of twenty-five prairie chickens/day in 1878) had been initiated.

Other developments occurring about this same time were designed to maintain some of the fast disappearing wilderness. In 1872 Yellowstone National Park, often considered to be the first national park in the world, was established. (Actually Hot Springs, Arkansas was the first national park formed in the U.S.) In 1887, the Rocky Mountain Parks Act gave Canadians their first national park. Whereas the Yellowstone Park Act had prohibited only the "wanton destruction" of wildlife, the Canadian equivalent provided for the "protection and preservation of game, fish, (and) wild birds generally." The inherent strength of the latter statement ensured a sounder legislative base for wildlife protection in the Canadian national parks system. In 1894, Yellowstone Park had to be closed to hunting, and thus a precedent was established which has become generally pervasive in North America by the latter part of the twentieth century. However, U.S. legislation has opened at least some of the Alaskan national parks to public hunting and Grand Tetons Park continues to allow elk hunting.

The national parks system was not the only area of federal jurisdiction where policies differed between Canada and U.S. The U.S. Supreme Court had declared in 1842 that wildlife was held in trust for all citizens. This statement set the stage for U.S. federal government intervention and direct involvement in the protection and conservation of wildlife. As trustee of wildlife, the U.S. federal government has successfully met numerous challenges from state governments, and although a doctrine of state ownership of wildlife has developed, U.S. federal wildlife law continues to expand. Its influence is most noticeable in the western states with their extensive federal lands. There the federal government controls the habitat and the state governments the regulations. Canada's jurisdiction over wildlife was never clearly stated in the original constitution (the British North America Act). By default, the actual Canadian situation has divided federal and provincial responsibilities based on interpretation and ad hoc arrangements. Provinces may opt in or out of federally funded wildlife programs. Unlike the U.S. where many states have significant percentages of their land area in federal lands, the Crown lands are under provincial, not federal control. It is only in the international area and through treaties such as the Migratory Bird Treaty of 1916 and the enabling legislation of the Migratory Bird Convention Act of

1917 that the Canadian federal government obtained responsibility for wildlife management, in this case for waterfowl and other migratory birds.

Despite the great differences in governmental systems and the extent of federal influence, in practice the areas of federal influence do not differ greatly between the two countries. The major difference is the degree of U.S. federal intervention in state activities as a result of extensive federal land holdings. This is still a contentious issue in many states and was the basis for the "Sagebrush Rebellion" of the 1980's. Some of the southwestern states witnessed citizens' movements designed to bring about the transfer of control from federal to state jurisdiction.

In addition to national parks, habitat protection took the form of bird and game sanctuaries or refuges both public (Lost Mountain Lake: Canada 1887; Pelican Island: U.S. 1903) and private (Weber's Pond: Wisconsin 1891; Jack Miner's Game Sanctuary: Ontario 1907).

Despite these efforts, wildlife stocks still continued to decline. Prohibition of market hunting, restrictive legislation, and creation of wildlife or wilderness sanctuaries were failing to reverse the trend. It took Theodore Roosevelt's idea of "conservation through wise use" and actions precipitated by Roosevelt's doctrine to reverse it. Roosevelt's doctrine was simple. He recognized wildlife as a renewable natural resource just as range and forest land already were recognized. He contended that wildlife stocks would last forever if they were harvested scientifically and not faster than they were being produced. Propagation, stocking, and habitat management were to become other cornerstones of wildlife management as the twentieth century progressed. The biological naiveté of the early 1900s which necessitated such statements as Roosevelt's may seen incredible today; but it is important to realize we still have too many managers who ignore the biological realities of the populations they are supposedly managing. Even now benign ignorance or continued adherance to outmoded or scientifically unsubstantiated ideas, too often blocks rational wildlife management.

Some Management Principles

What are the mechanisms the modern manager can employ? Manipulation of hunting seasons has been a favorite. Seasons can be opened early or extended in areas where the manager wishes to enlarge the harvest. Shortening a season to reduce harvest often backfires because the increased effective hunting pressure/unit time usually compensates for the decreased number of available days. Males-only seasons (especially for cervids), periodic harvest, and party permits all have been used or suggested as means to maximize recreational opportunity and license sales, sometimes without regard to the biological realities of the situation and social requirements of the species. Economic pressures can be the controlling factors when a management agency derives its income directly or indirectly from license sales.

If we were to have the best of all possible worlds in a management sense, how would harvest be controlled? First, the geographical area to be managed should be divided into ecophysical regions which describe the environmental realities of the area. Factors such as soils, vegetation, physiography, climate, water, human population, and access must be considered and boundaries determined primarily on ecological grounds. The species to be managed will determine whether sub-units are necessary. Ideally, if the data were available, management should be geared to a discrete population and its critical habitat requirements, be it a white-tailed deer wintering area or a garter snake hibernaculum.

Second, the manager should have sound population estimates for the management area, and because wildlife populations seldom show random distributions, he also needs knowledge of the distributional patterns of the species. Further necessary biological data include natural mortality and natality rates by sex and age class; sex ratios by age class, and factors responsible for any differential rates. Actually what is needed is a complete understanding of the population dynamics of the species.

Third, it is useful to have an idea of the public's demands. How many prospective users are there? What are their expectations? What types of use can be provided? What potential conflicts between users exist? This provides the socioeconomic frame for later management decisions.

Finally, a management plan must be developed with options ranging from the most practical to the most desired, offering logical and rational explanations of what the costs and benefits of each approach would be. The desired population levels and attendant use levels, be they harvest or viewing, are to be quantified and mechanisms for control detailed.

Even in our ideal world, there may be legislative restrictions to which one must adhere. What flexibility exists for management decisions? What are the political realities of the jurisdiction, and what mechanisms are available for selling the public and the administration on the value of the management program? What are the funding limitations?

Let's now look at two very different hypothetical examples in a less than ideal world.

Example 1—An Urban Nongame Species
    Desired uses:
    a. recreational viewing
    b. aesthetic component of urban areas

Viewing opportunities are limited to areas of open grassland interspersed with mature conifers and shrub patches, which are also the breeding and feeding habitat. Habitat requirements are usually met by city parkland and cemeteries but seldom by private homeowners. The species is migratory, so viewing opportunity is limited to spring and summer. Normal breeding density is 1 pair/hectare with approximately 10 hectares of prime habitat still available within the city. Naturalist groups and bird watchers are interested in viewing opportunities, but the species is sensitive to disturbance during the breeding season so productivity is highest (3 young/breeding pair) in cemeteries and lowest in public parkland (1 young/breeding pair). Demand is 10,000 viewer hours/year. No funds are available for management of this species. Conflict is possible among cemetery owners, bereaved individuals, and resource users. Longevity of the species, natural mortality, and reproductive rate clearly show that park populations are not self-sustaining and that recruitment occurs from the cemetery populations.

Management should be directed to protect the cemetery populations and improve viewing opportunities within the park system. Unless a problem develops, the cemeteries can be left alone. No publicity regarding the abundance of the species there should be made, and a discreet letter to cemetery managers suggesting they contact your agency if bird watchers begin to pose a nuisance should encompass the action (or inaction) requirements. Make parks' officials aware of the critical habitat requirements of the species and ask them to maintain those areas currently supporting breeding populations. See if parks officials and the naturalist groups are willing to fund viewing platforms to at least localize the impact of birdwatchers. Numbers required, siting of the structures, and some mechanism for determining the public response (and the birds' response) should be incorporated into the plan. Modifications are required only if demand and/or supply change drastically.

Example 2—A Big Game Species
    Desired uses:
    a. recreational viewing
    b. sport hunting

The species occurs in 75% of the management zones (40,000km$_2$) in the jurisdiction. Available winter range is critical and potentially limiting habitat. Population is estimated at 60,000 individuals and annual harvest at 20,000. The population has been declining and is currently below the predicted carrying capacity of 85,000 animals. Major mortality factors include poaching, winter starvation in some areas, predators (domestic and wild) and hunting. Nonresident hunters account for 10 percent of the harvest and 30 percent of the revenue from license sales. Forest industries have been reducing critical habitat at a non-replacement rate of 1000 ha/year. Demands for hunting opportunity and recreational viewing are increasing. The tourist industry demands that no season closures or reductions occur because of the potential economic impact on rural areas.

Management direction should allocate hunters and harvest in numbers more representative of regional conditions and population. If adequate management zones do not exist, they must be reorganized and used to distribute hunters more effectively. Impose quota systems to achieve harvest levels that will allow population growth in the underpopulated zones. Hunter opportunity will be reduced by these quotas, but some of the demand may be met by primitive weapons seasons (archery or muzzle-loading). Minimum season length should not be reduced below two weeks to avoid concentration of hunters and to meet tourism requirements. Consider dog and wild predator control programs for those areas where serious losses to predators occur and explore antipoaching programs such as hot line informer and reward systems.

Effective management of critical winter habitat areas must be achieved either through cooperative efforts with the forest industry (by cut restrictions and other forest management guidelines) or through land-use legislation to protect critical wintering areas, or by both of these.

License fees for nonresident hunters should be significantly increased (declining numbers of licenses sold are offset by increased cost so revenue remains relatively constant). Area specific licensing for residents achieves the required restrictions on hunter numbers. In areas of high demand, use party permits with one animal per two hunters as the legal limit.

Education is required to explain the need for these actions and assure the nonhunting public that managers are aware of their interests. Management programs can increase viewing opportunities. It is also helpful to consider creating nonhunting zones in those areas of highest nonconsumptive recreation activities.

While these two examples may seem somewhat simplistic or contrived, in reality they represent two extremes in wildlife management. Many nongame management situations are handled adequately by benign neglect or minimal intervention. By contrast management of popular game species often necessitates comprehensive micro-management.

Models Can Help

There has been a tendency in recent years to use computer modelling to aid in deciding which regulations to impose. These models plug in biological data and harvest trends and provide comparative scenarios for different regulatory decisions. To be useful the data bases must be sound. Many wildlife agencies do not have accurate survey records. For those that do, the data bases are short, covering only a few years. Effective simulation depends on a long and accurate data record.

In reality, there are two types of models that can be used: (1) stochastic or (2) deterministic. The former is based on complete information about a natural population change. Using the giant Canada goose as an example, De Angelis (1976) pointed out that natural fluctuations in wild populations are best described by difference equations with randomly varying parameters. This approach recognizes the interdependence of birth and death rates and is superior to a logistic approach, with independence assumed. A stochastic difference equation model is therefore better equipped to reflect the rapid fluctuations likely to occur in most natural populations.

Caughley (1977) considers that there are but three problems of populations management: conservation, harvesting, and control. Invariably though, the decision of which management practice to apply to the situation is dependent on basic life table information on the population. It is perhaps obvious that no effective management can be applied without an understanding of the biology of the species and a population's variability, current trends, and composition. Knowing this, a manager can decide at what level of harvest the population will increase, decline, or provide a sustained yield (SY).

SY is but a small proportion of a large population, so maximum sustained yield (MSY) has been used as the management objective by many wildlife agencies. By operating at MSY, the maximum output of individuals is reached and hunter satisfaction sustained by higher harvests. The problem with MSY is that if exploitation exceeds this value, precipitous population decline is a likely consequence, particularly with a low productivity species.

If an adequate data base exists, proposed management strategies can be modelled to predetermine their impact on a species. Unfortunately, such models sometimes have been misused in the past. To be effective, a model must be limited in application to the species and circumstances for which it was designed. The use of models has often been abused by overextending them or projecting data to inappropriate situations. The U.S. Fish and Wildlife Service's model for the mallard has frequently been used to predict impact of hunting regulations on other dabbling ducks, even though the biology and indeed the effect of the regulations are known to be different. Walters et al. (1974) developed a model of the population dynamics of the mallard duck in North America so that long-term predictions of population response to management activities related to habitat and harvest could be made. They concluded that the key value of their model was not its predictive power but its ability to serve as a focus for research needs.

Other models, such as that for the Yukon grizzly derived by Sidorowicz and Gilbert (1981), are simpler because the data base was limited. Much of the data had to be extrapolated from similar populations in other geographical areas; therefore the model reflects the most likely biological situation based on these data, not necessarily the real one.

Generalized models such as ONEPOP are used for many different species whose attributes satisfy the logic of the model. Managers can model deer, elk, moose, or other big game species as long as certain basic information is known about the populations and harvest values are available. Populations are delineated by geographical boundaries which represent the year round range. This minimizes the problem of immigration and emigration as confounding factors. The function of the model is to simulate the dynamics of the real population so that the effects of various management decisions can be predicted.

The major advantage of modelling is that it forces the manager to decide which population factors are most critical and to define clearly how those factors interact. The ability to determine management effects on simulated populations without a time delay or involvement of personnel is an important money saver.

The major disadvantage of modelling is that few data bases are complete enough for an acceptable level of predictability. Managers also may view models as a cure-all for their problems when they really are only valuable tools.

To receive maximum benefit from a model, the user must be familiar enough with it to understand the underlying assumptions, its strengths, weaknesses, and accuracy. Familiarity is best achieved by being involved in the development of the model. The manager can interact with the modeler by providing the data base and assisting in development of the model's conceptual framework. To use a model for management purposes without understanding the underlying assumptions is dangerous and can lead to costly errors. Starfield and Bleloch (1986) provide examples of model development in wildlife management and lead the reader through the vagaries of inadequate data and other confounding factors in model construction.

The basic assumption of most population models is that either the environment is homogeneous or the population exists in a vacuum. Most models are not sophisticated enough to cope with the natural environmental heterogeneity of the real world. More truly ecological models are in the process of development and will include dispersal, immigration, species interactions, social behavior, critical reproductive habitat (refuges), and patterns of hunter distribution and harvest rate. The new models will also reflect time and space factors. Once the data to power these models are in place, managers will have the predictive capacity necessary to make wise decisions.

Regulatory Management

Even the most sophisticated model is only an aid. The manager's control over the number of animals being harvested is the ultimate key to effective regulatory practice. Theoretically, the easiest way is to establish a harvest quota and cease the harvest once it is reached. The limitations here are primarily political but also practical. There must be some means of determining the actual harvest level. Those jurisdictions requiring registration within twenty-four to forty-eight hours after harvest can simply monitor the tallies from the registration stations. How then do you effectively close down hunting, trapping, or any form of harvest once the quota is reached? In an uncontrolled licensing system with no limit on the number of licenses sold, inequality of opportunity is likely to occur because of unpredictable season closure. When individuals pay the same fee, they expect the equivalency of opportunity a fixed season provides. At least everyone knows when the season will end in that situation.

In Maine, the 1971 white-tailed deer season was curtailed under the emergency powers of the Inland Fish and Game commissioner. A series of severe winters had drastically reduced populations in several management zones (management was actually on the basis of two hunting zones, even though biological data from eight management zones were collected and analyzed). Because Maine has a compulsory registration system for deer, it was easy to compare the actual harvest with safe harvest levels developed from population estimates and indices. The biological advice was to close three management zones because of pending overharvest. The commissioner had to weigh the following factors: (1) potential long-term damage to deer populations; (2) potential long- and short-term declines in hunting license sales in succeeding years; (3) adverse political response by the public, hunting camp operators, and legislators to the use of emergency powers previously only contemplated in years of extreme fire hazards; and (4) a credibility gap between the managers and public if the severity of the situation became known and nothing was done. Action taken in this sensitive situation was a masterpiece of political tightrope walking. The season was stopped with three days' notice in the northern *hunting* zone (not the management zones) and shortened slightly in the southern hunting zone. Closure on the basis of the long-established hunting boundaries, with sufficient notice for hunters already afield in the north and at least remnant hunting opportunity in the south, did much to temper any adverse response. There were some dissidents who wanted their license fees refunded, and there was a slight decline in license sales in 1972. The public generally accepted the wisdom of the commissioner's action.

In Vermont, though severe winter mortality losses suggested compensatory mortality was occurring, entrenched management regulations had long held sway over both deer management and public education policies. As a result of a long-standing bucks-only season, the Vermont range was drastically overpopulated, and the deer populations possibly were psychophysically disrupted as per Bubenik's theory (Chapter 3). In an effort to balance populations and reduce pressure on the range, a modest antlerless season was initiated based on the premise that these deer would die anyway. Maine on the other hand had shown that their managers were not prepared fully to accept compensatory mortality as fact in their state and warned that overharvest of Maine deer would be a potentially severe depressant to already climatically reduced populations. Vermont officials reacted differently. Unfortunately, the politics of management more often than not override sound biological judgement. The Vermont officials feared a potentially negative hunter response to their antlerless deer season which was justifiable in light of the ecological realities of their overpopulated range and disproportionate female to male sex ratio. They did not explain, or perhaps recognize, that the Maine and Vermont situations were biologically very different. Even among the Maine management zones, there were real differences. At least one zone bordering on New Hampshire was like Vermont's situation in that it was underharvested but it too had to be closed when the southern hunting zone was curtailed. This is just one small example of the biological and political complexities inherent in management that can result from very restrictive legislation. In essence, Vermont deer hunters opposed to doe harvests used the Maine closure to discredit their own deer managers in a way that was totally unjustified. In recent years Maine too has opted for male only seasons in part of the state and may find that it, like Vermont, has limited its management flexibility for the future.

Harvest quotas also can be achieved by limiting license sales or hunting opportunity per individual. If license quotas are established based on average success rate per hunter and loss by crippling, adjustment can be made the following year for the slight variations from average values that will occur. After discovering that shortening the deer season did little to limit harvest and the decline of their deer population, Minnesota experimented with a long season. The hunter selected a maximum of three hunting days within the thirty day season, but each day had a maximum number of hunters. This approach effectively distributed hunter pressure throughout the season and provided equality of opportunity.

Hunting opportunity can be allocated by type of hunting. Archery, muzzle-loading, quality or trophy, and wilderness hunting are examples. An allocation system is more subtle but it also serves to distribute hunting pressure. For example, Washington State now requires a hunter to choose a single weapon system per big game species. A hunter may take deer only with bow and arrow if this is his choice but may choose another type of weapon for elk. More hunters can be accommodated because many bow hunters formerly also hunted with rifles. Low success methods like archery, low density hunting, or "quality" zones, are means of reducing harvest in sensitive or overharvested areas. Less vulnerable areas are then left to bear the brunt of the general firearms hunting season.

Management problems can also result from underharvest, and there are mechanisms for enticing hunters to areas that can handle more of them. Some of the most useful ways to achieve better hunter distribution involve economic incentives. Lower license fees or increased bag limits are powerful ones.

Even within underhunted areas, hunter distribution can be a problem. It has been shown that hunters seldom move distances greater than 1.5 miles (2.4 km) from access roads, and the number of hunters generally decreases with distance from an access road or trail. Conversely, studies of animal distribution suggest they may avoid areas close to access roads. More favorable distribution of hunters can be achieved through a better access system. This can be partially accomplished by using either public or private funds to maintain forest roads after cutting. Private funds are user fees paid to the landowner. Road access must be carefully regulated because some species such as elk, grizzly bear and moose are vulnerable to disturbance caused by vehicles. Road closure has been used to reduce disturbance and hunting pressure on big game species—especially elk. This has the added benefits of promoting a higher quality hunting experience and reducing danger of hunting accidents in areas with too many access roads. Similarly, seismic grid patterns, which provide travel lanes for both moose and hunter, have necessitated controls on hunter access in places like Alberta and Alaska.

An innovative method of restricting waterfowl harvest was implemented by the U.S. Fish and Wildlife Service. Each species was allocated a point value according to sex, for instance male mallard, 25 points; female, 40 points. Species in difficulty for which managers wished to reduce harvest had very high point values, such as female canvasback, 100 points. A hunter may hunt until his accumulated harvest has reached or exceeded the designated point limit eg 100 points. He might then have to quit hunting if he shot a female canvasback. The logic behind this regulation is that hunters would concentrate on low point value birds to maximize the number of birds they could get. The system has been tried in at least twelve states, and although successful on this limited basis, it will take some time before general hunting can be controlled by this type of system. The hunter need only to identify the bird after it is shot, but it would be advantageous to him to be able to identify the bird on the wing. This should eventually result in a more knowledgeable hunter. Enforcement is likely to be a problem on a large scale, however, as hunters might be inclined to dispose of high count birds. The interesting outcome of preliminary testing is that the majority of hunters surveyed preferred the point system to the fixed bag limit, possibly because of the potential for increased harvest if the hunter uses the system judiciously.

The effectiveness of regulatory management has been demonstrated many times but perhaps nowhere as dramatically as in Newfoundland. In 1960 biologists determined that moose populations showing winter densities of twelve or more animals per square mile were causing severe damage to balsam fir and white birch regeneration in a central portion of the province. To attract hunters they instituted a long (fifteen weeks) season, a resident license fee at half the normal cost, and a bag limit of three moose of any sex or age (although a separate license was required for each moose taken). With these and other incentives a kill of thirteen moose per square mile was achieved in 1960. This harvest plus that of 1961 resulted in a population decline to less than six moose per square mile in the winter survey; a density level at which browsing pressure was insufficient to cause severe damage to forest regeneration.

One advantage of regulation, as opposed to habitat management or land-use planning, is the immediacy of control it offers. By wise use of liberal or restrictive mechanisms, harvest rates can be adjusted to the desired level. Historically, management agencies have usually been too conservative, probably in response to the massive declines in wildlife numbers in the late 1880's and early 1900's. This has resulted in overpopulations of some species such as white-tailed deer. Bucks-only laws instituted to protect stocks in states like Vermont, New York, and Pennsylvania did the job all too well. Range deterioration and agricultural damage often became problems. To be truly effective, regulatory management must be tied to biological reality. Data on age-specific birth and death rates, breeding ages of males and females, numbers of individuals, sex and age class, and carrying capacity should all be known. Carrying capacity is "the maximum number of animals of a given species and quality that can survive in a given ecosystem through the least favorable environmental factors within a stated time period" (Edwards and Fowle 1955). The most limited environmental element will also limit the number of individuals that can live on any area of land. Any management practice that increases the supply or improves the distribution of these elements will tend to increase the carrying capacity of the area up to the point where crowding initiates density-dependent control mechanisms. This concept provides the mechanistic base for habitat management (Chapter 5).

The fallacy of state or province wide uniform regulations should become apparent with the realization that animals and hunters are not distributed uniformly over the land area. Regional differences mediated by ecological factors have to exist. They must be acknowledged and regulations formulated accordingly. Characteristics of the hunters must also be known. Ideally managers should apprise hunters of the need for regulatory management changes and obtain their support. More effort is needed to improve the image of hunting and hunters. The best management scheme will fail if the hunting public ignores the program and continues to violate regulations. It is unfortunate that ethics cannot be legislated, for if all hunters were imbued with a land ethic and respect for life and property, anti-hunting sentiment would not be so strong.

We give a small example as a case in point. We approached young hunters as they fired their shot guns from a county road into our neighbor's property. We informed the hunters that they were breaking the law on two counts—firing from a roadway and trespassing—as the property into which they were shooting was posted. They replied, "We didn't know this was private property." At this point I indicated the obvious "No trespassing" signs, "But we were only shooting tweetybirds," they said. Our disbelief and anger must have been apparent because they decided they had better leave before we told them that this was yet another infraction of the law. Such events are unfortunately all too common. Those hunters who enjoy their sport and take care to obey the law and the rights of others are commonly associated with the far too many gun-carrying miscreants. This issue underlies a considerable amount of the anti-hunting sentiment and undermines the best efforts of many management agencies.

Hunting has often been considered by managers to be a compensatory mortality factor. The idea resulted from a misapplication of Errington's early work on such prolific species as muskrat and bobwhite quail, which were difficult to overharvest. When mortality occurs, species compensate by reducing the age of sexual maturity, increasing survival rates of embryos and young animals, and basically increasing overall productivity per female as the mean age of individuals in the population declines. However, for species with limited reproductive potential or in situations of extreme local harvest, hunting mortality becomes a prime additive factor; populations are reduced or even extirpated. It is vital to assess the impact on a population of all mortality factors, including hunting. These data indicate whether the population will be able to compensate and to what extent it can do so. Regulations and other management practices then may be framed accordingly.

The U.S. Fish and Wildlife Service recently has come under attack for having inadequate waterfowl harvest data to justify hunting seasons and bag limits. The current waterfowl harvest survey is not conducted in a random fashion with regard to hunters; instead it is a random selection of post offices selling duck stamps. With a biased sample and an overall response rate of 10–15%, serious errors in harvest estimates can result. The answer is to institute a federal migratory bird hunting permit that itself could be used as the basis of a statistically valid harvest survey.

Such deficiencies in primary data give fuel to those opposed to hunting, and this group represents almost a majority of the population. Kellert and Berry's (1980) information on adults and Westervelt and Llewellyn's (1985) study of fifth and sixth grade students confirm that 40–45% of the adults and about 80% of the students were opposed to sport hunting. Most adults were opposed to hunting on moral grounds (56.1%) or for some specific reason other than unethical behavior of hunters; only 5.6% of those surveyed mentioned hunting behavior. This survey shows the depth of anti-hunting sentiment and suggests that wildlife agencies wishing to perpetuate hunting as a management tool had better be prepared to defend their position on sound, biologically valid, data.

Bibliography

Bergerud, A. T., F. Manuel, and H. Whalen. 1968. The harvest reduction of a moose population in Newfoundland. J. Wildl. Manage. 32:722–728.

Bubenik, A. B. 1972. North American moose management in light of European experiences. N.Am. Moose Conf. Workshop. 8:276–295.

Caughley, G. 1977. Analysis of vertebrate populations. John Wiley Sons, New York, NY. 234 pp.

De Angelis, D. L. 1976. Application of stochastic models to a wildlife population. Math. Biosci. 31:227–236.

Edwards, R. Y., and C. D. Fowle. 1955. The concept of carrying capacity. Trans. N. Am. Wildl. Nat. Resour. Conf. 20:589–602.

Geis, A. D., R. K. Martinson, and D. R. Anderson. 1969. Establishing hunting regulations and allowable harvest of mallards in the United States. J. Wildl. Manage. 33:848–859.

Gross, J. E., J. E. Roelle, and G. L. Williams. 1973. Program ONEPOP and information processor: a systems modeling and communication project. Colorado Coop. Wildl. Res. Unit, Colorado State Univ., For Collins, Prog. Rep. 327 pp.

Kellert, S. R., and J. K. Berry. 1980. Knowledge, affection and basic attitudes toward animals in American Society. U.S. Fish Wildl. Serv., Washington D.C., Rep. by N.T.I.S., U.S. Dep. Comm., Springfield, VA. 178 pp.

Michener, J. A. 1978. Chesapeake. Random House, New York, NY. 865 pp.

Nelson, L., Jr., and J. B. Low. 1977. Acceptance of the 1970–71 point system season by duck hunters. Wildl. Soc. Bull. 5:52–55.

Rost, G. R., and J. A. Bailey. 1979. Distribution of mule deer and elk in relation to roads. J. Wildl. Manage. 43:634–641.

Sidorowicz, G. A., and F. F. Gilbert. 1981. The management of grizzly bears in the Yukon, Canada. Wildl. Soc. Bull. 9:125–135.

Starfield, D. M. and A. L. Bleloch. 1986. Building models for conservation and wildlife management. Macmillan Publ. Co., New York, NY. 253 pp.

Thomas, J. W., J. D. Gill, J. C. Pack, W. M. Healy, and H. R. Sanderson. 1976. Influence of forestland characteristics on spatial distribution of hunters. J. Wildl. Manage. 40:500–506.

Walters, C. J., and P. J. Bandy. 1972. Periodic harvest as a method of increasing big game yields. J. Wildl. Manage. 36:128–134.

Walters, C. J., R. Hilborn, E. Oguss, R. M. Peterman, and J. M. Stander. 1974. Development of a stimulation model of mallard duck populations. Can. Wildl. Serv. Occ. Pap. No. 20. 35 pp.

Westervelt, M. O., and L. G. Llewellyn. 1985. Youth and wildlife. U.S. Dep. Int., Fish Wildl. Serv., Washington D.C. 78 pp.

Williams, G. L. 1981. An example of simulation models as decision tools in wildlife management. Wildl. Soc. Bull. 9:101–107.

Recommended Readings

Starfield, A. M., and A. L. Bleloch. 1986. Building models for conservation and wildlife management. Macmillan Publ. Co, New York, NY. 253 pp.

A helpful guide to the development of models, how to use them and their limitations. A number of case histories from hypothetical African game reserves are used to illustrate methodology and ideology.

U.S. Fish and Wildlife Service's series of publications on the "Population Ecology of the Mallard" provides useful insight into the development of a data base and management protocols for the mallard duck in North America.

Verner, J., M. L. Morrison, and C. J. Ralph (eds.) 1986. Wildlife 2000. Modeling habitat relationships of terrestrial vertebrates. Univ. Wisconsin Press, Madison, WI. 470 pp.

Includes papers presented at a symposium in 1984. Deals with the development and application of models designed to predict wildlife responses to habitat modification. It is a thorough review of the state of the art in wildlife-habitat modelling.

V HABITAT MANAGEMENT

We have made considerable progress in recent decades in the development of management prescriptions for wildlife habitat. Anyone who has compared the first techniques manual of The Wildlife Society with the most recent fourth edition will attest to this progress. Despite considerable improvement in our capability to manipulate the environment for wildlife, we still do so primarily for single species and at times secondarily to other resource areas like forestry or agriculture. We are only beginning to think and act in terms of ecosystem management, to conceptualize the complex of physical and biological components that provide food, water, cover, and shelter for communities of wildlife species, and to integrate these needs into land-use activities that might otherwise destroy them.

This chapter does not provide management prescriptions but examines issues related to wildlife habitat management and elaborates on mechanisms for ensuring consideration of wildlife needs within the general planning process. It discusses methodologies developed for describing or assessing wildlife habitat and integrating this information into the planning procedure.

Habitat Evaluation and Land-use Planning

Habitat, literally the place where an animal lives, is often the factor most limiting to wildlife populations. With the increasing demand for land for agriculture, urbanization, water impoundments, and so on, the habitat for many species of wildlife is lost. A few tolerant and/or adaptable species have their habitats increased. With adequate planning, it is sometimes possible to mitigate the effects of land-use change and in some cases even enhance the natural environment. Large scale extraction of coal seams, oil shales, or oil sands presents an opportunity for habitat manipulation on a massive scale. European countries have had decades of experience with this, but in North

113

America the Appalachian rehabilitation of coal-mined areas is the first such major exercise. Development of the Alberta oil sands could create land forms and water bodies more varied and productive of wildlife than the muskeg found in much of the area now. Similar opportunities sometimes should be exploited by wildlife managers rather than always opposed for the short-term disadvantages involved. As managers, we should maintain a long-term ecological perspective and become actively involved in planning, or events will simply pass wildlife by and the very real opportunities for turning temporary environmental disaster into lasting ecological advantage will be lost.

In the past, wildlife habitat alteration has tended to be very species oriented. Management was practiced for individual species—for ruffed grouse, perhaps, or white-tailed deer—instead of considering the full ecological consequences of habitat manipulation. Such an approach does have validity when the manager is dealing with critical habitat elements, e.g., wintering range for cervids, staging areas for waterfowl, or when endangered or threatened species are involved. Habitat management should otherwise be balanced ecologically to meet the needs of as many different species as possible. Unfortunately, we often do not have data on all the habitat requirements of each species although much effort has been directed this way in recent years. Thomas (1979) introduced a planning framework for wildlife in forest environments that adopted a more holistic approach. Although the Pacific northwest and the managed forests of the Blue Mountains of Oregon and Washington provided the example, the methodological approach is valid for habitat management in most forested areas of North America. Wildlife management has to be integrated with forest and range management to be effective. Objective, quantifiable arguments must be presented to justify modification of forestry and range practices to meet wildlife habitat needs.

Thomas' approach is deceptively simple. As a first step, the plant communities and their successional stages are described for an area. Wildlife information is then extracted at four levels. Level 1 is the life form association i.e., the relationship of animal life forms to the vegetative associations for such functions as feeding and reproduction. For example, in the Blue Mountains a number of species feed and reproduce primarily on the ground without specific water or physiographic considerations (elk, dark-eyed junco, and western fence lizard are examples). This particular association describes a life form that includes the 3 species listed plus others. The advantage of this system is to reduce substantially the number of faunal units to be considered. In the Blue Mountains case, it meant 16 life forms represented 378 species (Table 5.1). It also means that forest managers can more readily evaluate the responses of wildlife to habitat types than if they had to consider each species independently. Level 2 describes the relationship of the individual species to the plant communities and their successional stages for feeding and reproduction (Figures 5.1 and 5.2). This approach is of particular value for endangered, threatened, or indicator (featured) species. The various species are grouped by life form to facilitate comparison with level 1. It becomes apparent as this is done that some forest communities are more productive of wildlife than others.

Level 3 gives a one line summary of key biological information for each species, and at level 4 references are listed for consultation if the information provided in the previous three levels is not sufficient. The adaptability of each species is scored by a versatility index (V) where

$$V = (C_r + S_r) + (C_f + S_f)$$
$$C = community$$
$$S = successional\ stage$$
$$r = reproduction$$
$$f = feeding$$

The more specialized wildlife have low V values. Special emphasis is also afforded particular habitat types such as riparian zones, edges, snags, decaying logs, cliffs, talus, and caves.

If featured species management is utilized, actual prescriptions to enhance habitat conditions can be provided. Thomas et al. (1979) give such details for elk and deer and in the process outline appropriate silvicultural options.

Verner and Boss (1980) developed these concepts into an extensive application for the western Sierra Nevada region of California. The data base is available in computer readable format so that prospective users can plug directly into the species matrices and make predictions on the effects of forest management practices or land-use alterations. Biological information provided by species includes: status, distribution/habitat, special habitat requirements, breeding, territory/home range, food habits, other pertinent and key references (Figure 5.3). Habitat is ranked by type as optimum, suitable, or marginal and season(s) of use are given. In effect, it is a valuable planning tool. The approach actually had its background in methodologies proposed to help conduct environmental impact assessments as required by NEPA (1976). See Whitaker and McCuen (1976) and Graber and Graber (1976) for examples of environmental evaluations with specific relevance to wildlife.

Attempts to standardize habitat evaluation by federal wildlife personnel resulted in studies by Ellis et al. (1978), who evaluated four methodologies for accuracy and repeatability, and by Baskett et al. (1980), who replaced the original "blue handbook" of the U.S.D.I. with the "yellow hand-book."

Table 5.1 Life Form Descriptions (Thomas, 1979)

Life form	Reproduces	Feeds	No. of species[1]	Examples
1	in water	in water	1	bullfrog
2	in water	on ground, in bushes, and/or in trees	9	long-toed salamander, western toad, Pacific treefrog
3	on ground around water	on ground, in bushes, trees, and water	45	common garter snake, killdeer, western jumping mouse
4	in cliffs, caves, rimrock, and/or talus	on ground or in air	32	side-blotched lizard, common raven, pika
5	on ground without specific water, cliff, rimrock, or talus association	on ground	48	western fence lizard, dark-eyed junco, elk.
6	on ground	in bushes, trees, or air	7	common nighthawk, Lincoln's sparrow, porcupine
7	in bushes	on ground, in water or air	30	American robin, Swainson's thrush, chipping sparrow
8	in bushes	in trees, bushes, or air	6	dusky flycatcher, yellow breasted chat, American goldfinch

Table 5.1 Continued

Life form	Reproduces	Feeds	No. of species[1]	Examples
9	primarily in deciduous trees	in trees, bushes, or air	4	cedar waxwing, northern oriole, house finch
10	primarily in conifers	in trees, bushes, or air	14	golden-crowned kinglet, yellow-rumped warbler, red squirrel
11	in conifers or deciduous trees	in trees, bushes, on ground, or in air	24	goshawk, evening grosbeak, hoary bat
12	on very thick branches	on ground or in water	7	great blue heron, red-tailed hawk, great horned owl
13	in own hole excavated in tree	in trees, bushes, on ground, or in air	13	common flicker, pileated woodpecker, red-breasted nuthatch
14	in hole made by another species or in a natural hole	on ground, in water or air	37	wood duck, American kestrel, northern flying squirrel
15	in burrow underground	on ground or under it	40	rubber boa, burrowing owl, Columbian ground squirrel
16	in burrow underground	in air or water	10	bank swallow, muskrat, river otter
		Total:	327	

[1]Species assignment to life form is based on predominant habitat-use patterns.

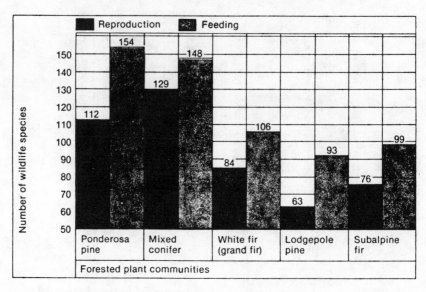

Figure 5.1   Number of wildlife species oriented to forested plant communities for feeding and reproduction (Thomas, 1979)

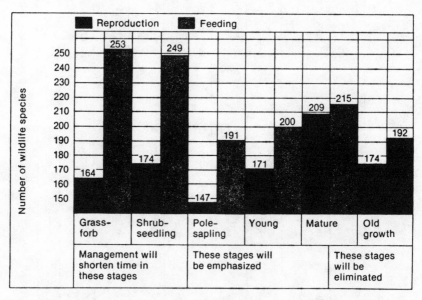

Figure 5.2   Number of wildlife species oriented to forestry successional stages and the potential effect of intensive timber management (Thomas, 1979)

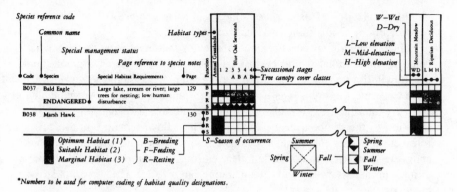

Figure 5.3   The key to elements in the species/habitat matrix given in a bald eagle example (Verner and Boss, 1980)

Although the latter study occurred in Missouri, the procedure outlined was proposed as suitable for other areas as well. The basic elements of the approach are:

1. The wildlife species to be considered on each study site are selected and the handbook material on life requirements read.
2. The study site is walked through, the characteristics mentioned in the handbook are noted, and a field form is used to ascertain the scores that can be given. Each characteristic is then subjectively scored. Some of these habitat characteristics are very important to the species and have a maximum score of ten for good conditions; less critical characteristics have a maximum score of five. If a particular characteristic is not applicable or does not occur, "NA" is put on the form.
3. Measurements of such vegetative characteristics as tree size class (based on dbh of overstory trees), canopy closure and cover percentages are made on site.
4. Using low-level aerial photos, measurements of distance factors—to water, cropland, other woodlots, forest, and other habitat types—are made from the center of the study unit.
5. Habitat unit values are derived from the above and the overall value for the site is computed, compensating for the NA characteristics.

If sufficient sites have been evaluated, the relative value of any one site can be determined. If a site has particular value for certain species, it should also show up with this approach. In cooperative efforts with a number of provinces, the Canadian Wildlife Service has used the Golet Wetland Classification system to inventory areas and assign a score for their value to wildlife production. This provides a means of assigning priority to land units for protection, acquisition, or management.

Habitat evaluation procedures are intended to document what is there, what could be there, what would be lost, and the relative value of a given land unit to wildlife populations. In Maine, for example, a system to set priorities for deer wintering areas was used based on number of deer overwintered, size of wintering area, distance to nearest wintering area, and relative contribution to the regional deer population. This allowed managers to decide forest cutting practices within individual "yards." The outcomes ranged from complete protection to controlled clear-cutting. Inventories of habitat conditions are necessary not only for planning but also for actual manipulative practices: i.e., management.

Increasingly, remote sensing is being used to classify habitat. Aerial and satellite imagery provide the opportunity for mapping and classifying land on a scale not previously possible. Variables commonly used in the classification process include plant associations, land forms, surface topography, soils, aspect, slope, and moisture condition. In Canada, the Canada Committee on Ecological Land Classification provided a focus for wildlife managers attempting to develop uniform methodologies for wildlife habitat classification. No comparable group exists in the United States, but important contributions have been make by using Landsat and aerial imagery. Geographical information systems (GIS) have been an off shoot of remote sensing activities. These systems generally provide a means of overlaying detailed information on a land classification system usually based on wildlife habitats or vegetative communities. The information generated provides both overview and site-specific means of examining the existing data bases. A GIS is a powerful management tool and invaluable for decision-making over larger land areas. One such use has been for so-called "Gap Analysis." In this application areas of maximum biodiversity are compared with protected areas to determine where major regions of biodiversity are not included within land holdings assuring their protection. The basic concept is that long term maintenance of the most richly productive wildlife habitats in reasonably protected status is the best option for minimizing future species extinctions. Currently mapping is underway for much of the United States.

With few exceptions, most of the methodologies in use are general in nature and not related solely to game species. This is partly due to the land-management planning policy of the U.S. National Forest Management Act and the Resources Planning Act and explains the forefront activity of the U.S. Forest Service in comprehensive wildlife habitat management. Wildlife is thus an inclusive term representing all species of vertebrates other than fish. Management agencies have been scrambling to fill the void that exists relating to the habitat requirements for many bird, amphibian, reptile, and small mammal species. Examples are the proliferation of nongame programs within state and provincial wildlife agencies and the number of workshops and symposia that have been held recently on nongame habitat management procedures. Management of wildlife habitat is becoming increasingly sophisticated and more indicator species-oriented, sometimes unfortunately.

Perhaps of greatest importance to wildlife managers is the question, ''How do you preserve wildlife habitat?'' Other than direct purchase, there are a number of techniques that have been used. We describe three of them.

Land-use Planning Controls

These procedures are based on extant legislation that controls or regulates the use of land. Land can be categorized as natural area or wildlife habitat if such classifications exist. Washington State's Environmental Policy Act of 1971 (SEPA) allows cities and counties to designate environmentally sensitive areas (ESA'S). SEPA applies in these ESA'S to some activities which are normally exempt from procedural review, but which could have significant adverse impact such as some forest practices, maintenance dredging and water rights issuances. The Massachusetts Wetlands Protection Act includes wildlife habitat as a function of wetlands to be protected, although the act only protects certain habitats such as riparian and flood plain. Many states have Forest Practices Acts that protect riparian habitat.

Official plan designations, zoning bylaws, and transfer of development rights also can be used to protect wildlife habitat. The transfer of development rights has been used to separate the right to develop property within the existing legislative frame from the other rights of land tenure or ownership. The owner is compensated by being given a certain number of development credits which can be transferred and used on another designated area or sold to another party.

With particular reference to wetlands, the 404 Permit Program in the United States, under the Federal Clean Water Act, requires all developers proposing to dredge or fill in wetlands to apply to the Army Corps of Engineers for an approval permit. The granting of permits, in turn, is monitored by the Environmental Protection Agency (EPA) and by conservation groups. The EPA can veto any approval if it feels the land should not be altered from its natural state. The impact of private interest groups on this process has ensured that proposed wetland developments have received considerable public scrutiny when important wildlife habitat is to be impacted. The growing federal initiative to protect wetlands will place increased emphasis on the 404 Permit Program as one of the mechanisms for achieving such protection. At the time of printing of this book, proposed changes to the 404 Permit Program would severely limit this oversight capability.

Purchase of Property Rights

Protection can be given to wildlife habitat by buying the partial rights to property in order to place restrictions on the land use. One method is to make an outright purchase, place restrictions or protective covenants on the property title, and resell the land, but often this approach is too expensive.

A *conservation easement* is the purchase of partial rights to a property. Under the terms of such an easement there is a servient tenant who retains the right to use and enjoy the property, subject to the rights of the second party, the dominant tenant, who places restrictions on the use of the property. Compensation or payment for the easement is usually determined by subtracting the assessed value of the land with the specified development restrictions from the assessed value with no restrictions. An example of this type of easement entails restriction of tree cutting on a given piece of property. The cost of the easement generally reflects the lost commercial value of the unharvested trees. The Nature Conservancy in the United State has effectively used this method in its national wetlands program to protect large watersheds like the Brule River in northern Wisconsin. Many states, including Montana, Oregon, Missouri, and Washington, have enabling legislation for conservation easements. Recently The Nature Conservancy has begun acquiring water rights for important sites in the arid west as a means of protecting critical water flows and maintaining riparian and aquatic habitats.

Long-term-leasing has also been used to preserve wildlife habitat. The Canadian Wildlife Service entered into many such leases with prairie farmers to prevent drainage of potholes that were valuable to waterfowl. The problem with lease arrangements is that they have definite time limits. Although the government, as tenant, retains exclusive possession or control of the property for the fee paid, upon termination of the lease the landowner is free to do as he pleases with the land. Many prairie farmers entered into ten-year lease agreements not to drain potholes which they had never intended to drain. In the face of such attitudes, considerable money can be spent to achieve little. This may also by the case for the 1985 and 1990 U.S. Farm Bills, which contain provisions for conservation reserves. The 1990 bill allows farmers to sell the federal government a conservation easement on their wetlands and toughens the conservation compliance component by requiring farmers to implement plans to prevent soil erosion. Highly erodible agricultural land can be placed under contract with the federal government for a ten-year period and planted to grasses or trees. Wildlife habitat is one recognized objective. The farmer is paid for removing the land from production, but at the end of the ten-year period he is free to do whatever he wants with the land unless the sodbuster provisions, which are linked to the erosion potential of the land, are invoked. This would prevent conversion of the new grasslands or young forests back to croplands. Otherwise the end result would be farm subsidy and not conservation. The 1990 bill includes provisions which would deter conversion to cropland by means of penalty payments. Nonetheless, evidence that the primary function of the conservation provisions in the 1985 Farm Bill was to reduce commodity production rather than conserve soil or provide wildlife habitat mounted as farmers were allowed to harvest hay from, or graze cattle on, reserve lands during the 1988 drought and other incursions were allowed in 1989 and 1990. The 1990 bill appears to be more environmentally sound than its 1985 counter part.

Management agreements require an agency to perform certain management services provided the landowner does not take certain actions such as posting the land against hunting.

Incentive Programs

The United States Department of Agriculture administers a number of programs that serve to enhance or protect wildlife habitat. The Water Bank Act provides payments to landowners who sign an agreement not to drain their lands. It is similar in nature to the leasehold agreement. The Soil Conservation Service (SCS) will provide trees and shrubs free or at low cost to prevent soil erosion and provide wildlife habitat, an added benefit. The SCS also provides wildlife habitat plans for agricultural lands when requested by a farmer. *Preferential tax treatment* can be used as a financial incentive to preserve or produce wildlife habitat. Either property or income tax incentives are offered. In the case of property tax, the landowner may be given an exemption or deferment for maintaining the property in its natural state. Once the property is developed, the exempt status is lost and all deferred taxes have to be paid. Income tax incentives encourage the donation of land to public agencies by allowing it as deduction from income. Another financial incentive that has been proposed in Canada is the use of *Loan guarantees and reduced interest rates* to encourage environmentally sound farming practices and wildlife habitat preservation especially in the prairie provinces. In such an arrangement, federal and provincial mortgages and loans would include the incentives if the land-use activities for which the money was being borrowed were shown to be sustainable without environmental damage. A *special designation*, although not financial, can provide incentive for a landowner to protect natural habitat. Many of the early bird sanctuaries and nature preserves were private lands whose owners made such designations in order to receive recognition by the government in the form of special certification, publication of the owner's name, or posting of the property. This has worked successfully for many agencies, public and private, in natural resource areas, a good example being the Tree Farm Program. Tree Farmers post their land with distinctive signs, adhere to sound principles of forest land management, and are confirmed by professional foresters free of charge to the landowner.

Declining Wildlife Habitat—Old-Growth Coniferous Forest as an Example

Although most forests in North America are the second or third commercial growth on the same site, there are still areas in western Canada, Alaska, and the Pacific northwest where considerable acreage of old-growth (>180 years) forest remain. Some of these are within wilderness areas or national parks and are thus protected from commercial exploitation, but most of this habitat type outside of such areas is programmed for harvest by the turn of the century. Wildlife species like Vaux's swift, spotted owl, lynx, red-tree vole, Olympic salamander, Oregon slender salamander, and black-tailed deer, that appear partially or wholly dependent on this habitat for survival, will see further population reductions as the amount of old-growth forests continues to decline. The unique habitat features of old-growth forests, other than the large conifers themselves, are large snags and large dead falls on land and in streams. The forests are structurally complex with multiple vegetational layers and substantial amounts of ground cover. Soil building occurs predominantly within old-growth types. The microclimate produced by the vegetation is suitable for fungal growth that promotes decomposition and provides food for many organisms, including a number of small mammals. Crown and ground dwelling lichens are major sources of nitrogen, and lichen has been suggested as a key winter habitat requirement for woodland caribou populations.

To envision the decline in wildlife fauna possible if reduction in old-growth to current planning goals occurs, we need only look at one dependent species, the spotted owl. As recently as 1982, projected populations totalled 1,365 pairs and the planning goal was 375 pairs; a 75 percent reduction. As the result of an effort to enumerate the species and determine minimum viable population size, the Forest Service later set new objectives to maintain 1030 pairs (530 In Oregon and Washington) out of the existing population of perhaps 3,000 pairs. Thus a population reduction of about 65 percent was proposed in national forests. The habitat standard set was 1000 acres per breeding pair, although research had indicated that as much as 2000–2500 acres per breeding pair of spotted owls may actually be needed. Unless the habitat standard was increased, it may be well have been impossible to save the species except within the national parks and wilderness systems. The proposed spotted owl guidelines in the draft supplement to the final EIS for an amendment to the Pacific Northwest Regional Guide (U.S. Forest Service) would have provided at least 550 spotted owl habitat areas. Although each habitat area (SOHA) might include about 2,200 acres, only 1000 acres would be protected from timber sales. Litigation by environmental groups forced reconsideration of the spotted owl for listing as an endangered or threatened species after the U.S. Fish and Wildlife Service had initially declared there was no justification for such status. In the meantime, timber sales that were being blocked by court injunctions proceeded under Section 318 of FY 1990 Appropriations Act for the Department of the Interior and Related Agencies, which established measures that the Forest Service must follow to minimize the effect of timber harvest on spotted owls. This compromise agreement allowed 7.7 billion board feet to be sold from Oregon and Washington National Forests. The Forest Service also established advisory boards consisting of environmental, business and community interests in the 13 National Forests known to be occupied by the northern spotted owl. These boards reviewed and made recommendations related to timber sale designs. An Interagency Scientific Committee chaired by Jack Ward Thomas and with other scientifically qualified personnel from the Forest Service, Fish and Wildlife Service and the Bureau of Land Management was established to: review the biological basis of the Fish and Wildlife Service criteria for review of timber sales and the basis for conference opinions; determine whether current land management strategies of the agencies are reserving options that will allow for long-term conservation of the northern spotted owl; provide recommendations to preserve options from now until the conservation strategy is completed; define habitat relationships for long-term conservation of northern spotted owls; suggest options to achieve the amount and configuration of habitat needed for long-term conservation of the northern spotted owl throughout its range; and evaluate current research, monitoring, and inventory programs to answer critical questions and track the adequacy of management strategies. The Thomas Report, as it is known, recommended that Habitat Conservation Areas (HCA's) replace the SOHA's. The HCA system allows management for clusters of at least 20 breeding pairs of owls and avoids the fragmentation that SOHA's would allow. But the extent of the lands to be "locked up" in the HCA's caused anguished outcries from industry, loggers, truckers, and governments in the timber dependent communities of the Pacific northwest. The battle between owls and economics was fully joined after the species was listed as threatened by the Fish and Wildlife Service. President Bush stated that a "balance" must be found between protection of owl habitat and concern for jobs. Congress would be asked to pass legislation to (1) allow the BLM to implement its own owl protection plan rather than the Interagency

Scientific Committee's and do so without court challenge being possible, (2) adopt an interim management plan developed by an interagency task force for Forest Service lands and also disallow court challenge and (3) expand the mandate of the Endangered Species Committee (a politicized vehicle of the President) to allow it to develop a long-term forest management plan for federal lands. In effect, the administration's reaction was to do whatever was possible to ensure the Thomas Report would not be implemented and the power of the Endangered Species Act would be weakened. Although the final outcome was unknown at the time this book went to press, it will establish a precedent that will affect policy and wildlife management for the immediate future.

A related political controversy has surrounded the Tongass National Forest in southeast Alaska. Here the old growth hemlock, cedar and spruce provide critical winter habitat for Sitka black-tailed deer. Congressional action has resulted in decreased harvest targets and greater consideration of non-commodity values.

Habitat availability and quality are but two factors that will decline with a significant reduction in the old growth forest type. Another major factor is the distributional pattern of those remnant old-growth forests. Although we have no definite knowledge of the best distributional configurations to maintain maximum wildlife values, biogeographical theory clearly predicts that fragmentation or isolation of the remnant old-growth forests will result in local and regional faunal extinctions and an overall decline in species diversity and abundance. Therefore, it will be the pattern of cutting and degree of isolation of the remaining patches of old-growth forests that become critical elements in determining the impact such habitat loss has on wildlife. This realization has led to landscape level studies and a renewed emphasis on bio-diversity as a goal in forest planning and environmental impact analyses. The U.S. Forest Service has adopted an ecosystem approach to forest management in the western coastal states that embraces the maintenance of biological diversity and sustainable outputs of goods and services.

Other examples could have been used to illustrate the same ecological realities of declining and increasingly fragmented wildlife habitat—the loss of bottomland hardwoods in the Mississippi River, the loss of wetland habitat, or the loss of short grass prairie. Each situation suggests that at some stage the remaining habitat will no longer be able to support given wildlife species because of size or distance considerations. Newmark (1987) provides strong corroborating evidence from the U.S. National Parks where parks in the 1,000–3,000 square kilometer size range (eg. Mount Rainier and Sequoia-King Canyon) have lost up to 32 percent of their original species. When habitats of sufficient size are no longer available and new ones cannot be reached, those species dependent upon them will inevitably become extinct. It is merely a question of time.

Habitat Management—Can It Be Achieved?

Activities posing the greatest threat to wildlife habitat are development (urban, industrial, utilities, mining), agriculture, and forestry. Wildlife management needs to be integrated with these enterprises if we are to maximize the potential of other land uses to produce wildlife habitat or at least to mitigate the impacts. Better communication between government agencies is a first step toward consideration of wildlife values outside of wildlife departments. Interagency panels or committees to explore policies and programs that impinge on wildlife habitat and to whom wildlife managers can express their concerns will also help alleviate the situation. The mere existence of such committees, however, only permits communication; action is often dependent on the individuals involved. The economic and political components of greatest value often determine what policy or action is ultimately followed. Canadian federal and provincial governments offer incentives to farmers to drain wetland areas, then through other departments or ministries sometimes offer incentives to maintain wetlands as wildlife habitat. Such counterproductive actions could be prevented if a coordinated interagency program were developed to provide some means of giving priority to wetlands based on wildlife values. Drainage assistance would then be allowed only for those sites of low value for wildlife and high value for agriculture. The political reality is that agricultural interests have the greatest clout and wildlife habitat suffers as a result. There often is no meaningful attempt even to set up committees to address the issues. Still, there is hope that attempts to establish a sustainable land management ethic in Canadian agriculture will overcome the decades of countervailing forces.

Wildlife managers at times have been their own worst enemies. The Ontario Chapter of the Canadian Society of Environmental Biologists (formerly Canadian Society of Wildlife and Fishery Biologists) in the mid-1970s had a committee develop a brief on agricultural land-use effects on wildlife for submission to the provincial government. That committee included representatives from a number of pertinent ministries including Natural Resources (OMNR), Agriculture and Food (OMAF), and Environment, plus the academic community. The brief, when completed, made a number of useful recommendations for implementation of policy by both OMNR and OMAF. The executive, however, refused to transmit it to the government for fear it would be too controversial. Professional momentum lost, influence never gained, action never taken. Too often the litany of wildlife "professionals" has been just such inaction. As a profession, it is our responsibility to speak out clearly and strongly on issues that affect wildlife and the environment. Too not do so is to abrogate our responsibility.

Gravel extraction and other mining activities usually can be turned to advantage by rehabilitation which enhances wildlife habitat. There are now numerous examples in Europe and North America where agriculture, forestry, and wildlife habitat have been successful land uses after rehabilitation of mining sites. Again this demonstrates the need for negotiation and involvement in land-use planning by wildlife managers. Adequate habitat inventories are strong weapons in such deliberations because they mean the quantifiable information is available. When it is possible to document the losses occurring and the relative importance of categorical accruals, potent ammunition is added to wildlife habitat advocacy. When this can be translated to losses in animal numbers, economic values can be assigned; and when economic values are involved, wildlife managers are talking in terms that politicians can understand.

The need to preserve habitat to sustain wildlife population has led Canadian governments (*Guideline for Wildlife Policy in Canada*, 1982) to consider the following actions:

1. Ensure that policies and laws allow the conservation of any wild animals and their habitat.
2. Adopt a definition of wildlife that can include any species of wild animals.
3. Provide a basis in law for the integrated management of wildlife with wildlife habitat.

To maintain wildlife habitat, the following actions were to be considered:

1. Assess the capability of habitats to support wildlife, including the identification of existing constraints.
2. Assess the capacity of habitats to respond to changing land uses.
3. Formulate regional goals and objectives for the maintenance of wildlife habitat, particularly as inputs to land-use planning.
4. Conduct periodic surveys of the extent and quality of habitat to determine gains and losses.
5. Adopt measures to ensure that the use of ecosystems does not reduce their potential productive capacity in order to retain a maximum latitude for choice in making future decisions on land use and development.
6. Control the discharge of pollutants to minimize damage to habitat.

7. Establish systems of protected areas that include representative ecological types, giving priority to the protection of unusual habitats of limited extent, such as estuaries and old-age timber stands;

8. Conclude agreements between government agencies and with private corporations aimed at improving and extending wildlife habitat by integrating wildlife management with Agriculture: plan multiple-use strategies for certain ecosystems (e.g., grazing lands, wetlands); Forestry: harmonize forestry and wildlife objectives for forest lands and plan cutting and reforestation programs accordingly; Energy and mining: plan multiple-use strategies for lands altered by mining, seismic survey lines, roads, hydro-reservoirs, and other activities; Urban and recreation development: plan to maximize wildlife benefits and to minimize both risks to human safety and damage to property caused by wildlife.

The Canadian wildlife policy guidelines provide a blueprint for the development of meaningful policy; they do not ensure it. The guidelines will only become functional policy if the various jurisdictions actively pursue courses of action to implement the recommendations and if non-government agencies provide the political push to ensure that this is done. A wildlife manager cannot expect to achieve meaningful results by working in a vacuum. Interpersonal communications and mobilization of all interested parties are vital to success in the political arena.

As an outgrowth of the Wildlife Policy guidelines, the Canadian cabinet created [Wildlife] Habitat Canada in 1984 to be an agent of policy implementation, particularly as it relates to habitat acquisition. This represents the only federal agreement with the provincial jurisdictions involving private agencies such as Ducks Unlimited and the Canadian Wildlife Federation. This agency will have the major action role in assessing and developing wildlife habitat in Canada in the future. In 1990, the Wildlife Ministers' Council officially adopted "A Wildlife Policy for Canada" based on the 1982 guidelines. The goal of the policy is "to maintain and enhance the health and diversity of Canada's wildlife, for its own sake and for the benefit of Canadians." This would require: 1) maintenance and restoration of ecological processes, 2) maintenance and restoration of biodiversity and 3) sustainability of all wildlife uses. The policy is intended to be implemented and this is required reading for all Canadian wildlife managers.

The new push toward sustainable agriculture in both Canada and the U.S. offers promise for more environmentally sound land management practices in the agriculture sector. Perhaps the abuse of the land base seen this century will be stopped; we can only hope that the new government initiatives will be successful.

The Lakeshore Capacity Study

One illustration of an interagency approach to land-use planning was an effort by the province of Ontario managed through the Ministry of Housing's local planning policy branch. This interministerial study involved the Ministries of Housing, Environment, and Natural Resources. Wildlife was one component in an integrated study designed to measure the capacity of land and lake systems in central Ontario to support cottage development. The wildlife model was to predict quantitatively the impact of proposed development on wildlife and wildlife habitat. Songbirds, loons, raptors, deer, small mammals, mink, reptiles, and amphibians were all investigated as potentially sensitive indicators of change brought about by development of lakeshore areas. The disturbances associated with development include direct habitat loss or change due to clearings, buildings, pathways, and roads, and the indirect effects of noise, wave action (boats), and the presence of humans and their pets. Measures of disturbance were necessary so that cause-effect relationships could be ascertained and the model realistically would predict the effect of different types of development on wildlife populations and habitat. The most apparent effect of development is alteration of vegetation species composition and structure. By quantifying vegetational change associated with development and measuring differences in songbird and small mammal populations in relation to these environmental changes, a measure of impact was derived. LAKELIFE was the computer information system developed to provide that evaluation. The output predicts the changes in the existing wildlife community that will occur as a result of any particular development proposal. It is a powerful planning tool and when used in an iterative fashion can produce a development with an acceptable level of impact on wildlife communities. The primary inputs are total length of shoreline, length of developed shoreline, number of cottage lots, area of the lake, habitat types (by shoreline segment—usually 50 or 100m) and average lot size (frontage × 50m), segments that include deer wintering areas, littoral zone habitat type (by segment), offshore and onshore loon nesting sites (number by segment), number and location of suitable hawk nesting areas, number and location of suitable turtle nesting sites, and total number of streams (by segment). Impact values on small mammals, loons, mink, deer, streams, hawks, songbirds, and five fish species are then derived and used to evaluate whether development should occur and in what segments it should or should not take place. Lot size or location can be altered to reduce the impact. Two basic criteria were used to determine the acceptability of cottage development.

1. Wildlife populations must be maintained in self-sustaining communities that are as similar as possible to undisturbed shoreline communities, at least on some portions of the lake.
2. No species is to be extirpated from the shoreline community of any lake.

Unfortunately, the provincial government never implemented the findings of the study. Instead it was left to municipal and county planners to capitalize on the results.

A similar approach to vertebrate community assessment and an understanding of its dependence on the old-growth habitat types was undertaken in the Pacific northwest. This ambitious project was intended to compare the fauna in unmanaged young, mature, and old-growth stands in several physiographic regions. Although the research was terminated prematurely as funding priorities shifted, very few species were determined to be old-growth dependent when forests are regenerated after a natural catastrophic event such as fire. The effects of human intervention, especially logging, are the factors apparently limiting so-called old-growth related species.

More comprehensive studies of this type are needed if we are to achieve the necessary predictive capability to demonstrate the effects of habitat alteration and land-use decisions on wildlife populations. The agency controlling the policies for development or exploitation must then regard wildlife as a component to be considered along with water quality, aesthetics, board feet of timber, and agriculture. Often this only occurs when wildlife managers are vociferous enough to ensure that their resource gets equal consideration. Even persuasive wildlife managers can be thwarted by weak ministers, deputy ministers, assistant deputy ministers, game or wildlife commissioners or directors. Advocacy must transcend the organization and must be politically acceptable *within* the agency before it can be politically successful outside of it.

In Washington state, a consensus based mechanism has been adopted to avoid increasing the legislative restrictions of the Forest Practices Act. The Timber, Fish and Wildlife (TFW) Agreement facilitates timber management practices that are environmentally sound and protective of wildlife values. Industry, state and federal agencies, tribal groups, conservation organizations and universities are all represented on the coordinating board of TFW. This approach to habitat management is an appropriate model to emulate as it obviates the confrontational mode of conflict resolution. In fact, cooperative management is the norm for many species in northern Canada and Alaska with native Americans, agency personnel and local interests all represented and involved in concensus management.

A useful set of references for land-use planning decisions has been published by the U.S. Forest Service. These reports on wildlife habitats in managed rangeland cover natural (e.g. riparian zones) and man-made habitats. The series is very informative and provides excellent descriptions of the various habitats in southeastern Oregon rangeland.

The U.S. Fish and Wildlife Service, through the Habitat Evaluation Procedures Group, has been producing a series of habitat suitability index models. These too are designed for use in planning decisions and represent efforts to work with the species' existing biological data bases to provide information on what constitutes optimum habitat. Each model synthesizes the species' habitat-use information in such a way that index values between 0.0 (unsuitable habitat) and 1.0 (optimum habitat) can be generated for given environmental factors. Generally only those factors that can be related quantitatively to habitat suitability are selected for the model. Although not perfect, the models are intended to be updated as a result of their application in the field. One major failing of the habitat suitability models (HSI) is the assumption that all relationships between the suitability indices and the environmental factors are linear. Whether this developed as a convention based on the first models produced or whether it is used as a means of simplifying more complex relationships, it is an inappropriate response to "real world" situations. Despite this criticism, the HSI is a serious attempt to quantify the important relationships between wildlife and the environments that support it. In addition to the species models, guild (usually related to behavioral patterns that link otherwise dissimilar species) and layers of habitat models have also been developed. They allow consideration of broader ecological questions in the planning process. Finally, many states and provincial national resources, as well as quasi-governmental, agencies have developed criteria for forest management, transmission corridors, urban development, and other land use activities that are responsive to wildlife habitat needs.

Bibliography

Anonymous, 1990. A wildlife policy for Canada. Can. Wildl. Serv., Envir. Can., Ottawa. 29 pp.

Baskett, T. S., D. A. Darrow, D. L. Hallett, M. J. Armbruster, J. A. Ellis, B. F. Sparrowe, and P. A. Korte. 1980. A handbook for terrestrial-habitat evaluation in central Missouri. U.S. Fish Wildl. Serv. Resour. Publ. 133. 155 pp.

Cannon, R. W., F. L. Knopf, and L. R. Pettinger. 1982. Use of Landsat data to evaluate lesser prairie-chicken habitats in Western Oklahoma. J. Wildl. Manage. 46:915–922.

Clark, K., D. Euler, and E. Armstrong. 1983. Habitat associations of breeding birds in cottaged and natural areas of central Ontario. Wilson Bull. 95:77–96.

Cooperrider, A. Y., R. J. Boyd, and H. R. Stuart (eds). 1986. Inventory and monitoring of wildlife habitat. U.S. Dept. Int., Bur. Land Manage. Service Center, Denver CO. 858 pp.

Cringan, A. T. 1957. History, food habits and range requirements of the woodland caribou of continental North America. Trans. N. Am. Wildl. Conf. 22:487–501.

Crowell, J. B., Jr. 1982. Resource management thrusts and opportunities: fish and wildlife—a fuller dimension to improved resource management. Trans. N. Am. Wildl. Nat. Resour. Conf. 47:17–22.

DeGraff R. M., and N. G. Tilghman. 1980. Workshop proceedings: Management of western forests and grasslands for nongame birds. U.S. Dept. Agric. For. Serv. Gen. Tech. Rep. INT-86. 535 pp.

Dixon, R. S. 1981. Vegetation mapping the barren ground caribou winter range in northern Manitoba using Landsat. Manitoba Surveys and Mapping Branch, Remote Sensing Centre, Dept. Nat. Resour. TR 81–1. 49 pp. + maps.

Edwards, R. Y., and R. W. Ritcey. 1960. Foods of caribou in Wells Gray Park, British Columbia. Can. Field.-Nat. 74:3–7.

Ellis, J. A., J. N. Burroughs, M. J. Armbruster, D. L. Hallett, P. A. Korte, and T. S. Baskett. 1978. Results of testing four methods of habitat evaluation. Rep. to Proj. Impact Evaluation Team, Div. Ecol. Serv., U.S. Fish Wildl. Serv., Ft. Collins, CO. 92 pp.

Franklin, J. F., and R. H. Waring. 1980. Distinctive features of the northwestern coniferous forest development, structure and function. Proc. Annu. Biol. Colloq. 40:58–86.

Graber, J. W., and R. R. Graber. 1976. Environmental evaluations using birds and their habitats. Biol. Notes No. 97. Illinois Nat. Hist. Survey. 40 pp.

Gutierrez, R. J., and A. B. Carey, eds. 1985. Ecology and management of the spotted owl in the Pacific northwest. U.S. Dept. Agric. For. Serv. Gen. Tech. Rep. PNW-185. 119 pp.

Hagis, W., and W. Young. 1983. Methods of preserving wildlife habitat. Lands Directorate, Envir. Canada Working Paper No. 25. 34 pp.

Heimer, M. 1975. Bergkamen communal tip: extracts from the explanatory report to the landscape plan. Landscape Planning 2:249–264.

Isaacson, D. L., D. A. Leckenby, and C. J. Alexander. 1982. The use of large-scale aerial photography for interpreting digital data in an elk habitat-analysis project. J. Appl. Photo. Eng. 8:51–57.

Jennings, M., J. L. Alfonso, and W. Budd. 1988. Use of the environmentally sensitive areas rule by county governments in Washington state. Envir. Impact Assess. Rev. 8:63–70.

Jennings, M. D., and J. P. Reganold. 1988. Policy and reality of environmentally sensitive areas in Whitman County, Washington, U.S.A. Envir. Manage. 12:369–380.

Leckenby, D. A., D. L. Isaacson, and S. R. Thomas. 1985. Landsat application to elk habitat management in northeast Oregon. Wildl. Soc. Bull. 13:130–134.

Lynch, J. F., and R. F. Whitcomb. 1978. Effects of the insularization of the eastern deciduous forest on avifaunal diversity and turnover. Pp. 461–489, *In* Classification, inventory and analysis of fish and wildlife habitat. U.S. Govt. Printing Off. Washington, DC 604 pp.

MacArthur, R. H., and E. O. Wilson. 1967. The theory of island biogeography. Princeton Univ. Press, Princeton, NJ. 203 pp.

Maser, C., J. M. Trappe, and D. C. Ure. 1978. Implications of small mammal mycophagy to the management of western coniferous forests. Trans. N. Am. Wildl. Nat. Resour. Conf. 43:78–88.

Maser, C., J. W. Thomas, I. D. Luman, and R. Anderson. 1979. Wildlife habitats in managed rangelands—the Great Basin of southeastern Oregon manmade habitats. U.S. Dept. Agric. For. Serv. Gen. Tech. Rep. PNW-86. 40 pp.

Newmark, W. D. 1987. A land-bridge island perspective on mammalian extinction in western North American parks. Nature 325:430–432.

Racey, G. D. and D. L. Euler. 1982. Small mammal and habitat response to shoreline cottage development in central Ontario. Can. J. Zool. 60:865–880.

Racey, G., and D. Euler. 1983. An index of habitat disturbance for lakeshore cottage development. J. Environ. Manage. 16:173–179.

Racey, G. D., T. P. Clark, J. A. McDonnell, and D. L. Euler. 1981. LAKELIFE user's manual. A lake planner's guide to the assessment of impact on wildlife and fish habitat. Wildlife Component Lakeshore Capacity Study Part II mimeo report. 28 pp. + appendices. Ontario Min. Nat. Resour. November 1981.

Robbins, C. S. 1988. Forest fragmentation and its effects on birds. Pp. 61–65 *In* Managing north central forests for non-timber values. T. E. Johnson (Ed). Soc. Am. For. Publ. No 88–04.

Ryder, J. P. and D. A. Boag. 1981. A Canadian paradox—private land, public wildlife: can it be resolved? Can. Field.-Nat. 95:35–38.

Samson, F. B. 1980. Island biogeography and the conservation of non-game birds. Trans. N. Am. Wildl. Nat. Resour. Conf. 45:245–251.

Schoen, J. W., O. C. Wallmo, and M. D. Kirchhoff. 1981. Wildlife forest relationships: is a re-evaluation of old-growth necessary? Trans. N. Am. Wildl. Nat. Resour. Conf. 46:531–544.

Scott, J. M., B. Csuti, D. Stoms, and F. Davis. 1991. Remote sensing for nongame wildlife habitat management. Trans. N. Am. Wildl. Nat. Resour. Conf. 56:134–140.

Sims, R. A., W. D. Towill, K. A. Baldwin, and G. M. Wickware. 1989. Field guide to the forest ecosystem classification for northwestern Ontario. Ont. Min. Nat. Resour. Thunder Bay, ON. 191 pp.

Svedarsky, W. D., and R. D. Crawford. 1982. Wildlife values of gravel pits. Symposium proceedings. Univ. Minn. Agric. Exp. Stn. Misc. Publ. 17–1982. 249 pp.

Thomas, J. W. 1979. Wildlife habitats in managed forests. The Blue Mountains of Oregon and Washington. U.S. Dept. Agric. For. Serv. Agric. Handbook. No. 553. 512 pp.

Thomas, J. W., C. Maser, and J. E. Rodiek. 1979. Wildlife habitats in managed rangeland—Great Basin of southeastern Oregon—riparian zones. U.S. Dept. Agric. For. Serv. Gen. Tech. Rep. PNW-80, 18 pp.

Thomas, J. W., H. Black, Jr., R. J. Scherzinger, and R. J. Pederson. 1979. Deer and elk. Pp. 104–127, *In* J. W. Thomas ed. Wildlife habitats in managed forests, the Blue Mountains of Oregon and Washington. U.S.D.A. For. Serv. Agric. Handbook. No. 553.

Thomas, J. W., E. D. Forsman, J. B. Lint, E. C. Meslon, B. R. Noon and J. Verner. 1990. A conservation stratgy for the northern spotted owl. Rep. Interagency Sci. Comm., Portland Or. 427 pp. + maps.

Verner, J. and A. S. Boss. 1981. California wildlife and their habitats: western Sierra Nevada. U.S. Dept. Agric. For. Serv. Gen. Tech. Rep. PSW-37 439 pp.

Whitaker, G. A., and F. H. McCuen. 1976. A proposed methodology for assessing the quality of wildlife habitat. Ecol. Model. 2:251–272.

Whitcomb, B. L., R. F. Whitcomb, and D. Bystrak. 1977. Three longterm turnover and effects of selective logging on the avifauna of forest fragments. Am. Birds. 31:17–23.

William, G. L. 1988. An assessment of HEP (Habitat Evaluation Procedures) applications to Bureau of Reclamation projects. Wildl. Soc. Bull. 16:437–447.

Recommended Readings

Bunnell, F. L. 1989. Alchemy and uncertainty: what good are models? U.S. Dept. Agric. For. Serv., Gen-Tech. Rep. PNW-GTR-232.

A thorough examination of why wildlife-habitat models often fail and what must be done to make them work.

Canadian Symposia on Remote Sensing
These proceedings contain a number of papers relevant to classification of wildlife habitats using remote sensing techniques.

Committee on Agricultural Land Use and Wildlife Resources. 1970. Land use and wildlife resources. Natl. Acad. Sci., Washington DC 262 pp.
Although concentrating on agriculture-wildlife interrelations, this book not only explores the problem areas but also looks at mechanisms for resolving the points of conflict.

Committee on the Role of Alternative Farming Methods in Modern Production Agriculture. 1989. Alternative agriculture Nat. Res. Council. Natl. Acad. Press. Washington, DC. 448. pp.
Because agriculture is the largest non-point source of water pollution, and because antibiotic and pesticide residues can be found in food, and because soil erosion, soil salinization and aquifer depletion are continuing problems associated with agriculture, this report was designed to examine alternative production systems that would reduce the adverse environmental effects. The report summarizes the economic and scientific viability of alternative production systems.

Harris, L. D. 1984. The fragmented forest. Island biogeographic theory and the preservation of biotic diversity. U. Chicago Press, Chicago, IL. 211 pp.
A thorough discussion of the old-growth forest issue with proposals for management of the remnant stands based primarily on the situation in the Pacific northwest.

Hoover, R. L., and D. L. Wills, eds. 1984. Managing forested lands for wildlife. Colorado Div. Wildl. in cooperation with U.S. Dept. Agric. For. Serv., Rocky Mtn. Reg., Denver, CO. 459 pp.
One state's attempt to provide information for managing forested lands using silvicultural practices that would improve wildlife habitat.

Ruggiero, L. F., K. b. Aubry, A. B. Carey, and M. H. Huff (tech-coord.). 1991. Wildlife and regulation of unmanaged Douglas-fir forests. U.S. Dept. Agric. For. Serv. Gen. Tech Res. PNW-GTR.
Presentation of community studies in unmanaged Douglas-fir forests of various ages in the western United States.

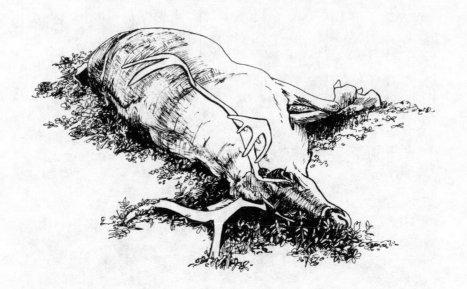

VI SPECIES MANAGEMENT

Although the concept of this book has been predicated on a general description of management procedures as they apply to wildlife, this chapter will take a more in-depth look at management at the species level. Seven examples representing different groups of wildlife will be given and the management techniques and political problems associated with each outlined in some detail.

1. Ungulates—Caribou *(Rangifer tarandus)*

Barren-ground and woodland caribou both occur in North America. Most research has been concentrated on the former (by the Canadian Wildlife Service in the Northwest Territories and the Alaska Fish and Game Department in Alaska). More recently woodland caribou populations have received increased attention for several reasons. The woodland caribou of the Ungava region of eastern Canada (George River herd) are increasing at a rapid rate. In contrast, populations elsewhere, in Ontario, Alberta and British Columbia, appear to be declining and the Selkirk herd in northern Idaho and Washington and southeastern British Columbia is considered endangered in the U.S. In Newfoundland, where woodland caribou have traditionally been a major big game species, studies are underway to assess the impacts of hydroelectric development, predation, and hunting on the species. Although woodland caribou currently offer interesting areas of investigation, this discussion will concentrate on the barren-ground form.

Evidence from aerial surveys in the 1940s and 1950s suggested a substantive and rapid decline in caribou numbers was occurring throughout the Canadian north. The primary cause of the decline was hunting, with harvest and crippling loss equaling or exceeding annual recruitment. However, for sociological, political, and logistical reasons, it was not practical to control the human kill of caribou. Although regulation seemed reasonable in light of the inventory data, inadequate enforcement meant that the traditional disregard of the law by native and white hunters, which resulted in excessive, wasteful killing of the caribou, could not be stopped. Treaty Indians were not required to obey hunting regulations (except in the provinces outside their reserves) and some native peoples were truly dependent on caribou meat for sustenance and clothing.

As caribou numbers continued to decline rapidly, what was previously a caribou economy had by 1955 reached a point where alternate economic strategies were necessary to prevent starvation of some caribou-dependent people. This occurred despite attempts to curb caribou mortality by hunting (elimination of sport hunting) and predators (estimated annual loss to wolves was 5 percent). Poison baits (alkaloidal strychnine and sometimes 1080 in frozen meat) to kill wolves were placed primarily in caribou wintering areas.

As predator control continued into the 1960s, the rate of decline of the herds slowed and populations appeared to stabilize; by the mid-sixties there were unsubstantiated claims that the caribou herds were growing rapidly. The political pressure generated by these reports caused the Northwest Territories Game Management Service to relax its restrictions on caribou hunting by white residents, and commercial exploitation of the herds followed further liberalization in 1968. A 1967–1968 caribou survey showed, however, that no substantial population increase had occurred since the 1955 census and the liberalized hunting was not justified. This problem of survey accuracy and the inability to directly compare very different results has plagued caribou managers into the 1980s.

The Kaminuriak herd has received particular attention from biologists and managers. It winters in northern Saskatchewan and Manitoba and summers primarily in the Northwest Territories and transcends three different jurisdictions (four, if the federal government's interest is included). Studies on the biology of these caribou have shown that calf mortality seems to be the primary limiting factor to population growth. Causes of high calf mortality include poor condition of the mother (inadequate milk production), hypothermia (bad weather conditions during the calving period and shortly thereafter), and predation (wolves). A caribou working group (Caribou Management Board) involving representatives of all interested parties (provincial, territorial, and federal governments, plus native peoples) has been working out a management strategy for the Kaminuriak and Beverly herds since 1982. The credibility of government managers who were trying to reduce harvest by use of quotas was severely weakened in 1982 when an improved census showed a population 40 percent above the predicted value. The census findings were duplicated in 1983 showing a population of 100–140,000 animals compared to earlier estimates in the 40,000 animal range.

Possible reasons for the dramatic increase would relate to the survey technique, immigration into the Kaminuriak herd from another herd, missed calving grounds in previous censuses, or the return of a segment of the Kaminuriak herd that had altered its migration patterns a decade earlier. Whatever the reason(s) for the increase, it left managers in the difficult position of explaining the policy changes necessitated by such a different data base. Nonetheless, a formal agreement was signed in 1983 between the respective governments (Manitoba, Saskatchewan, Northwest Territories, and the federal government represented by the CWS and the Department of Indian and Northern Affairs) and the native peoples. A thirteen person board with eight native people supplementing five government representatives makes management recommendations for the caribou. This Beverly and Kaminuriak Caribou Management Board and its authorized publication, Caribou News, have succeeded in opening discussion on caribou management and establishing mutually agreed upon management strategies. In addition to a detailed long-term management plan, the Board has developed an educational program for use in community schools throughout the caribou range, and set up a scholarship fund for post-secondary students studying caribou management. The Board also recommended that the Northwest Territories government set commercial quotas for the sale of caribou meat as a subsistence food resource. The Board has strongly opposed mining development and other activities which would disturb caribou habitat. The Board now serves as an outstanding example of cooperative management and has spawned a number of similar groups in northern Canada.

The Alaskan herds by 1980 had also declined by more than 50 percent since the mid-60s. Overhunting was the primary factor, with predator-caused calf mortality also being important. Insufficient recruitment occurred to replace the adult losses caused by hunting. Caribou managers in Alaska were unsuccessful, according to Bergerud (1978), because they believed that large herds could not be overharvested; they underestimated predator caused calf mortality, and they thought that caribou populations had to be hunted heavily to prevent overgrazing of the range. Alaska has recently begun a program of predator control, opting to reduce calf and adult mortality due to predators rather than substantially reduce harvest. Although popular with Alaskan hunters, this management approach has brought severe criticism from the public in the lower forty-eight states.

Predator control, particularly on a selective basis, appears to be increasingly used by big game managers as they realize they are dealing with additive rather than compensatory mortality. The agencies' clientele is the hunting fraternity, and restriction of predator numbers is often more expedient and easier to obtain politically, especially in more rural jurisdictions, than restrictions on harvest or hunter numbers. Therefore, Canadian and U.S. caribou managers both support predator control programs especially as the programs have proven to be successful in increasing caribou numbers.

Because caribou move such great distances and the summer and winter use areas are so large, habitat management is basically nonexistent. Forest fires on the winter range have been thought to cause a loss of vital habitat, and fire suppression to protect lichen rich mature forests has been supported in Alaska and the Northwest Territories. However, Skoog (1968) questioned the dependency of caribou on lichens, as their diet even in winter is seldom more than 50 percent lichens. A recent study for Coats Island showed that unavailability of lichens in the winter diet contributed to caribou mortality, especially of calves during severe winter conditions (Adamczewski et al. 1988). If the species does indeed require lichens in the diet, it must be considered that it takes thirty to fifty years for lichens to reach reasonable biomass levels following a fire.

In recent years, there has been a shift in thought toward fire management instead of fire suppression. In support of such management action for caribou, Maikawa and Kershaw (1976) concluded that the occurrence of spruce-stereocaulin woodland in the south-central Northwest Territories was dependent on cyclic burning. Without fire, the spruce canopy closes and lichens are replaced by mosses. However, the reburn cycle of about one hundred years in the area studied assured a continuance of suitable caribou winter range. Fire is important in maintaining extensive barren-ground caribou range. Kelsall et al. (1977) caution that this type of statement should be qualified. Fires have been so universal in recent times in areas of major human settlement and mining exploration and development that little if any mature forest remains over large geographical areas. Fire management would be appropriate in these latter areas, with natural wildfire allowed to occur only in remote, noncommercial forests. Furthermore, recent studies by Dan Thomas of the Canadian Wildlife Service show lichens making up 75–90 percent of a caribou's diet in winter and the heaviest use of regenerated forest habitat occurring 50–250 years after a fire. These findings have significance because they suggest a longer period of optimal winter range for caribou than predicted in earlier studies.

Another area of controversy has been the effect of northern development, especially of oil and gas resources, on caribou populations. Klein (1971), reporting on studies of Scandinavian reindeer, suggested that highways and railroads would not generally create barriers to movement of caribou. The main problem would be mortality due to collisions with motor vehicles and trains. (In North America, though, improved access also would mean increased mortality from hunting—legal and illegal.) Johnson and Todd (1977) substantiated these generalizations with a study of mountain caribou in southern British Columbia (the Selkirk herd mentioned earlier), where the animals continued to use a traditional movement route despite mortalities from collisions with vehicles and poaching. It is still possible that increased traffic by trains or motor vehicles on these linear routes ultimately will result in decreased use or abandonment of range. It may also split the population into two units which may be more vulnerable because of smaller unit size. Whitten and Cameron (1983) showed that caribou avoid moving through the Prudhoe Bay industrial area even though such movements were common prior to 1975.

The effect of pipelines is another concern. In northern Alaska, the trans-Alaska pipeline resulted in some documented avoidance by caribou. It now appears that the Porcupine herd is splitting into two units as suggested above. In contrast, the Nelchina herd continues to cross the pipeline at preconstruction points and that population has increased substantially. Barriers to traditional migration or movement routes can be caused not only by such transportation corridors but also by impoundments resulting from hydroelectric developments. The areas flooded often have been important calving areas, especially in woodland caribou range.

Preliminary work by Miller and Gunn (1979) suggested that harassment of caribou by low flying aircraft might mean added energetic expenses, particularly to cows and calves, and that calving areas should be avoided by such aircraft.

A management scenario developing from all this is contingent on better knowledge of caribou movement patterns, productivity, mortality factors, energetics, and population size (see Chapter 3). In varying locales it means predator control, increased enforcement to prevent illegal hunting, curtailment of hunting opportunity, cooperation of native peoples-especially treaty groups-and mitigation of impacts resulting from development activities. Caribou is a species primarily restricted to primitive or wilderness areas and must be managed by a modern approach despite being symbolic of a wildness that no longer exists except in the minds of many North American city dwellers. This means that caribou, as the "sacred cows" of the Inuit and Indian and a talisman of wilderness to the urbanite, generate their own political realities (another recurrent theme in this book) which must be understood and sometimes addressed by the manager. Decisions made to manage caribou in Alaska and the Northwest Territories are scrutinized in San Francisco, Toronto, and other urban centers. Bad press generated by public outcries far removed from the location of the management activities often dictates what managers can or cannot do. Predator control to enhance caribou populations and oil development in the Arctic National Wildlife Refuge are such issues. The input of public controversy is probably best illustrated in our next example, where the best of biological data and management schemes ultimately proved ineffective against a concerted public outcry a continent away.

Bibliography

Adamsczewski, J. Z., C. C. Gates, and R. J. Hudson. 1988. Limiting effects of snow on seasonal habitat use and diets of caribou (*Rangifer tarandus groenlandicus*) on Coats Island, Northwest Territories, Canada. Can. J. Zool. 66:1986–1996.

Bergerud, A. T. 1978. Caribou. Pp. 83–101 *In* J. L. Schmidt and D. L. Gilbert, eds. Big game of North America. Stackpole Books, Harrisburg, PA.

Boertje, R. D., W. C. Gasaway, D. V. Grangaard, and D. G. Kelleyhouse. 1988. Predation on moose and caribou by radio-collared grizzly bears in east central Alaska. Can. J. Zool. 66:2492–2499.

Cameron, R. D. and K. R. Whitten. 1980. Influence of the Trans-Alaska Pipeline corridor on the local distribution of caribou. Pp. 475–481, *In* Proceedings of the Reindeer/Caribou Symposium E. Remers, E. Gaare and S. Skjenneberg, Eds. Direktoratet for Viltog Ferskvannskisk, Trondheim, Norway.

Carruthers, D. R., R. D. Jakimchuk, and C. Linkswiler. 1984. Spring and fall movements of Nelchina caribou in relation to the trans-Alaska pipeline. Ren. Resour. Consulting Serv. Ltd., Toronto. 101 pp. plus 7 photos.

Dauphine, T. C., Jr. 1976. Biology of the Kaminuriak population of barren-ground caribou. Part 4: Growth, reproduction and energy reserves. Can. Wildl. Serv. Rep. Ser. No. 38. 71 pp.

Gasaway, W. C., R. O. Stephenson, J. L. Davis, P. K. Shepherd, and O. E. Burris. 1983. Interrelationships of wolves, prey and man in interior Alaska. Wildl. Monogr. 84. 50 pp.

Johnson, E. A., and J. S. Rowe. 1975. Fire in the subarctic wintering ground of the Beverly caribou herd. Am. Midl. Nat. 94:1–14.

Johnson, D. R. and M. C. Todd. 1977. Summer use of highway crossing by mountain caribou. Can. Field-Nat. 91:312–314.

Kelsall, J. P. 1968. The migratory barren-ground caribou of Canada. Can. Wildl. Serv., Queen's Printer, Ottawa. 340 pp. plus maps.

Kelsall, J. P., E. S. Telfer, and T. D. Wright. 1977. The effects of fire on the ecology of the boreal forest, with particular reference to the Canadian north: a review and selected bibliography. Can. Wildl. Serv. Occ. Pap. No. 32. 58 pp.

Klein, D. R. 1971. Reaction of reindeer to obstructions and disturbances. Science. 173:393–398.

Maikawa, E. and K. A. Kershaw. 1976. Studies on lichen-dominated systems.

XIX. The postfire recovery sequence of black spruce-lichen woodland in the Abitou Lake region, N.W.T. Can. J. Bot. 54:2679–2687.

Miller, F. L. 1974. Biology of the Kaminuriak population of barren-ground caribou. Part 2: Dentition as an indicator of age and sex; composition and socialization of the population. Can. Wildl. Serv. Rep. Ser. No. 31. 88 pp.

Miller, D. R. 1976. Biology of the Kaminuriak population of barren-ground caribou. Part 3: Taiga winter range relationships and diet. Can. Wildl. Serv. Rep. Ser. No. 36. 42 pp.

Miller, F. L., and A. Gunn. 1979. Responses of Peary caribou and muskoxen to helicopter harassment. Can. Wildl. Serv. Occ. Pap. No. 40. 90 pp.

Parker, G. R. 1972. Biology of the Kaminuriak population of barren-ground caribou. Part 1: Total numbers, mortality, recruitment, and seasonal distribution. Can. Wildl. Serv. Rep. Ser. No. 20. 95 pp.

Scotter, G. W. 1964. Effects of forest fires on the winter range of barren-ground caribou in northern Saskatchewan. Can. Wildl. Serv. Wildl. Manage. Bull. Ser. 1. No. 18. 111 pp.

Scotter, G. W. 1967. Effects of fire on barren-ground caribou and their forest habitat in northern Canada. Trans. N. Am. Wildl. Nat. Resour. Conf. 32:246–254.

Scotter, G. W. 1971a. Fire, vegetation, soil and barren-ground caribou relations in northern Canada. Pp. 209–230 *In* Proceedings fire in the northern environment, a symposium. Pacific Northwest For. Range Exp. Stn., Portland, OR.

Scotter, G. W. 1971b. Wildfires in relation to habitat of the barrenground caribou in the taiga of northern Canada. Proc. Annu. Tall Timbers Fire Ecol. Conf. 10:85–106.

Scotter, G. W. 1991. The Beverly and Kaminuriak Caribou Management Board: an example of cooperative management. Trans. N. Am. Wildl. Nat. Resour. Conf. 56:309–320.

Skoog, R. O. 1968. Ecology of the caribou (*Rangifer tarandus granti*) in Alaska. Unpubl. Ph.D. thesis, Univ. Calif (Berkeley), Berkeley. 699 pp.

Whitten, K. R., and R. D. Cameron. 1983. Movements of collared caribou, *Rangifer tarandus*, in relation to petroleum development on the Arctic slope of Alaska. Can. Field-Nat. 97:143–146.

2. Marine Mammals—Harp Seal *(Pagophilus groenlandicus)*

The "white-coat," or newborn pup, of the harp seal is one of the most familiar visages of wildlife. The large, sad, brown eyes set in a cuddly countenance and the off-white pelt have made this species an attractive symbol of the anticommercialization forces as well as groups like the Animal Welfare League and Defenders of Wildlife. The Canadian government reacted to growing public pressure against the east coast seal hunt in the 1970's by funding considerable research on the harp seal to ensure appropriate quotas were set to maintain populations at a level sustaining an annual harvest of 180,000 animals. To understand the management strategies, some background is necessary.

There are three separate and distinct breeding stocks of harp seals in the North Atlantic. The largest stock occurs off the east coast of Canada within the Gulf of St. Lawrence and on the Front (off the coast of Labrador). The adult females spend January-March in this area and give birth before returning to the Canadian Arctic and the waters off west Greenland for summer breeding. All three stocks have been exploited commercially for centuries, but concern mounted because harvests of the Gulf and Front stock during the 1950s and 1960s were responsible for major declines in harp seal numbers. In 1961, the establishment of opening and closing dates was the first regulatory management step to be taken. In 1965, adult females on the whelping patches were protected; Norway stopped sealing in the Gulf, and Canada imposed a quota of 50,000 seals on Canadian sealers operating there. By 1970, the stock was only 33–50 percent of the 1951 level. Pressure from humane groups such as the International Fund for Animal Welfare was growing. In 1971, the Canadian government acted by imposing quotas for both the Gulf and Front and establishing an independent Committee on Seals and Sealing (COSS) composed of scientists, veterinarians, and executive members of Canadian and international humane societies. COSS was to examine the economic, sociological, ecological, and humanitarian aspects of the seal hunt and recommend to the government any changes in regulation that might be needed.

The quotas established were done so under the International Commission for the Northwest Atlantic Fisheries (ICNAF) Harp Seal and Hood Seal Protocol, which since 1961 had assumed management responsibilities for the international (Canada, Denmark, and Norway) hunt. The 1971 quotas were 200,000 harp seals to be taken by sealing ships and 45,000 by landsmen. In 1972, the allowable take was sharply reduced to 150,000 animals (120,000 by vessels, 30,000 by landsmen) and remained at this level through 1975 while scientific studies on the actual status of the population were under way. The population model developed projected a population of more than 1.2 million animals/year that would produce about 320,000 pups in 1977. The model assumed a carrying capacity of about 3.7 million seals with a Maximum Sustained Yield (MSY) of 1.6 million animals. The Sustained Yeild (SY) for the 1977 population was projected at 190,000 animals, with a total allowable catch of 170,000 animals suggested to permit the stock to reach the MSY in ten to fifteen years. The 1977 quota of 170,000 animals was considerably higher than the 1976 quota of 127,000.

Within a year, through scientific agreement that natural mortality values used in the model were too high and should be set at 11 percent, the SY estimates ranged from 227,000 to 245,000 seals. Pup production estimates were 310,000 to 350,000. The Minister of Fisheries set a management strategy for 1978 that would restrict harvest to a maximum 75 percent of SY, thus allowing continued population growth. A quota of 180,000 seals was set for 1978. Although conflicting views from the scientific community continued, there was no dispute that the population should progress toward the MSY level with the target allowable catch value.

Following 1978, Canada took a more independent role in determining seal management and accepted ICNAF recommendations only if they were deemed satisfactory. This stance occurred in conjunction with a political move that extended jurisdictional responsibility to 200 miles offshore instead of the old 12 mile zone.

COSS continued to make recommendations that were generally adopted to upgrade the humaneness of the sealing operations. Although alternatives were examined, the regulation bat or club was found to fulfill the requirements of humane slaughter. Emphasis was placed on educational programs for the sealers and biological studies, particularly of the behavior and energetics of the harp seal.

It appeared that significant progress was being made toward scientific management of harp seals which would make the harvest acceptable to the public. Canadian public opinion began to shift in favor of the hunt in 1980. Then in 1981, ice formed offshore of Prince Edward Island and landsmen had direct access to the breeding stock. Although quotas were not exceeded, the gore of the slaughter and the unprofessional attitude of the amateur sealers were viewed nationally and internationally on television. Public opinion was drastically influenced. This event fed the anti-seal hunt lobby, giving it added momentum and heightening the European response that eventually led the European Economic Council in 1983 to ban importing of seal skins or products. The 1983 quota was meaningless, for very few sealers bothered to harvest. The primary economic market had disappeared; the commercial nature of the hunt and the economic factors that had previously driven it became apparent to all. The political reality was that all the biological knowledge and reasonable management criteria which had been developed for this species were meaningless when the consuming public deemed the exercise to be cruel and inhumane.

Even without a commercial market, harp seals will still be killed, just as grey seals are, when their activities, directly or indirectly (such as feeding, net fouling) affect fishermen's work. The economic future of native communities formerly dependent on the seal hunt is bleak. A number of the smaller settlements have been abandoned.

Bibliography

Herscovici, A. 1985. Second nature: the animal-rights controversy. CBC Enterprises, Toronto, Canada. 254 pp.

Lavigne, D. M. 1978. The harp seal controversy reconsidered. Queen's Quart. 85:377–388.

Lett, P.f., R. K. Mohn, and D. F. Gray. 1979. Density-dependent processes and management strategy for the Northwest Atlantic harp seal population. ICNAF Select. Pap. 5:61–80.

Malouf, A. H. (chairm.) 1986. Seals and sealing in Canada. Report of the Royal Commission 3 Vols Can. Govt. Publ. Ottawa, Canada. 1366 pp.

Mercer, M. C. 1977. The seal hunt. Inform. Branch, Dept, Fish Environ. Ottawa. 24 pp.

Ronald, K., J. Selley, and P. Healey. 1982. Seals Pp 769–827 *In* Wild mammals of North America. J. A. Chapman and G. A. Feldhamer (Eds.) John Hopkins Univ. Press, Baltimore, MD.

3. Furbearers—Beaver *(Castor canadensis)*

The beaver is one of the primary North American furbearing species in terms of value (averaging about $15 million annually in the 1980's). In fact, its fur value led to extirpation throughout much of North America by 1900. Stringent or total protection or the species was law almost universally by 1915. The focus of early management during this century was to restore populations throughout much of the former range. Beaver were live-trapped from remnant populations and transplanted successfully to many new locations. Beaver now occur over virtually all their historical range. Only two jurisdictions within the beaver's distributional range, Rhode Island and Delaware, do not have trapping seasons for the species.

The resurgence of beaver populations was not without its problems. Many southern states found that considerable economic losses were being sustained by timber growers and agricultural interests. While such problems are not limited to the south, the fur value of southern beaver (Georgia, Alabama, Mississippi) is low, and there is often little incentive to trap the animals. Alternate forms of population control are needed. Some extreme methods have included consideration of alligator releases to reduce beaver populations by predation. Dispersal of alligators and/or beaver limits the effectiveness of the approach. Generally the most that can be accomplished without trapping

Table 6.1 Beaver Land Capability Classification System (Slough and Sadleir 1977)

	Class	No. of beaver colony sites per shoreline mile	
No.	Description	Lakes	Streams
1	No biophysical limitations affect beaver production	3+	6+
2	Sight limitations	2-<3	4-<6
3	Moderate limitations	1-<2	2-<4
4	Severe limitations	<1	<2
5	Limitations preclude beaver production	0	0

is control of the water level by drains in the impoundments created by beaver. This is useful where such activities would otherwise flood roads. Fences have been used successfully to prevent clogging of culverts and dams have been dynamited to eliminate flooding—after the beaver have been removed by trapping.

Trapping in North America is either by registered trapline, harvest quota, license quota, or on an area restriction basis. The trapper using a registered trapline usually has a harvest quota established by the management agency. Registered traplines are on Crown or other public land; the area is limited geographically and may be censused by the agency to ensure the quota is appropriate. Censusing consists of flying over the area just before freeze-up to count the food piles (thought to represent active lodges) and multiplying by the number of beaver per colony (usually about 4.0). This method overlooks den or bank beaver and requires an accurate determination of actual number of animals per active lodge. It may overestimate actual population size as recent evidence suggests that smaller food piles often are not associated with active lodges.

Much of northern North America is too remote to conduct censuses economically. In such cases, the land capability system for beaver developed by Slough and Sadleir (1977) or some related methodology may have real applicability. By using remotely sensed images of the area and comparing habitat characteristics to beaver requirements, a measure of the land's capability to produce beaver can be obtained. The regression model developed by the above authors resulted in a classification system with subclasses representing limitations and special considerations (Tables 6.1–6.2). The equations for estimating beaver numbers are:

$$Y(\text{lakes}) = {}^-3.84 - 0.781(P_L) + 1.43E^-3(A_L) + 0.555$$
$$(A_L^{1/2}) - 5.10E^-4(R_L^2) + 1.24(W_L) + 1.79(TA_L^{1/2}) + 6.32(N_L)$$

and

$$Y(\text{stream sections}) = 74.2 + 2.41(L_s) - 0.554(L_s^2) - 98.5$$
$$(L_s^{1/2}) + 56.2(\log_{10}L_s) - 2.43\,E^-4(W_s^2) + 4.42(G_s^{-1}) + 0.954(TA_s)$$
$$+ 0.600(NS_s^2)$$

where

P_L = perimeter
A_L = area
R_1 = area:perimeter
W_L = water level stability index
TA_L = length of aspen shoreline
N_L = length of non-productive brush shoreline
Ls = length
Ws = width
Gs = gradient index
NSs = length of nonproductive brush and swamp shoreline

Similar models can be used for all wildlife species when we have enough valid information on the habitat requirements of the species.

Table 6.2 Descriptions of Beaver Land Capabilities Classification System Showing Limiting and Special Subclasses (Slough and Sadleir, 1977)

	Symbol	Subclass description
		Limiting subclasses
Lakes	S	Shoreline configuration allows buildup of waves
	O	Outlet not regulated by beaver dam(s)[a]
Streams	W	Width restricts damming[a]
	G	Gradient restricts damming[a]
Both	F	Absence of major food and construction species (aspen, willow, and alder)
		Special subclasses
	H	Human disturbance of shoreline (e.g., roads, railways, land clearing)
	T	Natural topography limiting as above
	D	Lake depth limiting. Freezes to bottom in winter

[a]These factors result in water level instability. Limitations imposed by stream gradient (i.e. flow rate).

Most of the larger Canadian provinces have some form of registered trapline or fur block (Saskatchewan) system whereby specific trappers are licensed to trap specific areas. The vast majority of North American jurisdictions sell only resident trappers licenses that permit them to trap on their own property, any private property for which they can obtain permission, and sometimes public property. The competition on unregulated public lands in such jurisdictions can be extreme. Ontario has a management system whereby the number of trappers on private lands are limited by zone. To obtain a license, a new trapper must operate in a zone where vacancies exist or if the quota is filled go on a waiting list for his trapping area of preference. This system provides more control over trappers and harvest and is aimed at eliminating the possibility of overexploitation that became evident when fur prices soared in the late 1970s.

Closed seasons exist except in those areas where beaver are considered an economic liability. The open season is generally sometime between November and March, coinciding with primeness of the pelt. Often a royalty or stamp fee is paid to the management agency, and the pelt is stamped. This allows a record to be kept of the number of pelts, individual trapper performance, and marketing activities through fur dealers and auction houses. The actual trade in fur can be estimated from mail surveys, inspection of fur buyers' records, shipping permit records, and pelt tagging records.

Many jurisdictions now require novices to take a trapper education course that deals with the proper sets to use for given furbearers, how to use traps safely and effectively, landowner trapper relationships, skinning and casing procedures, and more recently, how to trap and kill an animal as humanely as possible. Some trappers' associations hold workshops to keep their members informed of the latest developments in legislation, public opinion, trapping methods, and trap development. It should be evident that management effectiveness depends to a large extent on the cooperation of the trappers. Many associations have developed their own trapper education programs when jurisdictions do not have compulsory ones. Trappers are vulnerable to public criticism because of the commercial nature of their profession and the perceived cruelty of devices used to catch animals (see Chapter 7). Associations often provide an effective political buffer to this antipathy just by being organized and using the management agency as their political lever.

Two diseases are particularly relevant when discussing furbearers—rabies and tularemia. While rabies seldom occurs in beaver, tularemia, caused by the bacterial agent *Francisella tularensis*, can be an important disease of beaver. Tularemia causes white spots on the internal organs, especially the liver and spleen, which also become enlarged. The spots are sites of focal necrosis caused by the bacterial toxins. The disease may be endemic in small rodents and has decimated beaver populations, particularly in high density areas where disease transmission between individuals is easily facilitated. Bacteria are transmitted in water, the obvious route of beaver epidemics, but also by direct contact with the fur and tissues of infected animals, inhaling dust contaminated by feces of diseased animals, eating insufficiently cooked, contaminated meat, and by the bites of bloodsucking invertebrates. The risk of infection is high for trappers and wildlife managers who may be handling contaminated live animals, carcasses or fur.

Bibliography

Arner, D. H., C. Mason, and C. J. Perkins. 1981. Practicality of reducing a beaver population through the release of alligators. Pp. 1799–1805, *In* Worldwide Furbearer Conf. proc. Vol. III. J. A. Chapman and D. Pursley, Eds. Frostburg, MA.

Boettger, R. W., and M. Smart. 1968. Beaver flowages converted from liabilities to assets. Maine Fish Game. 10(3):5–7.

Broschart, M. R., C. A. Johnston, and R. J. Naiman. 1989. Predicting beaver colony density in boreal landscapes. J. Wildl. Manage. 53:929–934.

Novak, M. 1987. Beaver Pp 283–312 *In* Wild furbearer management and conservation in North America. Novak, M., J. A. Baker, M. E. Obbard and B. Mallorh, Eds. Ont. Min. Nat. Resour., Toronto, Canada.

Osmundson, C., and S. Buskirk. 1991. Dynamics of beaver food caches and cache size as a predictor of colony size in Wyoming. 9th Midwest Furbearer Workshop, Custer, SD (abstract only).

Slough, B. G., and R. M. F. S. Sadleir. 1977. A land capability system for beaver (*Castor canadensis* Kuhl). Can. J. Zool. 55:132–1335.

4.   Waterfowl—Black Duck *(Anas rubripes)*

For the Atlantic flyway, the black duck is the most important bird in the hunter's bag. The species apparently has been declining in numbers, however, and by 1982 had shown a 60 percent decline from 1955. Recent winter survey information suggests that the rate of decline has slowed but the reliability of this major indicator of population trends has been questioned even though Christmas bird counts tend to confirm the trend (70 % decline from 1949–50 to 1982–1983). What is responsible for this massive decline has been the subject of considerable speculation.

Although there appears to be suitable unoccupied breeding and winter habitat available, there have been massive die-offs from starvation in New Jersey. This suggests that wintering habitat may be declining in some areas because of loss of salt marshes. Biologists have been able to increase brood production by liming dystrophic lakes. The many lakes that appear suitable for black duck breeding purposes may simply be unproductive bodies of water because of their pH, and all suitable breeding habitat may be saturated. If this is so, the acid precipitation problem is likely to make more lakes unsuitable, and breeding habitat may be a key limiting factor.

Toxic chemicals such as DDT and PCBs have been found in high concentrations in black duck eggs. DDT and its metabolites decreased in importance as PCBs increased. Both groups of chemicals can, and do, cause eggshell thinning. Measurements of black duck eggshell thickness in 1964 averaged significantly less than in eggs collected prior to 1940. Eggshell thickness has increased with the decline in use of DDT, but is still below the pre-1940 value. Thin eggshells can lead to cracking during incubation. The hen will then remove any defective eggs or abandon the nest. If environmental contaminants are a major cause of decline, one would expect to find decreased productivity per female, but a study of brood size and production from 1956–1981 failed to reveal any meaningful changes.

Genetic swamping by mallards has been supported by a number of biologists as a cause of the decline. Black ducks and mallards readily hybridize, and wing samples had shown 13 percent hybrids by 1980. The rate of hybridization is estimated at 3–5% per year. The release of mallards by states and private organizations in the Atlantic flyway has contributed to this problem. Black duck characters are replaced by mallard characters so that the hybrids tend to be more mallard-like, and over time this genetic mixing alone could doom the black duck, especially when studies have indicated that male mallards dominate male black ducks when both compete for the same female.

Despite these other factors, it appears that overhunting may be most responsible for the black duck decline. Managers often have looked at hunting as a compensatory mortality factor, and this concept viewed overhunting as simply not possible, whether it be for deer or ducks. In waterfowl this concept was based on mallard data and in reality was a relatively recent change in philosophy from the additive approach. Hunting is known to cause 50–60 percent of the annual mortality in black ducks. With liberal regulations in the mid 1950s large kills were made that may have exceeded productivity despite the high duck population. By 1959 when the black duck population was obviously reduced, the more restrictive regulations were insufficient to halt the decline. The smaller kills were still proportionately too large to allow a population increase. In 1983–1984, restrictive regulations were imposed which should show a reversal in the decline if hunting is the key mortality factor responsible. While such a result did occur considerable controversy still surrounds hunting effects on black duck survival rates. Nonetheless, the black duck population does appear to be stabilizing and perhaps even rebounding to a certain extent.

What should have been the management reaction? Season closure is an ideal candidate. Yet the black duck is the major bag species on the flyway, and management agencies derive their revenue primarily from the sale of licenses. Many waterfowl hunters are after black duck, and a season closure would result in loud complaints from hunters and significant declines in revenues to state agencies. Not only was there no closure, but in 1970 the USFWS actually liberalized black duck hunting regulations.

Beginning in 1972 and continuing each year until 1975, minor restrictions were imposed, but seasons were still more liberal than those in 1968. By 1982, states like Maine and Massachusetts were considering season restrictions or closure because of alarming statistics showing large short-term declines in black duck numbers and a link between hunting and the decline.

Although waterfowl management is ultimately a federal responsibility, states are empowered to impose more restrictive regulations than the federal ones. Maine biologists recommended unilaterally closing the season in that state in 1982. But the politicians decided it would be unfair to Maine hunters unless the other states were also closed. Some states, including Maine, adopted their own restrictions to reduce harvest, but the Atlantic Waterfowl Council put off consideration of any flyway restrictions until 1983. At the same time, the Humane Society of the United States, the Maine Audubon Society, and a private citizen filed a lawsuit to block the 1982–1983 black duck season. It was rejected. In the winter of 1983, the inventory of black ducks was the lowest ever recorded. A 1983 management objective was to achieve a 25 percent reduction in state kill for those states harvesting 5,000 or more black ducks annually. This would achieve an overall kill reduction of 12 percent in the Atlantic Flyway when Canada was included. This level of reduction was adopted not because modelling indicated it would reduce kill sufficiently to allow the population to stabilize and recuperate, but because it was the minimum measurable reduction that biologists thought could be made. It also was the maximum reduction state fish and game directors in the flyway would accept.

Are we then managing the resource for the resource's sake or for political goals that may ultimately deplete the resource? In truth we do both, and this is the real conundrum of wildlife management. When the two conflict we may fail to respond as quickly as we should because the political costs are too high, but by failing to respond quickly, the long-term economic and biological costs may be higher than the immediate ones (cf. Chapter 4 Maine deer example).

We are learning more about the black duck as a result of the controversy, but we still are unsure of the proper management responses as the roles of the various factors are still unclear because the data are often conflicting.

Bibliography

Anonymous. 1980. Important resources problem strategy paper: black duck-coastal mid-Atlantic (IRP No. 504). Habitat preservation Reg. 5. U.S. Fish Wildl. Serv., Newton Corner, MA.

Anonymous. 1983. Public information package concerning black ducks. U.S. Fish Wildl. Serv., Washington, DC (mimeo).

Blandin, W. W. 1982. Population characteristics and simulation modelling of black ducks. Unpubl. Ph.D. thesis, Clark Univ, Worcester, MA.

Conroy, M. J., J. R. Goldsberry, J. E. Hines, and D. B. Stotts. 1988. Evolution of aerial transect surveys for wintering American black ducks. J. Wildl. Manage. 52:694–703.

Conroy, M. J., G. R. Costanzo, and D. B. Stotts. 1989. Winter survival of female American black ducks on the Atlantic coast. J. Wildl. Manage. 53:99–109.

Grandy, J. W. 1983. The North American black duck (*Anas rubripes*): a case study of 28 years of failure in American wildlife management. Int. J. Study Anim. Problems 4(4): Suppl. 35 pp.

Feierabend, J. S. 1984. The black duck: an international resource on trial in the United States. Wildl. Soc. Bull. 12:128–134.

Heusmann, H. W. 1982. The black duck situation (and what to do about it). Mass. Wildl. (May-June):14–19.

Krementz, D. G., M. J. Conroy, J. E. Hines., and H. F. Percival. 1988. The effects of hunting on survival rates of American black ducks. J. Wildl. Manage. 52:214–226.

Martinson, R. K., A. S. Geis, and R. I. Smith. 1968. Black duck harvest and population dynamics in eastern Canada and the Atlantic flyway. Pp. 21–52, *In* The black duck evaluation, management and research: a symposium. P. Barske, Ed. Atlantic Waterfowl Council and Wildl. Manage. Instit.

Nichols, J. D., and F. A. Johnson. 1989. Evaluation and experimentation with duck management strategies. Trans. N.Am. Wildl. Nat. Resour. Conf. 54:566–593.

Rusch, D. H., C. D. Ankney, H. Boyd., J. R. Longcore, J. K. Kingelman, and V. D. Stotts. 1989. Population ecology and harvest of the American black duck; a review. Wildl. Soc. Bull. 17:379–406.

Spencer, H. E. 1982. Black ducks—a state of concern. Maine Dept. Inland Fish Game, (4/19/82). 3 pp plus appendices.

5. Upland Game Birds—Ruffed Grouse *(Bonasa umbellus)*

The ruffed grouse is the most ubiquitous of the North American grouse. There are excellent descriptions of the species and its management in Johnsgard (1973), Bump et al. (1947) and Atwater and Schnell (1989).

The ruffed grouse is one of the species that many wildlife managers consider to be immune to hunting pressure. Fischer and Keith (1974), reporting on a central Alberta population where they banded 1,132 birds, concluded that although fall hunting increased total annual mortality in certain cohorts, (territorial males), it had no measurable effect on spring population levels. Their study echoed the findings of numerous other researchers and has helped support the concept that hunting is a compensatory mortality factor for this species. One important aspect of Fischer and Keith's study and another by Gullion (1970) was the finding that hunting kill decreased with increasing distance between banding site and the nearest road or access trail. This means that in large continuous tracts of habitat with limited road access hunters are unlikely to influence the population sufficiently to offset the normally large reserve of juveniles. However, in much of eastern North America ruffed grouse habitat is no longer continuous, and those small patches open to public hunting may receive such high hunting pressure that local populations can be affected. What allows them to rebuild is the decreasing return effect. As the population is effectively reduced by hunting, the return to hunters per unit effort decreases until it reaches the point that they abandon the area. With decreased hunting pressure, the remnant population or immigrating birds can build the numbers back up. It is apparent that small tracts (100–200 acres) can have the local grouse populations wiped out if hunting pressure is severe enough.

The drumming log is an important component of ruffed grouse habitat. Forest management practices can have a substantial influence on ruffed grouse by affecting this component of the male's territory. The drumming stage itself is needed, but it will not be used by the male if stem density and canopy coverage in the shrub layer are insufficient. When the shrub layer is removed within an area of 50m^2 centered on a previously active drumming site, it renders that site unacceptable as a display location. Thus forest plantations with little or no shrub layer and clean forest practices (removal of downed material) mean the loss of potential drumming stages. When birds do select these sites, they become more vulnerable to avian predators. There is a critical balance between sufficient shrubby material to screen the bird from potential predation and sufficient openness to allow the grouse to see at least six meters in all directions. During periods of population depression, this ideal habitat is the only place where birds are found.

The most consistently used male territories contain a number of acceptable display locations and are near the middle of an aggregation of territories, a pattern similar to the lek, or territorial dancing ground of other grouse species such as the sharp-tail grouse, sage grouse, black grouse, and prairie chicken. Because of the nearly ideal habitat conditions, they are used by long-lived birds. This reservoir of breeding animals serves as the focus for re-populating more marginal habitats which, because of biological or physical constraints, are less preferred or less safe and are "home" to more transitory populations.

Ruffed grouse show seasonal shifts in habitat use. Deciduous habitat types are preferred in spring and summer, but as temperatures drop the animals make increasing use of conifer cover. During periods of snow cover the birds are likely to be found in conifer stands. The birds still move to the deciduous trees to feed on buds in the winter and must do so on a regular basis because they carry very small fat reserves. The lower critical temperature for the species measured at $6.0°$ C in February and $0.3°$ C in March near mid latitude of the eastern distributional range in Massachusetts indicates that the animal must either ingest considerable energy or conserve it in some fashion.

Plasma glucose levels increase during the winter in grouse while plasma lipid levels remain stable. The increased glycogen levels in liver and pectoral muscles suggest that shivering thermogenesis could be enhanced and that the animal responds to energy needs glycolytically, not lipolytically. Because the birds use snow burrows (which reduce radiative and convective heat loss) and have excellent plumage insulation, the lower critical temperature is probably seldom reached except when the birds are feeding. During feeding, they are able to select the most nutritious and highest energy buds, and as the feeding bouts are short (fifteen to twenty-five minutes) and infrequent (two per day) the energy costs of feeding are kept as low as possible. It is important from a management perspective to have sufficient male aspen or other budding trees (white birch, black cherry) available to provide the birds with good winter forage.

With this species, habitat management assumes greater value than regulatory management except in those situations where heavy hunting pressure impacts small localized populations. The only political question is usually associated with hunter access and landowner complaints. Grouse hunters usually use shotguns, so landowners are not as concerned about safety problems. The ruffed grouse has shown considerable resilience to man's activities and has been relatively easy to manage. Many early management efforts such as small forest clearings and seeding log landings and roads to clover were more effective in making the birds available to hunters than increasing populations. The ruffed grouse is thus an example of an uncontroversial species for which considerable biological and management knowledge exist. It can be difficult to hunt because it flies well, is generally in brushy areas, and becomes more flighty as hunting pressure increases although some races apparently never become flighty and thus are especially vulnerable. It also is widely distributed, yet can be easily studied and so serves as an exception to most game species for which management action is more critical.

Bibliography

Atwater, S., And J. Schnell. (eds). 1989. Ruffed grouse. Stackpole Books, Harrisburg, PA. 370 pp.

Boag, D. A. 1976. The effect of shrub removal on occupancy of ruffed grouse drumming sites. J. Wildl. Manage. 40:105–110.

Boag, D. A., and K. M. Sumanik. 1969. Characteristics of drumming sites selected by ruffed grouse in Alberta. J. Wildl. Manage. 33:621–629.

Bump, G., R. W. Darrow, F. C. Edminster, and W. F. Crissey. 1947. The ruffed grouse. Life history. propagation. management. N.Y. State Conserv. Dept. 915 pp.

Dorney, R. S., and C. Kabat. 1960. Relation of weather, parasitic disease, and hunting to Wisconsin ruffed grouse populations. Wisconsin Conserv. Dept. Tech. Bull. 20. 64 pp.

Fischer, C. A., and L. B. Keith. 1974. Population responses of central Alberta ruffed grouse to hunting. J. Wildl. Manage. 38:585–600.

Gullion, G. W. 1970. Factors influencing ruffed grouse populations. Trans. N. Am. Wildl. Nat. Resour. Conf. 35:93–105.

Gullion, G. W., and W. H. Marshall. 1968. Survival of ruffed grouse in a boreal forest. Living Bird. 7:117–167.

Johnsgard, P. A. 1973. Grouse and quails of North America. University of Nebraska Press, Lincoln. 553 pp.

Pietz, P. J. and J. R. Tester. 1982. Habitat selection by sympatric spruce and ruffed grouse in north central Minnesota. J. Wildl. Manage. 46:391–403.

Rasmussen, G., and R. Brander. 1973. Standard metabolic rate and lower critical temperature for the ruffed grouse. Wilson Bull. 85:223–229.

Robel, R. J. 1972. Possible function of the lek in regulating tetraonid populations. Proc. Int. Ornith. Congr. 15:121–133.

Svoboda, F. J., and G. W. Gullion. 1972. Preferential use of aspen by ruffed grouse in northern Minnesota. J. Wildl. Manage. 36:1166–1180.

Thomas, V. G., H. G. Lumsden, and D. H. Price. 1975. Aspects of the winter metabolism of ruffed grouse (*Bonasa umbellus*) with special reference to energy reserves. Can. J. Zool. 53:434–44.

Thompson, F. R., and E. K. Fritzell. 1989. Habitat use, home range, and

survival of territorial male ruffed grouse. J. Wildl. Manage. 53:15–
23.

6. Raptors—Peregrine Falcon *(Falco peregrinus)*

The peregrine falcon showed tremendous declines in populations throughout the Northern Hemisphere beginning in the 1940s and continuing into the
1970s. Pesticides, particularly DDT, were responsible for eggshell thinning
and hatching failure. The species disappeared from much of its former range
but like the bald eagle, the osprey *(Pandion haliaetus)*, and other raptors
affected by environmental contamination by persistent pesticides, populations
were expected to increase with the reduced use of DDT. This has happened
even though relatively recent studies of eggs in Oregon have still found DDT
metabolite levels above those known to cause hatching failure. It is likely
that some birds are picking up these DDT metabolites on their wintering
range where many countries continue to use the pesticide for agricultural
purposes, or are feeding on migratory birds with high contaminant loads as
is suggested for New Jersey falcons.

Action was precipitated by a conference held in 1965 in Madison, Wisconsin. Raptor experts from North America, Europe, and Great Britain met
solely to discuss the plight of the peregrine falcon. In 1970 the Canadian
Federal-Provincial Wildlife Conference (an annual meeting of senior personnel from provincial, federal, and territorial wildlife agencies) authorized the
Canadian Wildlife Service (CWS) to initiate a captive breeding program for
the peregrine (jurisdictionally within the provinces' area of responsibility).
The function of the program was to raise sufficient birds to allow reintroductions in their former range. At about the same time as the CWS's project,
Cornell University was also involved in a peregrine breeding program. Cornell
birds were the first to be released into the wild, in 1974. As the number of
releases increased it became apparent that avian predators such as great horned
owls *(Bubo virginianus)* and golden eagles *(Aquila chrysaetos)* could cause
havoc by preying on the young peregrines. Control measures are needed or
releases have to be made in areas where these other avian predators are not
a threat.

Releases are generally made at historical eyrie sites where human disturbance is minimal. In natural areas, eyries are usually found on cliffs with
ledges for perching, roosting sites, plucking and feeding areas. High rise
buildings in urban areas previously served as nesting sites for peregrines and
successful releases have been made in such cities as Montreal, Baltimore,
New York, Spokane, and Edmonton where the birds feed primarily on pigeons
and English sparrows. The ledges of the buildings meet all the biological

requirements of the species just as well as natural rock ledges. The release of young birds is achieved by a process known as hacking. The birds are kept in an artificial nest box and fed until they are ready to fledge. The food source is gradually eliminated as the birds learn to fend for themselves. The management hope is that the birds will successfully migrate and return to the release site in future years to breed. This has occurred in Edmonton and Baltimore, among other locations. Citizens and visitors in both cities have had the rare opportunity of observing, through a closed circuit video system, the whole process of incubation, hatching, and rearing the young on a ledge of one of their high rises. The public relations value has been superb and much of the populace now considers the birds to be "their peregrines."

The lack of disturbance sought at release sites has not been the norm for much of the remaining wild population. Egg collectors, falconers seeking new birds, private individuals with their own captive breeding programs, and naturalists observing or photographing raptors are all sources of disturbance that tend to deplete natural recruitment and the wild breeding population. Raptors are still persecuted by hunters and ranchers. Trapping, poisoning, and shooting, although illegal in most jurisdictions, take a considerable toll of species such as the peregrine.

Legislation has been passed in the United States to make raptor propagation permits available under the Migratory Bird Treaty Act. The permit allows propagators and certain other people to purchase, sell, or barter captive-bred raptors for scientific, educational and falconry purposes if corresponding state regulations are passed. The legislation toughens the restrictions on endangered or threatened raptors listed under the Endangered Species Act although it allows continued trade in these species if the animals were in captivity prior to 1978. An intended primary function of the legislation is to reduce pressure on wild raptor populations. Without increased enforcement, the more restrictive legislation by itself is unlikely to have a significant impact on the illicit trade in falcons. A "sting" operation known as "Operation Falcon" ended in 1984 after 3 years of investigation. It resulted in indictments charging more than 400 violations of federal statutes. Included were nest robbing, egg smuggling and commercial sales of peregrines as well as other species used in falconry.

Management efforts for the peregrine falcon have been similar to those for other endangered nongame species. Captive breeding, reintroduction, and protection of existing eyries from disturbance, coupled with a public education program to prevent unwanted mortality and to sensitize the public to the birds' precarious status are the prime components. The peregrine falcon management effort has been successful and can be used as the model for other raptor species management. Nonetheless, the whole program would have been doomed to failure if the connection between persistent hydrocarbons such as DDT and the disastrous decline in population level had not been made and government action taken to reduce or eliminate use of the culprit chemicals in the environment. Volume 104 Number 2 of the Canadian Field-Naturalist (1990) features the peregrine falcon and contains several excellent articles on the species' status and environmental contaminants.

As managers, we must continue to use wildlife species as sentinels or early warning signals of declining environmental quality and must alert the public and governments to the consequences of continued contamination, despoilation, or incorrect resource extraction procedures that may be accounting for the problem. If this necessitates linking the potential consequences to human populations, we should do it. If the data are adequate and the public is convinced it is in its collective interest to seek a ban on the use of certain chemicals, to reduce sulphuric acid in the atmosphere, to reduce massive clear-cutting operations, and to stop draining wetlands, then the chance of political success increases. We should capitalize on those symptoms of our declining natural heritage to point out the long-term ecological consequences of a man controlled environment. Our dominance must be made to reflect the need for sustaining the diversity of life forms we have been fortunate enough to inherit. Future generations may well look back on this generation as the one that met or failed its responsibility to maintain an ecologically sound human interface with the life support system of this planet. If we fail, they will reap the disastrous consequences.

Bibliography

Fyfe, R. W., and R. K. Olendortf. 1976. Minimizing the dangers of nesting studies to raptors and other sensitive species. Can. Wildl. Serv. Occ. Pap. No. 23.

Henny, C. J., and M. W. Nelson. 1981. Decline and present status of breeding peregrine falcons in Oregon. Murrelet. 62:43–53.

Hickey, J. J., and D. W. Anderson. 1968. Chlorinated hydrocarbons and egg shell changes in raptorial and fish-eating birds. Science. 162:271–273.

Peakall, D. B. 1976. The peregrine falcon (*Falco peregrinus*) and pesticides. Can. Field-Nat. 90:301–307.

Peakall, D. B., T. J. Cade, C. M. White, and J. R. Haugh. 1975. Organochlorine residues in Alaskan peregrines. Pestic. Monit. J. 8:255–260.

Ratcliffe, D. A. 1967. Decrease in eggshell weight in certain birds of prey. Nature. 215:208–210.

Steidl, R. J., C. R. Griffin, L. J. Niles, and K. C. Clark. 1991. Reproductive success and eggshell thinning of a reestablished peregrine falcon population. J. Wildl. Manage. 55:294–299.

7. The Black-footed Ferret *(Mustela nigripes)*

The most endangered mammal species in North America probably is the black-footed ferret. Once distributed over much of the western plains of Canada and the United States, the species was considered extinct in 1974 when the only known population in South Dakota disappeared and captive breeding proved unsuccessful. Because the ferret is dependent on prairie dog colonies for both prey and shelter, its fate was inextricably linked to that of the prairie dog. As the prairie became cropland and eradication programs were conducted on the prairie dog colonies, both species' futures were impacted early in this century. Poisoning of prairie dogs was widespread and successful; the loss of prey base and secondary poisoning resulted in precipitous declines of black-footed ferret numbers.

In 1981, a population of black-footed ferrets was discovered near Meeteetse, Wyoming; that event initiated a saga which exemplifies the best and worst of endangered species management in the United States. In the west, there are strong public vs. private lands and federal vs. state jurisdictions conflicts. The Sagebrush Rebellion, as one example, in reality combined aspects of both. The Endangered Species Act clearly identifies the U.S. Fish and Wildlife Service as the responsible agency for listed terrestrial wildlife, but there was only one known population of ferrets and it occurred within the state boundaries of Wyoming. That state thus considered it part of its resident wildlife and claimed responsibility for the species' management. (A similar situation existed with the California condor in the state of California.) Additionally, the critical prairie dog colonies were primarily on private land; although much of that belonged to a cooperative rancher, the private landowners were more wary of the "Feds" than they were of the state people and thus were less likely to approve of federal intervention although clearly the weight of the law would support federal action. What happened was that the Fish and Wildlife Service rapidly delegated its responsibility to the Wyoming Game and Fish Department. The Department then set up a Black-footed Ferret Advisory Team (BFAT) consisting of a private rancher, representatives from the Department, the Bureau of Land Management, the Forest Service, the Fish and Wildlife Service, the Wyoming State Lands Board and the University of Wyoming. Another complicating factor was an ongoing research effort by Idaho State University and a consultant firm, Biota, funded in part by a major conservation agency, the Wildlife Preservation Trust. This ultimately resulted in representation of wildlife conservation agencies on BFAT by the National Wildlife Federation. The stage was set for interaction, positive and negative, between federal and state management agencies, private landowners, conservation interests and researchers.

BFAT moved cautiously, but a coordinated research program involving federal, state and university biologists was soon underway. Censusing and radio-collaring of ferrets, predator competition studies, prey base analysis, and discussion of recovery procedures all proceeded as part of BFAT's agenda of study. While the highly intrusive field research could be justified on the basis of the paucity of knowledge on the species, early concerns that the Meeteetse population was vulnerable to catastrophic events and that captive breeding should have a high and immediate priority were too easily set aside. BFAT did agree that at some point ferrets should be brought into captivity but, although planning for this event was conducted, there was no sense of urgency in the advisory team's actions. A workshop was held in 1984 in Laramie to present information on the ferret's biology, the basic tenets of conservation biology, and considerations important to a captive breeding program. Still, there was an atmosphere that it was necessary to explore all the potential pitfalls before committing to captive breeding. Much emphasis was placed on the failure of the Patuxent captive breeding effort using South Dakota ferrets, even though that population exhibited severe genetic problems which likely precluded successful breeding.

In 1985, disaster struck. Die-offs in the prairie dog colonies from sylvatic plague caused concern about loss of the prey base for the ferrets. Prairie dog burrows were treated with Sevin (active ingredient carbaryl) to kill the fleas that transmit the bacteria. BFAT agreed to plans to capture three pairs of ferrets for a captive breeding program to be conducted by Wyoming Game and Fish at the Sybille Research Unit. During all these events, some of the researchers at Meeteetse raised concerns that the ferret population seemed to be in decline and the program to capture six ferrets might be too little, too late. BFAT and Wyoming Fish and Game were considering whether the wild population was large enough to capture additional ferrets for another facility, the Front Royal Wildlife Research and Conservation Center in Virginia. The interest was to protect the Meeteetse population by not removing too many animals. One of the six ferrets captured for Sybille died of canine distemper on 21 October and the mark-recapture count at Meeteetse resulted in a population estimate of 31 animals, down from 130 animals in the 1984 census. It was evident that distemper was in the wild population and that ferret numbers were declining rapidly. The initial capture group succumbed to the disease but a decision was made to capture as many of the remaining wild ferrets as possible and this time take preventative measures such as isolation to stop the spread of the disease from infected animals. The worst case scenario had occurred. The pleas of researchers that captive breeding should have been the first priority of BFAT now had the weight of a prophecy of doom come true.

By 1986, all that remained of a once thriving wild population, the only known population of black-footed ferrets, were 18 animals all in captivity. A captive breeding advisory committee was formed and now the research was geared to maximizing production from the captive remnants of the Meeteetse population. Fortunately, at the time of printing, the captive population had grown to about 200 animals housed at three captive breeding sites with a fourth to be added for the 1991 breeding season. Zoos in Nebraska and Kentucky had supplemented the Sybille and Front Royal locations. Furthermore, plans were underway for the first reintroduction of the species at Shirley Basin/Medicine Bow in Wyoming in 1991.

At the time of crisis, full cooperation of the interest groups was finally achieved. The politics of management prior to the crisis may have ensured its occurrence. The rivalry between agencies and conservation interests, and the reluctance of the Fish and Wildlife Service to apply its jurisdictional rights and employ the full power of the Endangered Species Act may have been unavoidable. There is a lingering suspicion that other colonies of ferrets exist in the wild in Wyoming but they are on private land. If any government agency had exerted its power over the ranchers at Meeteetse, rather than cooperating with land owners and in essence operating at their largesse, any other ferret populations were doomed. The last thing that the independent Wyoming ranchers would tolerate would be the threat of government intervention on their land because of an endangered species. What is even more disturbing is the knowledge that the habitat for this species is so readily defined. The species exists only in large complexes of prairie dog colonies. Protect the prairie dogs and you protect black-footed ferret habitat. Ranchers don't like prairie dogs. It is felt that the prairie dogs compete with cattle for the limited forage and that there is a risk that cattle or horses will damage their limbs if they accidently step in a burrow opening, and equipment may be broken if a burrow system collapses under its weight. There is little evidence to support competition, indeed some studies show that forage for cattle may actually be increased by the presence of prairie dogs. The arguments appear economically based but in final analysis they are not. At the time, the Fish and Wildlife Service was unwilling to invoke the habitat protection component of the Endangered Species Act, possibly because it would have resulted in a challenge to the Act and a potential weakening of it. It has been left to the spotted owl to see how great an economic challenge is necessary to set aside consideration for endangered species.

Having witnessed the black-footed ferret saga, there are two relevant conclusions. The first is that wildlife professionals have vested political interests that may mitigate against effective and appropriate wildlife management activities. The second is that in times of crisis, it is possible to see the best of wildlife managers and management as personal, or agency, interests are set aside for full consideration of the resource's needs. The pattern is not unique to wildlife management. The current debates over global warming, the ozone layer's depletion and acid precipitation are mechanisms that effectively delay meaningful or appropriate actions until the crises are at hand. Wildlife managers are no better, or no worse, than human beings in other walks of life. Perhaps this is the fatal flaw in our own species which may someday make us endangered.

Bibliography

Clark, T. W. 1989. Conservation biology of the black-footed ferret *Mustela nigripes*. Wildlife Preservation Trust. Spec. Sci. Rep. 3. 175 pp.

Forrest, S. C., T. W. Clark, L. Richardson, and T. M. Campbell III. 1985. Black-footed ferret habitat: some management and reintroduction considerations. Bureau Land Management (Wyoming) Wildl. Tech. Bull. 2. 49 pp.

Seal, U.S., E. T. Thorne, M. A. Bogan, and S. H. Anderson (Eds). 1989. Conservation biology and the black-footed ferret. Yale Univ. Press, New Haven CT. 302 pp.

Ubico, S. R., G. O. Maupin, K. A. Fagerstone, and R. G. McLean. 1988. A plague epizootic in the white-tailed prairie dogs (*Cynomys leucurus*) of Meeteetse, Wyoming. J. Wildl. Dis. 24:399–405.

VII SOME SPECIALIZED AREAS of MANAGEMENT

In past years the art and science of wildlife management have been primarily concerned with five major principles. The first was protection, complete or partial, normally applied through regulations and their enforcement. The second was predator control, for if man was not the only responsible critter, what other animal may add to the mortality of prey? Of course, the fox, the wildcat, and the "hawk." Third, if neither protection nor predator control was adequate to increase populations, perhaps establishing an inviolate area for the wildlife to reproduce in would do the trick. Fourthly, if none of these approaches worked, maybe raising animals in captivity and releasing them into the wild would do it. This last activity was referred to by sportsmen as stocking. It was and still is very popular in some jurisdictions. The fifth and final idea to come of age was the concept of habitat improvement (Chapter 5). As we have seen, however, management is daily becoming more complex, and there are a myriad of specialized wildlife areas and concerns the manager must be aware of. In this chapter we present a few we feel are among the most important.

Protected Areas

The original concept behind establishing protected areas was to provide sanctuary (refuge or asylum) for one or more species to reproduce without harassment from human activities. Many people also felt that progeny from these protected areas would venture forth and repopulate extensive ranges outside the protected zone. This latter hope, as we now understand things, depends upon the home range and dispersal of the species as well as upon the size of the protected area. We have noted (Chapter 1) that the concept of setting aside areas for wildlife protection is not new; both Henry VIII and

167

James I did so. It should be recalled also that although these areas were set aside, they were protected from everyone except these same two gentlemen. Private parks for deer and exotic birds were present prior to 1900, principally on lands of the wealthy in Europe and North America. In this century, man has designed an amazing variety of areas, protected to some degree, for wild things, plants as well as animals.

Sanctuaries are public or private tracts of land which in their true form protect animals and plants within their boundaries. Certain elements of systems within a sanctuary may be removed to maintain either habitat conditions or animal populations at a particular level. Refuge is another term for sanctuary. These protected areas may be under federal, state, provincial, county, or municipal jurisdiction in North America. Some may be privately owned if trespass legislation or more specific legislation is present.

Parks are usually sanctuaries for wildlife although fishing is normally allowed. Parks also exist within the several levels of jurisdiction in North America. There are federal, state, provincial, county, and municipal park systems in the United States and Canada.

Designated wilderness areas on federal lands in the United States also provide protection to many wildlife species. These areas are roadless and thus less vulnerable to public use. Restrictions on motorized vehicles and land-use activities ensure preservation of natural conditions.

Management areas inherently admit to human intervention although they may provide some protection for specific purposes (nesting, brood areas) or for certain species. Federal and/or provincial and state law with attendant regulations applies in all protected areas, however, and specific legislation for various protected areas often is present in separate statutes.

The largest refuge (sanctuary) system in North America and probably in existence anywhere is the U.S. Wildlife Refuge System (USFWS), which encompasses over 37.5 million hectares (90 million acres). These areas have been established primarily to protect either waterfowl, other migratory birds, or larger mammals but also have been created since passage of the Endangered Species Act to protect threatened or endangered species. The refuge concept in North America began in 1893 with George Bird Grinnel and Theodore Roosevelt, and the first refuge was Pelican Island, Florida, established in 1903 (Chapter 4). The acquisition authority for the waterfowl refuge system was provided in 1929 under the auspices of the Migratory Bird Conservation Act. The Migratory Bird Hunting Stamp Act of 1934 assured a steady source of funding but also assured that the primary emphasis would be on waterfowl and that there would be pressure for hunting within the refuges. Amendments to the Conservation Act now allow hunting on up to 40 percent of the total area of any refuge if compatible with the major purpose(s) for which the area was established. Management on the refuge areas may be restricted to protection or may involve the production of grain crops for food, water level control, plant-water interspersion maintenance, reseeding, reforesting, and game harvesting. In the latter instance, muskrats and other furbearers have sometimes been trapped in the Montezuma Wildlife Refuge (New York) and the Horicon Marsh Refuge (Wisconsin) to aid in maintaining near optimum ratios of cover and open water for waterfowl. The overall administration and management of the U.S. Wildlife Refuge System and its units have been considered by Giles (1978) and Drabelle (1985).

In Canada, the first sanctuary was established in 1887 by Edgar Davidney, who was at the time lieutenant governor of the Northwest Territories. This was the Lost Mountain Lake area 130 kilometers northwest of Regina. Today, there are some 82 federal migratory bird sanctuaries in Canada totaling about 11.4 million hectares (about 28 million acres). Many of these areas serve to protect mammals, reptiles, and amphibians as well as birds.

Hot Springs (Arkansas) was the first national park (1872) in the U.S., and Banff (originally Rocky Mountains National Park) the first in Canada (1885). National park policy throughout the world today generally protects wildlife within park boundaries. Wildlife, by definition, now usually also includes vertebrates other than birds and mammals, some invertebrates, and plant life. Wildlife management within national parks has always been somewhat controversial; for if the park represents natural ecological conditions, apart from man's intervention, how do managers account for the establishment of the park as an inviolate area when it is itself an intervention? Inviolate areas are subject to population increases of many game species because neither direct nor indirect action by humans reduces their numbers. Some species actually learn to avoid harassment by not venturing outside. Such is the case with elk and white-tailed deer, which during open hunting seasons may repair to areas where they are not disturbed—often parks or sanctuaries. Park managers and interpreters also require roads, open areas for public use, buildings, and trails for access as well as areas for camping, administration, recreation, and interpretation. Roads and trails, in particular, often provide ecotones and open grazing areas that not only allow the public to view animals feeding but also increase the carrying capacity of the protected area. Transmission lines may provide additional interspersion especially valuable in producing food plants for grazing and browsing wildlife and for songbird nesting habitat. Faced with such changes, managers often have had to act to reduce game populations either through live trapping and removal or by shooting excess animals in order to help reduce both damage to vegetation and increased erosion. Elk were removed from Yellowstone for stocking elsewhere, and deer were killed to reduce the population density in Acadia National Park in Maine. A control program has been developed for the mountain goat, a species introduced to Olympic National Park in Washington. The Yellowstone elk problem has been controversial for many years, but it serves as an excellent example of the kind of problem ungulates may present when protection is provided. Harvests by hunters outside the park have removed thousands but have brought the wrath of members of the public who despise the "slaughter." Harvests by park authorities have also accounted for many animals, but even when the carcasses are distributed and wisely used, the public complaints and costs are high. The expense of live trapping and translocating is even higher, of course.

Should the matter of the elk be left to its natural conclusion, allowing range deterioration and perhaps a repeat of the massive die-off of 1914? Such a complex question must be carefully studied by park wildlife staff and state wildlife managers to maintain both the integrity of the park and sound, socially acceptable species management within budgets provided. We must also realize that what happens inside a park also affects land areas outside. Houston (1982) and Chase (1986) provide contrasting views of the elk situation in Yellowstone.

Management of wildlife within parks is most often restricted to habitat. Roadside, open area, and power line management to encourage the growth of palatable, nutritious plant species while discouraging others through hand labor (cutting them out), herbicides, seeding or planting native varieties is often possible. In other situations, winter feeding may be necessary (and responsible) on occasion to get animal populations of marginally high densities over brief periods of food shortage. In still other cases, the removal of animals by live trapping or culling will be necessary.

Wildlife managers in parks can also play a major role in advising on road and trail placement, service area locations, campground layouts, and various day-use or seasonal facilities to the benefit of wildlife and for better wildlife viewing. Advice on the use of salt on highways, fertilization, erosion control, speed limits, the location of garbage dumps, and many other concerns may involve the wildlife manager; and of course, he must also cope with nuisance wildlife that can pose many problems.

Perhaps no nuisance has reached such proportions as the bear-human interface. Black bears are attracted to dumps and people are attracted to black bears. The presence of grizzly bears in areas of even low human activity can be a major safety problem. The dump concern may not confront wildlife managers often in the future, however, because park dump locations should be determined at the planning stage so that humans are not allowed access to them. The grizzly bear situation is not so easy. These bears require extensive range areas and protection. Bear country can never be considered high density use areas for humans. Other nuisance wildlife such as skunks, porcupines, or rodents are usually thought of as part of the natural environment for park visitors to accept on the animals' terms. Only the beaver that floods the road may have to be moved.

Management areas may be within federal, provincial, or state jurisdiction and may go by different names. They allow for multiple use activity by humans within the bounds of the necessary management for one or more species in each area. Even hunting may be allowed. Canada has forty-four national or cooperative (joint federal-provincial management) wildlife areas. With less management involved, the waterfowl production areas and coordination areas administered by the USFWS also qualify as management areas, if for no more than habitat maintenance and seasonal protection. States and provinces also have their wildlife management areas. Some are managed specifically for wildlife and others are management areas in name only and are used almost entirely for other purposes. Such is the case with the Tobeatic Wildlife Management Area of Nova Scotia, which is primarily for forest management. Land use and motor vehicle access are both controlled by industry.

Private sanctuaries exist by virtue of land trespass legislation in many jurisdictions. The landowners take advantage of protection offered under statute, suitably mark the property, and refrain from killing the animals. Such areas are common in parts of North America but few are true private sanctuaries, known to the public and recognized as such. One very successful private sanctuary is located at Kingsville, Ontario. The story of the Jack Miner Bird Sanctuary began in 1904 when Miner, a pioneer conservationist, woodsman, and sportsman first lured four Canada geese to his home pond and clipped their wings. With this beginning of four live decoys he eventually wintered thousands of Canada geese and wild ducks. Jack Miner's work was continued by his son Manly, and the Kingsville sanctuary is still open to visitors, human and avian, from October to April each year.

Other early examples of private sanctuaries for wildfowl are those along Maryland's eastern shore. In the 1930's W. P. Chrysler, J. J. Raskob, and others, planted food and released propagated birds. They created highly successful protected areas even though limited hunting took place on some of them. Winter feeding became necessary and upwards of 4000 bushels of corn were fed one winter on one property alone. These areas also provided an element of protection for quail and pheasant. An interesting variation in protected area management is described from Connecticut (Bishop, 1949). It began in 1940 and was one of the earliest controlled hunting experiments in the eastern United States. Permits were required of hunters, bag limits established, areas divided into coverts for hunting, pheasants stocked, and wild birds (or stocked escapees) totally protected in blocks of 75 hectares (180 acres) to 177 hectares (424 acres) within the management unit. These protected areas were known as seed-stock refuges. Since then, a number of states have passed legislation allowing landowners to establish managed hunting areas with some degree of protection included for various species (for example, the New York State Fish and Wildlife Management Act). In North America today, refuges or sanctuaries for wildlife are very successful and of most consequence for two groups of animals; waterfowl and endangered species. The waterfowl (migratory bird) refuge system and the international migratory bird legislation allowing waterfowl to be managed on a flyway basis have been of paramount importance for ducks and geese. Protection of breeding and nesting areas, brood areas, and staging areas hold the highest priority in current and future management. For many endangered species, protected areas hold out the only hope for their continued survival; even protected areas may not be all that is required for such as the severely endangered California condor.

The size and most particularly, the actual boundaries of most protected areas are usually determined by socio-economic and political factors rather than biological or ecological ones. Nevertheless there are a number of factors which, under ideal conditions, the wildlife manager should consider prior to establishing a protected area. In relation to the land, the carrying capacity for the target species at the time of establishing the reserve should be assessed. In relation to the target species involved, their populations, breeding behavior, productivity and mobility are all factors that should be related to the size of the area and location of boundaries of the area. Adjacent land areas and land use should also be assessed relative to their contribution to protected area populations and vice versa. If both populations and the land area can be managed, the manager should attempt to maintain the estimated or theoretical optimum population sizes for survival of each protected species (Schonewald-Cox, 1983).

We should not leave the subject of protected areas without talking about wilderness, which may or may not be protected. Sometimes extensive, remote wilderness areas are protected only by legislation restricting certain types of access (float planes). At other times, smaller wilderness areas are established as inviolate refuges or sanctuaries. In the U.S., wilderness areas are generally roadless, and machines are not allowed unless traditional use areas have been established. Grazing is often permitted. Since World War II, planet-wide concern has been expressed for the retention of wilderness. Of the IUCN's three main objectives in its World Conservation Strategy, two may eventually be possible only if wilderness is preserved: the maintenance of essential ecological processes and the preservation of genetic diversity. For the wildlife manager, these objectives are important in dealing with wild animals, plants, and ecosystems on an everyday basis. Attempts to deal with them on an extended basis have been only partially successful. The International Biological Program (1964–74) was a cooperative project among the International Council of Scientific Unions. As one of its mandates, it attempted to describe, list, and reserve through legislation representative terrestrial communities worldwide. This program did result in an increase in terrestrial community preservation. In the future, it seems likely that it will become far easier to maintain several small areas under wilderness conditions than to protect a few large ones. Those species able to maintain genetic diversity within small ecosystem units will obviously be most favored for survival. Wilderness is increasingly threatened. "Once our master, then our enemy and now, finally, it has become our pensioner" (Gaston, 1982). The wildlife manager's decisions will regularly protect or destroy wilderness.

Bibliography

Bishop, J. S. 1949. Seed-stock refuge investigation. PR-4R, Connecticut State Board of Fisheries and Game. 34 pp.

Chase, A. 1986. Playing God in Yellowstone: the destruction of America's first national park. Atlantic Monthly Press. Boston, MA. 446 pp.

Drabelle, D. 1985. The national wildlife refuge system. Pp. 151–179 *In* Audubon wildlife report 1985. Natl Audubon Soc. New York, NY.

Gaston, T. 1982. Wilderness: the passing of a dream. Northern Perspectives 10(4):9–11.

Giles, Robert H., Jr. 1978. Wildlife management. W. H. Freeman and Company, San Francisco, CA. 416 pp.

Houston, D. B. 1983. The northern Yellowstone elk: ecology and management. MacMillan Publ. Co., New York, NY. 474 pp.

Leopold, A. S., S. A. Cain, C. Cottam, I. N. Gabrielson, and T. Kimball. 1963. Wildlife management in the National Parks. The Leopold Committee Report. Rep. from American Forests, April, 1963. 6 pp.

Levi, H. W. 1952. Evaluation of wildlife importations. The Scientific Monthly, LXXIV No. 6, pp. 315–322.

Miner, J. 1977. Wild Goose Jack. Paper Jacks, Markham, ON. 318 pp.

Schonewald-Cox, Christine M. 1983. Guidelines to management: A beginning attempt. *In* "Genetics and Conservation." Schonewald-Cox, Chambers, MacBryde, and Thomas, Eds. Benjamin/Cummings, Menlo Park, CA. 722 pp.

Trefethan, James B. 1961. Crusade for wildlife. The Telegraph Press, Harrisburg, PA. 377 pp.

Exotic Species

Mankind has always been interested in that which is unusual or exotic in nature, and animals foreign to one's native land are unusual—at least until they become easily recognizable and eventually common in a new home. For many people, the sight of an unusual foreign bird or mammal provides an aesthetic experience somewhat greater than a similar experience involving an indigenous animal. Similarly, the sportsman often gains more pleasure from hunting an introduced species than he does from seeking out a local animal as a target. Then too, there are the examples of immigrants to a new area who long for the presence of a part of the natural system to which they once belonged. They may want an animal for food or perhaps to make them feel more comfortable in their new homeland. As Teer (1979) has noted, "From his earliest beginnings, man has taken plants and animals with him wherever he went."

Because we are prone to like the unusual as well as the animals we are used to, we have hundreds of examples of exotic introductions into most parts of the world visited and settled by humans from distant homelands. Sometimes when a landmass was observed not to have many animals using it, its new human inhabitants got carried away. In New Zealand, of some 45 species of mammals introduced, about 25 became established. King (1984) nicely chronicles the impact of introduced mammalian predators in New Zealand on the native fauna. Because most avian niches were already filled, however, only around 24 of 130 species of introduced birds were successful. Usually, the number of exotics introduced has been fewer than the New Zealand example, but most jurisdictions in the industrialized world have dealt with new animals. Only a small percentage of the introductions have been successful in the past, and today's approach to the use of exotics is more cautious than it was years ago.

There are several questions the manager must be concerned with when he deals with a potential exotic introduction into the wild. Will the newcomer create a disruption in the system? Will diseases or parasites brought in be damaging to native species, or will diseases and parasites already present affect the exotic? Are all habitat requirements present and is a trophic niche available? Is the source stock viable and is the reproductive potential of the exotic capable of ensuring success?

In the case of system disruptions, we cannot always be sure what will happen, but we can take precautions. We know, for instance, that niche segregation among indigenous animals functions to reduce competition except under certain conditions which may alter the habitat either on a seasonal basis (winter; the dry season) or during protracted habitat stresses (long term droughts). In the case of red deer (*Cervus elaphus*) introduced into New Zealand in 1851, the animals were confronted with lush vegetation and no other mammals (except bats), so there was no niche segregation. Other species were soon introduced, but over the next seventy years the red deer increased with essentially no controls and became an agricultural pest of great proportions. Their feeding not only hurt the farmer but it modified the range to the detriment of other species and to man. We cannot blame the red deer, for the New Zealand story is one of man's failures, and more recently, successes. Harvests did not begin until the late 1920s, and soon after that hunters (cullers) were paid to kill red deer to reduce the populations. These cullings became commercial, and now meat and antlers produced on game ranches are significant components of the New Zealand GNP. The introduction of red deer into New Zealand was certainly successful, but it was also detrimental as were the successful introductions of the cavity nesting starling (*Sturnus vulgaris*) into the United States in 1872 and the burrowing European rabbit (*Oryctolagus cuniculus*) into Australia. The last two are competitive species with high comparative reproductive rates and diverse feeding habits. In these and many other cases we might have been able to predict what would happen, but the effects of introducing the grey squirrel (*Sciurus carolinensis*) to England and the snowshoe hare (*Lepus americanus*) to Newfoundland might not have been predictable even with today's knowledge and techniques. The grey squirrel competed successfully with the native red squirrel (*Sciurus vulgaris*) and became a forest pest of considerable proportions. The snowshoe hare increased following release, allowing high lynx densities to follow, which in turn reduced the Arctic hare (*Lepus arcticus*) numbers to low levels in restricted habitat.

Usually a quarantine period prior to release will ensure that diseases and parasites of birds are not introduced, but for mammals susceptible to organisms such as rabies with long and variable incubation of six to twelve months, a quarantine alone might not be adequate. In the United States, only the offspring of big game mammals held in captivity may be released into the wild. All industrialized countries have restrictions on the importation of exotics. Usually it is the health and agriculture agencies that are involved, but in North America, there may also be both federal and provincial or state legislation preventing importation for any purposes, except by permit. The United States has had the State-Federal Cooperative Foreign Game Program in operation since 1950. This program has three objectives:

1. To provide a reservoir of sound ecological and life history information to individuals and government agencies against which to evaluate foreign species suggested for trial acclimatization
2. To discourage unwise introductions by making these facts available to all concerned
3. To provide an alternate course of action by meeting the recognized need for filling vacant or drastically understocked habitats by a sci-

entifically conceived and executed program of research and trial introductions (Bump, 1968)

One of the keys to success or failure based on the objectives listed is understanding why, in objective (3), for example, the habitats are understocked. Why are indigenous species not present? For highly developed jurisdictions such as in Europe and North America, land-use changes have so altered our native habitats that many species already have been lost or their numbers severely reduced (Chapter 8). Replacing these habitats we have new ones, habitats that prevent natural succession and keep lands in crop production year after year. In forestry we also eliminate stands and often prevent natural succession through intensive management using fire, herbicides, reforestation, and the several mechanized and hand-labor tools of the forester. In essence, we have created habitats dependent upon human management of an intensive nature where exotics are sometimes better suited than are our native species. We find in eastern Washington that three of the four upland game birds present in non-forested habitats are pheasant, gray partridge, and chukar partridge (*Alectoris chukar*), all exotics. It is true, however, that both release site habitats and source sites require intensive study. It may be that we do not have to match them exactly to allow for success, but cover and food types for the requirements and behavior of the animal must be present, whether identical or not.

In addition to available habitat with an available niche, we also have to concern ourselves with the population from which we will take our animals for release. For a plastic species that may differ throughout a native range in ability to withstand various weather conditions, we should obviously obtain stock from areas with weather similar to that of the release site. Both mean minimum and maximum temperatures may be important, as are snowfall, ice, precipitation, and other weather factors. The animals must be from viable stock relative to survival and should reflect as well optimum reproductive rates for the species.

Animals released into new habitats may exhibit any of several different population patterns. They may increase to reasonable numbers compatible with their habitat, at or below carrying capacity; they may increase to a point above carrying capacity and then decline rapidly (boom-bust); or they may exist in low numbers for an indefinite period. The causes that eventually trigger success or failure may be obvious or unknown to us. Each instance is different and requires its own approach by managers.

Usually it is wise to afford newly released animals as much protection as possible from both man and opportunistic predators. It is also wise to monitor movements of released animals, for sometimes dispersal from release sites is rapid and wide ranging, yet we cannot expect one species from one source area to do the same thing in two different release sites. During ruffed grouse releases in Newfoundland, we had birds staying in the release site area and establishing a population in some cases and dispersing rapidly and widely from preselected release sites in others.

Of course we also need to keep in mind the breeding behavior of the animals we are dealing with. If a critical number at one site is a factor, such as in sharptails (*Pedioecetes phasianellus*), then both the sex ratio and the number of birds available in one small area will be important. With birds like ruffed grouse which do not require a social gathering place for more than two individuals, the number of birds released may be less critical than the sex ratio, which should favor females. The question of "how many" depends greatly on the behavior of the species, its dispersal, its courtship and breeding behavior, its reproductive potential, and its overall plasticity. One additional factor of importance is cost. Thousands of gray partridge were released in upstate New York and thousands of pheasants were released in many different states and in Canada, in Ontario and Nova Scotia, but the entire present population of Newfoundland moose resulted from no more than six animals. The cost-benefit ratios in these cases are considerably different. Exotics are imported into North America for zoos, sportsmen and nonsportsmen, to fill vacant or understocked niches and for commercial hunting programs. In this latter circumstance, large mammals have been successfully introduced into several states from Europe, Asia, and Africa. As far as it is possible, the wildlife manager must, however, accept the responsibility of maintaining the integrity of the native ecosystems. Where feasible, native species should be used before exotics.

Reintroductions are often successful if the original factors responsible for the decline and loss of the population are now absent or under control and if the habitat is still present. Translocations or transplantations are also often successful. Turkey (*Meleagris gallapavo*) have been successfully reintroduced into areas of New York, Idaho, Washington, and New England and beaver have been successfully moved in many jurisdictions. Sea otter (*Enhydra lutris*) translocations on North America's west coast from Alaska to Oregon have been more successful in the north than in the south.

Sometimes exotics may be used for "put-and-take" management purposes. In this approach, animals are released in the knowledge that they will survive in the wild at very low rates if at all and that a great many will be shot. The purpose is to provide targets for the hunter, and for economic feasibility, as high a proportion of animals as possible should be taken. Pheasants have often been used (as in Michigan, Ontario, Washington, and Maine) on a put-and-take basis although the practice is viewed today with less favor by the public and managers than it was in the past.

In releasing exotics into the wild or in releasing native species into the wild in areas away from their normal range, the manager may employ variations of two basic approaches. In the violent release approach, the animals are released with no opportunity to become familiar with their new surroundings. Early introductions were usually of this type. In the gentle release approach, animals are held in enclosures on the release site for a period of time prior to release, and in some cases, only the young born to these animals are released. The behavior of the animal being introduced and its known tolerance to variable habitat types are two of the parameters to consider in deciding on a release approach.

Outside of wildlife management but impinging on management in the countries of origin, exotics are used in medical research and to help sustain a gigantic pet industry. Colombia has been and remains a leading supplier of primates used for the study of malaria, cancer, and other human maladies. The pet industry uses many tropical and subtropical species of birds, reptiles, and some mammals. Of course captives also reproduce and help maintain stocks. The trade in exotic animal products is sometimes controlled in the market place (Chapter 8). Products of animals not listed in the CITES appendices may be purchased, and there is also a limited domestic market for all products in the countries of origin.

Bibliography

Bergerud, A. T. 1967. The distribution and abundance of arctic hares in Newfoundland. Can. Field-Nat. 81(4):242–248.

Bump, G. 1968. Exotics and the role of the State-Federal Foreign Game Investigation Program. *In* Symposium: Introduction of exotic animals: ecological and socioeconomic considerations. Ceasar Kleberg Research Program in Wildlife Ecology, College Station, Texas. 25 pp.

Jameson, R. J., K. W. Kenyon, A. M. Johnson, and H. M. Wight. 1982. History and status of translocated sea otter populations in North America. Wildl. Soc. Bull. 10(2):100–107.

King, C. 1984. Immigrant killers. Introduced predators and the conservation of birds in New Zealand. Oxford Univ. Press, New York, NY. 224 pp.

Levi, H. W. 1952. Evaluation of wildlife importations. The Scientific Monthly, LXXIV No. 6, pp. 315–322.

Parker, Richard L. 1968. Quarantine and health problems associated with introductions of animals. *In* Symposium: Introduction of exotic animals: Ecological and socioeconomic consideration. Caesar Kleberg Research Program in Wildlife Ecology, College Station, TX. 25 pp.

Pimlott, Douglas. 1953. Newfoundland moose. Trans. N.Am. Wildl. Conf. 18:563–581.

Schonewald-Cox, Christine M. 1983. Guidelines to management: A beginning attempt. *In* "Genetics and Conservation." Schonewald-Cox, Chambers, MacBryde, and Thomas, Eds. Benjamin/Cummings, Menlo Park, CA. 722 pp.

Teer, James G. 1979. Introduction of exotic animals. Pp. 172–177, *In* Wildlife conservation, principles and practices. R. D. Teague and E. Decker, Eds. The Wildlife Society, Washington D.C.

Vale, Robert V. 1936. Wings, fur and shot. Stackpole Books, Harrisburg, PA. 199 pp.

Shooting Preserves and Put and Take

Shooting preserves have been around for a long time. In fact Leopold (1933) suggests that Henry VIII may have used one when he protected pheasants, herons, and partridges near Westminster Palace. Kozicky and Madson (1979) indicate that shooting preserves "have been around for about 70 years and are as American as quail and cornpone." Shooting preserves are far less common in Canada than in the U.S., although legislation providing for them occurs in several provinces. Private pay-to-hunt preserves are successful in Ontario and Nova Scotia, for example. A shooting preserve definition is given by Kozicky and Madson as "an area owned or leased for the purpose of releasing pen-reared game birds for hunting over a period of five or six months." The benefits that are seen to exist are:

a. Legislation provides a longer season and thus an extended period of recreation.
b. Quality, uncrowded hunting is provided near high density human population centers.
c. The use of preserves by a proportion of the hunting public relieves pressure on public lands.
d. Preserves provide a place to hunt in areas where public access for the purpose of hunting may be denied on private lands.

A few released birds may escape to areas outside and survive to reproduce. Some knowledge and expertise concerning the biology and management of the species used is also gained.

As human populations continue to increase, as lands become less available for wildlife and to the hunting public, and as we ease further away from the extensive management (muddling through) approach in North America toward intensive management, shooting preserves may play an increasingly important role in wildlife management. This will probably hold true even though a high proportion of the public opposing hunting sees the shooting preserve as one of the worst examples of blood sports.

A large number of birds and mammals are popularly advertised as available on preserves or "resorts," as they are referred to in Texas. Various species of Asian and North American ungulates, wild boar (*Sus scrofa*), quail (*Colinus virginianus*), turkey, mallard ducks, gray partridge, and ring-necked pheasant are among the scores of animals raised under captive or semicaptive conditions and hunted on private preserves for profit. The pheasant, however, is the most important target wherever preserves exist within its range. Upland game birds used must flush readily and fly high and fast, providing a good-target for the hunter. Recovery rates of released birds must also be high to ensure a reasonable profit. Birds raised in captivity must also lend themselves well to captive conditions and offer high survival rates in captivity while retaining their wildness.

Hunters who do not favor shooting preserves may disagree with the put-and-take concept or simply feel that artificially propagated birds are too tame. Others may be displeased as a matter of class distinction or income level, because they are not able to afford artificial hunting and do not approve of it because of the class or cost factor. Feelings sometimes run high, which shows that all hunters are not of similar mind when it comes to all hunting practices.

The shooting preserve concept is a natural extension of two management principles, stocking and protected areas. Stocking of both exotic and native species has a long history (Chapter 1). It has long been a mainstay in fishery management and during the twenties and thirties was a popular element in approaches to wildlife management. *Forest and Stream* ran a column called "Practical Game Breeding," written by G. C. Corsan for years, and although game breeding was in the title of the column, stocking and area protection were often discussed with mention of private sanctuaries, including Jack Miner's, occurring commonly. Since the stocking of exotics, reintroduction, and translocations are mentioned generally elsewhere, we are concerned here only with put-and-take stocking, which is used most efficiently on preserves. The obvious reason is that the releases of birds are coincident with known hunting pressure. Preserve management combines the skills of habitat management, propagation, and business acumen. Cover types and feeding and roosting areas are maintained specifically for upland game birds in such areas. Habitats are as close to the optimum for the birds as possible yet natural for hunters and dogs. Although some escapees or even wild stock may be present from time to time, the majority of birds harvested are released from the pens forming the game farm portion of the preserve. In some situations, the preserve and game farm may operate independently, with birds purchased and released at regular intervals. In the case of pheasants where hunting may be restricted to males, depending upon the legislation, many more males than females are released. Females are occasionally retained for sale as meat birds, if the law allows. For species such as gray partridge, both sexes are released and harvested. The use of one upland game species over another depends upon a number of factors including break even costs, hunter choice, habitat available on the preserve, and the availability of birds. Since it is the recovery rate that is important on preserves and survival of pen-reared birds in the wild is low in most cases, the viability of the stock is not important here although it is of obvious importance in other forms of stocking. Put-and-take stocking is used on public lands in some instances, but public lands are even now inadequate to provide hunting opportunities close to many metropolitan areas. The put-and-take stocking efforts can never be as efficient on such lands as they are on preserves because of costs involved and because neither hunting pressure nor hunter distribution can be strictly controlled.

Besides wildlife agencies, the North American Game Breeders and Shooting Preserve Association of Goose Lake, Iowa, is the most up-to-date source of regular information for both game breeding and shooting preserves. Wildlife managers should be familiar with the legislation in the jurisdiction where they work and the major problems of game breeding for species most commonly used. They must also understand the basic concepts of preserve management.

Bibliography

Byers, S. M., and G. V. Burger. 1979. Evaluation of three partridge species for put and take hunting. Wildl. Soc. Bull. 7(1):17–20.

Kozicky, E. L. and J. B. Madson. 1979. The shooting preserve concept. Pp. 156–160, *In* Wildlife conservation, principles and practices. The Wildlife Society, Washington D.C.

Leopold, A. 1933. Game management. Charles Scribner's Sons, New York, NY. 449 pp.

Ratti, J. T., and G. W. Workman. 1976. Hunter characteristics and attitudes relating to Utah shooting preserves. Wildl. Soc. Bull. 4(1):21–25.

Schreiner, Charles, III. 1968. Uses of exotic animals in a commercial hunting program. *In* Symposium: Introduction of exotic animals: ecological and socioeconomic considerations. Caesar Kleberg Research Program in Wildlife Ecology, College Station, TX. 25 pp.

Migratory Animals

Migration has always fascinated biologists. The *why* question has been answered for most species but the *how* still remains a question for many. Among the mammals, the barren-ground caribou in North America and the reindeer of the USSR (both *Rangifer tarandus*) move for food and calving purposes. In savannah-land areas of Africa, ungulates move for food as periods of rainfall and drought alter the availability of grasses and forbs. In mountainous regions, ungulates may undertake altitudinal movements for food and comfort. Migration in birds is a subject that has kept the interest of naturalists and researchers high for hundreds of years. Some species like the crow (*Corvus corax*) may move short distances while others, like most warblers (family Parulidae), fly thousands of kilometers. Where man has not disrupted the process, migration allows mammals and birds to escape periods of cold or drought, to produce their young at the most propitious times in relation to weather and climate, and to have food for them. Like hibernation, migration has evolved over millions of years and provided selective advantages that have allowed for the successful existence of hundreds of species.

Regular (or nearly so) movements of animals, whether fish, reptiles, amphibians, birds, or mammals provide certain unique problems to the wildlife manager for only a part of the year. Perhaps this will be summer or the dry season. In winter or during the rains, another manager may be concerned with the species. As long as the animals remain within the boundaries of one jurisdiction, management usually can be coordinated rather well. With animals of limited mobility there is little chance that political boundaries will be crossed because they move short distances; but this is not true of most migratory species. In North America, coordinated, cooperative management was made possible through the migratory bird treaties and implementing legislation in Canada, the United States, and Mexico. For certain marine mammals like whales, some cooperative management has also been possible, although not always effective. For many species, however, cooperative arrangements without the support of legislation have had to develop and the problems have often been complex. Such is the case today, for example, with the Kaminuriak caribou herd in Canada.

Recently, international concern has been apparent in relation to migratory species. Beginning about 1962 a series of intergovernment conferences on wetlands considered the topic from many points of view and for many purposes, one of which was for waterfowl habitat. In 1971, the "Convention on Wetlands of International Importance Especially as Waterfowl Habitat" was adopted at a conference in Ramsar, Iran. Parties to this intergovernmental treaty accept two major obligations:

1. To recognize the international importance of at least one wetland within its territory by placing it on the convention list
2. To formulate and implement planning to promote the conservation of wetlands so listed and wise use in general of wetlands within their territory

Prior to this convention only the regulatory management of waterfowl and other migratory birds was possible under international legislation in North America. The protection of habitats and reservation of lands was accomplished on a national, state, or provincial basis in Canada, the United States, and Mexico. Canada became a party to the Ramsar Convention in 1981 and by 1989 had listed eighteen wetlands with the convention because of their importance primarily to migratory birds. Some are staging areas, some are stopover or breeding, nesting, and brood areas. Under the basic criterion of the convention, one percent or more of a regional population of a species must use the area at some time during the year. Although protection could, of course, be provided under national or provincial legislation, the listing under an international convention provides a sounder long-term guarantee of protection and opens the door to further international cooperation in management.

In 1979, the Convention on the Conservation of Migratory Species of Wild Animals was held in Bonn, West Germany. This was an umbrella convention to provide agreements covering individual migratory species or groups of species throughout their twelve-month range(s). International conventions can serve to restrict national autonomy in the management of migratory species, and it may be for this reason, as stocks of fish in particular became the focus for international conflict in resource management, that North American jurisdictions have not rushed to become party to the Bonn convention. Nevertheless we can look to the increased effectiveness of international conventions in restricting national domination over resources in the future, for this is really the only way in which resources of the "commons" and migratory animals can be properly managed on a world wide basis.

The IUCN supported by the United Nations Environmental Program was responsible for authoring the draft agreement for the Bonn conference that was signed by twenty-two nations, many of them underdeveloped countries. Some of the problems related to international conventions of this nature are noted by Johnson (1980), and it is significant that he notes lobbying by NGOs (nongovernment organizations) as being one of them. Many antihunting and other preservationist groups are among these NGOs. They argue primarily from moralistic and emotional positions and as Johnson notes " . . . nearly 70 lobbyist groups were represented at Bonn and some of these carry a great deal of political clout in their home countries. Only a few management groups attended or were represented.''

Here we see once again the potential for decision making by non professionals. Johnson (op. cit.) further urges that "Wildlife managers must increase their involvement in these matters.''

Bibliography

Johnson, M. 1980. New treaty arouses management issues. Wildl. Soc. Bull. (2):152–156.

Vontobel, Roy, ed. 1982. Man and wildlife in a shared environment. Can. Wildl. Serv., Ottawa, ON. 54 pp.

Urban Wildlife

There is a growing realization that urban centers can be made more natural and contain at least some wildlife components that will allow the human residents to understand more readily the ecological ties that bind us all. While this realization has come almost too late for some inner city areas, there have been welcome successes in many urban cores—from the hacking of peregrines on downtown office buildings in Montreal, Baltimore, and Edmonton to architectural designs that include roof and ledge gardens for avian habitat.

The city generally has been antithetical to nature and to man's psyche. Puri (1974) pointed out that the stresses and tensions in people living in cities cause numerous mental and psychosomatic disorders. Many of these problems of urban living cannot be treated successfully with conventional medicine. Instead, relaxation is one of the major sources of relief. How often have you found the solace of an urban park to be sufficient to ease the tension of noise, pollution, and the masses of humanity and concrete that defile our earthly base? How often did you think that it was not just the vegetation—the trees, shrubs, flowers—that was achieving this relaxation but the animals also— the squirrels, pigeons, robins, and sparrows? Geist (1975) echoed this sentiment when he stated that "the management and support of wildlife in urban areas is in the final analysis an exercise in preventive medicine.'' The late Constantinas Doxiadis (1975) looked at the problem of declining natural areas at the global level and felt there was only one solution and that required an "overset system" of wildlife and human settlements. In a global ecology context, there should be a balance between agriculture, industry, cities (settlements), and natural areas; there also should be intergradation so that natural areas literally invade urban complexes. Nature and wildlife must be part of the cities of the future if mankind is to avoid the mistakes of past civilizations that sought to remove or overpower nature and in the process created wastelands.

Perhaps the best mechanism for ensuring consideration of wildlife in urban areas is by specifically planning for it. Subject to management are open space and building design, the only two factors necessary to ensure both aesthetically pleasing human environments and wildlife habitat. Wildlife professionals too often avoid the urban scene for more rural surroundings. Wildlife management is first and foremost dealing with people, and about 80 percent of North America's people are found in cities. We have a responsibility for contributing to the urban planning process and lobbying effectively for natural ecological values; there is considerable public approval for such action. We have failed so far to capitalize on much of that latent political support.

What are some of the elements of wildlife management in an urban context? At the planning level it means advocating use of open space areas as wildlife habitat; designing corridors of habitat that link natural areas together. Often existing linear systems can be used to this end—railway and utility rights of way, streams, and even highway verges and medians. These corridors will tie together the urban ecological preserves and parks. Most cities already have natural or seminatural areas that are undeveloped (hazard lands) or have land uses of little impact (cemeteries). By linking these and providing access for viewing and educational purposes, Doxiadis' dream might be realized in every city! These areas need protection, however. If narrow belts of wildlife habitat or other sensitive places are adjacent to high density residential sections they are doomed to abuse and possible destruction. Adjunct land uses should be carefully controlled; low-density residential, hospital or convalescent homes, housing for the elderly, and light industry are appropriate.

Architectural designs that minimize or eliminate nesting or loafing areas for species like starlings, house sparrows, and pigeons can be incorporated into new construction. Landscaping with native shrubs and trees of high wildlife values and reducing the need for mowing (i.e., grassed areas) will encourage wildlife. There are now countless prescriptions for landowners on how to develop back-yard wildlife habitat. The U.S. Fish and Wildlife Service's Biological Services Program also has a document outlining methodologies for planning for wildlife in urban and suburban areas. The Urban Wildlife Research Center, Inc., founded in 1973, (now the National Institute for Urban Wildlife) serves as a storehouse of information for wildlife planning in cities. It also conducts research relating to "(1) effects of man's activities on wildlife and wildlife habitat; (2) environmental and wildlife planning and management for new residential, commercial and industrial developments; and (3) human-wildlife relationships in existing urban or other developed areas."

With the burgeoning interest in urban wildlife and its management, there is a growing need for wildlife managers committed to working within and improving metropolitan environments. Unfortunately, too many "wildlifers" are still attracted to the profession by the call of the wild and are trying to escape the city rather than improve it. Until our profession makes the necessary moves to ensure that a wildlife voice is heard in urban planning circles, we will continue to lose, not by malicious acts of planners but by the lack of consideration of alternate ways of doing things that are compatible with or enhance wildlife values.

A very important consideration is that most of the human population lives in cities, many of whose inhabitants have lost touch with their ecological roots; the educational system is not adequately geared to redress that deficiency. More direct understanding of nature and how our planet functions should be incorporated into elementary curricula. Too often field trips to natural areas or interpretive centers are considered luxury items and are dropped when school budgets are cut. Many inner core schools are within districts that do not have a strong tax base, so ecological field exercises become too expensive to be kept in the program. We should show that such experience at the elementary school level is essential to healthy mental development and enrichment as well as to understanding the complexity of life.

Project WILD has been developed by the Western Association of Fish and Wildlife Agencies and the Western Regional Environmental Education Council with the support of agencies such as the National Wildlife Federation and Defenders of Wildlife. It has been adapted for use in several states and provinces. This educational program uses wildlife examples pertinent to a child's understanding in diverse subject areas like mathematics and physics and is suitable in classes from kindergarten to high school level. It is hoped that by using examples from nature in courses other than biology or environmental studies the students who do not take these courses will at least get some exposure to ecological principles and to wildlife as real components of their "world." Project WILD is introduced to teachers through workshops conducted by the local wildlife and education agencies. In this way, it is expected to receive greater attention and use than if curricular guides were simply provided without proper instruction in their use.

Many of the problems associated with the management of wildlife species in cities have been addressed and adequately summarized in recent symposia. The reader should review these for more in-depth analysis of the particular attributes of this specialized wildlife management area (cf., Noyes and Progulske, 1974; McKeating, 1975; Euler et al. 1975; Anon. 1977; Adams and Leedy, 1987).

Bibliography

Adams, L. W., and L. E. Dore. 1989. Wildlife reserves and corridors in the urban environment. A guide to ecological landscape planning and resource conservation. Nat. Inst. for Urban Wildl., Columbia, MD. 91 pp.

Adams, L. W., and D. L. Leedy, eds. 1987. Integrating man and nature in the metropolitan environment. Nat. Inst. for Urban Wildl., Columbia, MD. 249 pp.

Anon. 1977. Children, nature and the urban environment. U.S. Dept. Agric. For. Serv. Gen. Tech. Rep. NG30. 261 pp.

Doxiadis, C. A. 1975. Wildlife and human settlements. Pp. 2–22, *In* Proceedings of the symposium—wildlife in urban Canada. D. Euler, F. Gilbert, and G. McKeating, Eds. Off. Cont. Ed., Univ. Guelph, Guelph, Canda.

Euler, D., F. Gilbert, and G. McKeating, eds. 1975. Proceedings of the symposium—wildlife in urban Canada. Off. Cont. Ed., Univ. Guelph, Guelph, Canada. 134 pp.

Geis, A. D. 1975. Urban planning and urban wildlife; a case study of a planned city near Washington D.C. Pp. 79–84, *In* Proceedings of the symposium—wildlife in urban Canada. D. Euler, F. Gilbert, and G. McKeating, Eds. Off. Cont. Ed., Univ. Guelph, Guelph, Canada.

Geist, V. 1975. Wildlife and people in an urban environment—the biology of cohabitation. Pp. 36–47, *In* Proceedings of the symposium-wildlife in urban Canada. D. Euler, F. Gilbert, and G. McKeating, Eds. Off. Cont. Ed., Univ. Guelph, Guelph, Canada.

Kelcey, J. G. 1975. Opportunities for wildlife habitats on road verges in a new city. Urban Ecol. 1:271–284.

Leedy, D. L., and L. W. Adams. 1984. A guide to urban wildlife management. Natl. Inst. for Urban Wildl., Columbia MD. 42 pp.

McKeating, G. B. 1975. Nature and urban man. Can. Nat. Fed. Spec. Publ. No. 4. Ottawa, Canada. 134 pp.

McKeating, G. B., and W. A. Creighton. 1975. Backyard habitat. Ont. Min. Nat. Resour., Toronto, Canada. 10 pp.

Noyes, J. H., and D. R. Progulske. 1974. Wildlife in an urbanizing environment. Univ. Mass., Planning and Resource Development Ser. No. 28., Amherst, MA. 182 pp.

Puri, G. S. 1974. The health hazard of stress in the urban-industrial environment of developed countries. Int. J. Ecol. Environ. Sci. 1:53–60.

Stenburg, K. and W. W. Shaw (eds.). 1986. Wildlife conservation and new residential developments. Proceedings of a national symposium on urban wildlife. Univ. Arizona, Tucson. 203 pp.

Thomas, J. W., R. O. Brush, and R. M. DeGraaf. 1973. Invite wildlife to your backyard. Natl. Wildl. Mag. (April-May). 12 pp. (reprint).

Depredations

Many wildlife species project contrasting images depending on which segment of the public is doing the viewing. Wolves are symbolic of wilderness to many, but to a livestock rancher they are vermin. Red-winged blackbirds are pretty birds to some, but to agriculturists they can be economically devastating if a farmer happens to grow corn, sunflowers, or any number of crops close to a summer or winter roost. These are the classic confrontations which, exclusive of the regulatory management of game species, have occupied a disproportionate share of attention in wildlife management. This has occurred because, as with game species, economic values can be assigned. Damage to food production, be the commodity sheep (coyote), honey (bears), fruit (small mammals and birds), or grains (small mammals and birds) totals in the billions of dollars and has focused attention on means of controlling populations of depredating wildlife. The U.S. Fish and Wildlife Service operated a predator control section that concentrated primarily on the coyote until 1986, when the Department of Agriculture assumed the responsibility. Prior to the 1960s the leg hold trap, M-44 ("coyote getter"), shooting, and toxicants such as 1080 were used to reduce coyote numbers—generally without significant success according to the carnivore catches from survey traplines. Some jurisdictions used bounties but they, too, usually have proven ineffective. Bounties are frequently paid for animals that would have been taken anyway. Biologically, it is difficult to find any cases where population levels of carnivores have been reduced as a result of bounties.

Two major reports on predator control have been submitted to the United States federal government. The first of these (Leopold et al. 1964) contained the conclusion that "All native animals are resources of inherent interest and value to people . . . (therefore) Basic government policy should be one of husbandry of all forms of wildlife." However, in situations where a species was causing significant damage to other resources or crops or where it endangered public health or safety (e.g., rabies), local population control was an acceptable and essential management tool. The authors cautioned that control had to be limited to the troublesome species, or preferably individuals, and to the locality where the damage or danger existed.

A second report (Cain et al. 1972) authorized through the Advisory Board on Wildlife Management (as was the Leopold report) recommended cessation of toxicant use. This was one of fifteen points intended to improve environmental safeguards associated with predator management. The committee included five wildlife ecologists, one plant ecologist, and one political scientist;

it was criticized strongly for not having representation from the livestock industries, especially when, a month after its report, an executive order was signed into law that restricted the use of toxicants on federal lands and in federal programs of mammal and bird damage control. In addition to the political repercussions from stockmen who tried to have predator control turned over to the states, this situation stimulated efforts to find alternative methods of coyote management; hence, new research was funded. The stockmen failed in their attempt to have more sympathetic management agencies (state agricultural departments) take over from the federal authority. If they had succeeded, it would have been antithetical to the concept that wildlife is the property of *all* the people and, therefore, should be managed by agencies responsible to a plurality of public values. A report prepared by the Mammalian and Avian Pest Management Committee on coyote predation in Ontario addressed this particular issue by suggesting that county predator control committees be formed in areas designated by a provincial predation control coordinator. The coordinator, an employee of the Fish and Wildlife Division of the Ministry of Natural Resources, was to work closely with the director of the Livestock Branch of the Ministry of Agriculture and Food. The Predator Control Committee would be given responsibility for directing management actions to prevent stock predation. The advantage of the system was that farmers and control agents were to operate through a local committee that should be more responsive and, therefore, more effective than a bureaucracy operating out of regional or headquarter offices. The committee representation was from the Ministry of Natural Resources (1 conservation officer), Ministry of Agriculture and Food (1 agriculture representative), municipal government (1), and producers. The committee, chaired by the agriculture representative, was to designate the location, intensity, and method of predator control, educate the producers, and coordinate local sportsmen and farmers to reduce the need for future control efforts. The provincial government never adopted this scheme; instead it continued to provide compensation to producers for documented livestock losses to wolves or coyotes.

A simulation model of coyote population control showed that the primary effect of killing coyotes was to stimulate density dependent changes in birth and natural mortality rates and that coyotes could thus sustain their populations except at the very highest levels of control. If 75 percent of a population were eliminated each year, it could be exterminated in slightly over fifty years. However, populations reduced by intensive control measures could recover to their pre-control densities in as few as three years once the control measures ceased. In effect, this supports the need for control efforts to be targeted at the problem individuals rather than the population as a whole, unless the control measures can be selective against pregnant females or females and their litters (a knowledge of the location of natal dens is required).

For the moment, management efforts are awaiting results of the research generated by the removal of 1080 and M-44s as control agents. Whether aversive conditioning (lithium chloride sheep collars), sterilization (diethyl stilbestrol), or repellents ever prove effective is a moot question. Perhaps better husbandry and more selective removal methods are all that are actually needed. 1080 has been recently approved for such selective use. Environmentalists are challenging the new EPA policy which would permit sheep collars with 1080 to be used subject to control by government agents.

Blackbird control poses another set of interesting management dilemmas. Some of the aversive conditioning agents like Avitrol (4-aminopyridine) have side effects that include nontarget species poisoning and distress vocalizations of the target species (which results in the aversive conditioning). The nontarget problem can be minimized or even eliminated by not treating the headlands and first rows of the crop, but the visual and auditory stimuli can be unpleasant or misinterpreted by an uninformed observer. This may not be a problem in agricultural areas. When the chemical was used in an urban situation (Toronto), the city folk did not take kindly to birds dropping out of the sky and flopping around on the lawns of a hospital. The use of Avitrol is only cost effective in certain situations, and movement of birds to different foraging sites may necessitate repeated applications. Therefore, this chemical agent and others such as methiocarb (3,5 dimethyl-4-(methylthio) phenol methyl-carbamate) did not offer the growers any real panacea.

Until recently, the U.S. Fish and Wildlife Service had conducted a program of population reduction at winter roost sites. A detergent (Turgitol) was used to break down the oil on feathers and destroy their insulating value when they were wetted. This resulted in hypothermia and death of the birds so treated. The approach had value in reducing disease and depredation problems associated with the roosts, but had little if any impact on summer populations and crop depredation near summer roost sites. Because Turgitol is effective at temperatures below 50°F (10°C), a postbreeding, summer roost population test program was proposed for a site where intensive studies of population, biology, and depredation had been conducted. Despite stringent environmental precautions and proposed water monitoring, pre- and post-spray, the provincial government did not give approval until *after* it had been reelected with a substantial majority. The lesson here is that potentially controversial wildlife management procedures probably should not be proposed or conducted close to election time. The proposal to kill a local population of blackbirds concerned an area where farmers (a small but vocal voting group) strongly supported the action. In terms of political realities, however, the proposal caused fear that the press might make an issue of it and thus generate a negative influence on urban voters. While all governments and politicians are not so sensitive, it is a truism that most are, especially if there is a precedent that resulted in bad press. Canadians, in particular, seem especially prone to such a reaction, possibly because of the harp seal issue and the strength of the antivivisectionist movement in that country.

Bibliography

Cain, S. A., J. A. Kadlec, D. L. Allen, R. A. Cooley, M. H. Hornocker, A. S. Leopold, and F. H. Wagner. 1972. Predator control—1971 report to the Council on Environmental Quality and Department of the Interior by the Advisory Committee on Predator Control. Univ. Michigan Press VIII, Ann Arbor, MI. 247 pp.

Connolly, G. E., and W. M. Longhurst. 1975. The effects of control on coyote populations: a simulation model. Dir. Agric. Sci. Univ. Calif. Berkeley. Bull. 1872. 27 pp.

Dolbeer, R. A. 1980. Blackbirds and corn in Ohio. U.S. Fish Wildl. Serv. Resour. Publ. 136. 18 pp.

Leopold, A. S., S. A. Cain, C. M. Cottam, I. N. Gabrielson, and T. L. Kimball. 1964. Predator and rodent control in the United States. Trans. N. Am. Wildl. Nat. Resour. Conf. 29:27–49.

Linhart, S. B., and W. B. Robinson. 1972. Some relative carnivore densities in areas under sustained coyote control. J. Mammal. 53:880–884.

Somers, J. D., F. F. Gilbert, D. E. Joyner, R. J. Brooks, and R. G. Gartshore. 1981a. Use of 4-aminopyridine in cornfields under high foraging stress. J. Wildl. Manage. 45:702–709.

Somers, J. D., R. G. Gartshore, F. F. Gilbert, and R. J. Brooks. 1981b. Movements and habitat use by depredating red-winged blackbirds in Simcoe County, Ontario. Can. J. Zool. 51:2206–2214.

Stickley, A. R., Jr., D. L. Otis, and D. T. Palmer. 1979. Evaluation and results of a survey of blackbird and mammal damage to mature field corn over a large (three-state) area. Am. Soc. Testing and Materials. Spec. Tech. Publ. 680. Pp. 169–177, *In* Vertebrate pest control and management. Philadelphia, PA.

Tyler, B. M. J., and L. W. Kannenberg. 1980. Blackbird damage to ripening field corn in Ontario. Can. J. Zool. 58:469–472.

Humane Trapping

It remains to examine one last emotional issue in wildlife management, that of trapping furbearing animals. Many humane organizations have focused their attention on the steel-jawed leg-hold trap, targeted because of the damage it causes to the animal, its general nonselectivity and its common use by trappers. In reality, much of their activity is overtly or covertly designed to eliminate commercial trapping altogether. As managers of wildlife, we have been remiss in supporting wildlife trapping without qualification. In Ohio, for example, blatantly false impressions were generated to defeat a proposed trapping ban. Instead of speaking out against the ludicrous claims that such diseases as rabies and bubonic plague will increase in prevalence without the use of the leg-hold trap, managers tacitly approved of the approach. This type of biased approach does little to enhance the profession's credibility even though it may help achieve policy objectives. Excellent biological arguments can be made for population management of such herbivores as beaver and muskrat and even for carnivores, such as fisher, which can be culled by means of careful management. Unfortunately, the management expertise needed to exact the proper age and sex quotas and the means selectively to trap individuals from populations are often lacking. Only recently have regulations been changed to protect adult, female fisher, which become increasingly vulnerable to trapping as the season progresses. With a January closing, harvest in Ontario is primarily restricted to juveniles and adult males. Without using live traps, which have the ancillary benefit of allowing the release of unwanted individuals, it is unlikely that the selectivity required for intensive management can be achieved—unless tremendous progress is made with pheromones or other chemical attractants or repellents.

Bearing this in mind, it is critical that traps and trap sets be made as selective as possible and that they either dispatch the animal humanely or hold the animal with minimal discomfort. Trapper education can be used to demonstrate the proper traps and sets for given species, but standards are necessary to ensure that traps meet some type of humane criteria. Recent improvements to leg holding devices include soft hold traps that have rubber jaws, leg snares, and triggers that can be set to different tripping pressures (and thus have a weight threshold to increase selectivity).

In Canada, the Federal Provincial Committee for Humane Trapping (FPCHT) submitted a final report in 1981 that contained a number of recommendations intended to maximize the "humaneness" in holding or killing furbearers. This government steering committee, created by the Federal-Provincial Wildlife Conference in 1973, grew out of the efforts of Canadian humane societies to focus public attention on the capture of furbearing animals. Along with sensationalist activities, like "They take so long to die," a film dramatizing the trapping of wild animals, objective efforts such as those by the Humane Trap Development Committee (HTDC) of the Canadian Federation of Humane Societies were undertaken. The HTDC made a performance evaluation of quick-kill traps from both mechanical and biological perspectives. Ultimately the FPCHT settled on a similar tack when a scientific and technical subcommittee became involved in determining policy and direction for the parent group.

A number of scientific studies were undertaken to determine the following:

1. The energy thresholds, by species, required to effect a humane death (humane killing by standard definition means rapid loss of consciousness followed by irreversible subsidence to death, but for the purpose of laboratory testing three minutes to loss of consciousness was the standard used);
2. The mechanical characteristics, including the energy output of traps;
3. The interface between traps and target species.

The end products of this research were that killing traps should strike the animal in the head/neck region of the body, that threshold graphs could be produced by species showing the impact and clamping forces (and combinations thereof) necessary to meet the humane criterion and that traps existed or could be modified to meet the mechanical criteria. The major deficiency of the FPCHT efforts was that virtually no field testing was undertaken to corroborate the research findings.

Examination of leg hold traps in "drowning" sets led to recommendations that they only be used for muskrat and mink and not for beaver. Similarly, snare studies showed that these devices did not meet the humane criterion established for red squirrels or canids. Needless to say, the recommendations were controversial for several reasons, not the least of which was that implementation would revolutionize how fur trapping was conducted in Canada. Some provinces such as British Columbia and Ontario adopted some of the recommendations relatively quickly because they were under the greatest pressure from the anti-trapping forces. But Canada now is moving rapidly toward more uniform trapping regulations that will restrict the use of leg-hold traps, reduce trap check times and set standards for killing and restraining trap devices. Trappers generally opposed restrictions on the use of snares and the steel-jawed leg-hold traps because these were the cheapest, and to them, most effective traps.

The FPCHT findings provided the basis for humane standards for killing traps established through the Canadian Government Standards Board. The Canadian government, in response to pressure from certain CITES nations that suggested sanctions against fur taken by inhumane means, proposed adoption of humane trapping by the international community. The action precipitated significant activity by the American National Standards Institute to establish a U.S. Technical Advisory Group (TAG) which would examine the issue within that country. This was an important step because many of the Canadian recommendations, which related primarily to killing devices, had little applicability in the U.S. Many jurisdictions there have banned the use of killing traps because of the danger to pets and fears for human safety in high population density areas. The U.S. TAG may also be able to help overcome the extremely polarized positions of the trapping (trappers, managers) and anti-trapping (humane societies, animal lovers) groups. A sufficient number of nations, including Canada and the United States, voted to establish an International Standards Organization Technical Committee on humane animal traps. Work began in 1986 to pursue meaningful international standards for killing and restraining trap devices. Another positive note is that Canada established the Fur Institute of Canada (FIC) in 1983 to continue the work initiated by the FPCHT. The FIC has embarked on a very ambitious research and public relations effort designed to offset the emotional approach of the many anti-trapping groups.

What seems like a simplistic question of "To trap or not to trap?" becomes in reality a more sophisticated association of questions: "How to trap? With what to trap? Who should trap? What should be trapped? and Why should it be trapped?" Again wildlife managers are forced into the scientific and political arenas before they can be effective as professionals. An ability to communicate honestly and at the proper level of technicality for the audience becomes a key asset for any manager. Protecting and managing the resource also requires educating, informing and consulting the public interested in that resource. Decisions cannot and probably should not be made solely by agency personnel, for to do so risks jeopardizing the scientific basis of management by exposing it to the emotional arena of politics. That is the responsibility of elected officials, not civil servants. As managers we must countenance, respect, and perhaps respond to those interests that may be different from our own but are nonetheless elements representing the general taxpaying public. A manager in reality only makes recommendations to government regarding action to be taken. If he has scientifically documented the rationale for his recommendations and has adequately shown the impacts on the resource and on the public, government must be prepared to act. It is more likely to act favorably if the management agency has made its case well to the public. Therein lies the secret to successful wildlife management. Scientific knowledge may be the underpinning, but the capability of "selling" a management scheme to politicians (and their electors) is equally crucial to success. What must be avoided is the temptation to circumvent this legitimate management agency role and this process.

Such was the case in a 1983 referendum in Maine to prohibit moose hunting. If the referendum had been successful, the moose management program would have been damaged and a precedent established to manage by public fiat rather than on the advice of professional scientists. If the public had been uninformed and the biological case for the moose season had not been made adequately, wildlife management in Maine would have suffered a serious setback. So in reality, the voters sustained the management decision because the management agency had been open and truthful with the public.

In a democratic system, we, as wildlife managers, must be prepared to defend sound management decisions in any forum, including the political one. Similar challenges are becoming more common-place. The American system allows for referenda to be placed on the ballot, which usurps the normal governmental process. If managers ignore this reality and operate outside the public arena, they must be prepared to accept the consequences. In California, wildlife management may have entered such a realm already. Voters have decided to close the mountain lion season despite managers' opinions that the population is growing and could support a harvest. Decisions by voter initiative are becoming commonplace in California, and it is possible that the voter may decide the fate of hunting in that state by this process in the near future.

Bibliography

Gilbert, F. F. 1991. Trapping an animal rights issue or a legitimate wildlife management technique. The move to international standards. Trans. N. Am. Wildl. Nat. Resour. Conf. 56:400–408.

Goodrich, J. W. 1979. Political assault on wildlife management: is there a defense? Trans. N. Am. Wild. Nat. Resour. Conf. 44:327–336.

Linhardt, S. B., G. J. Dasch, and F. J. Turkowski. 1981. The steel leg-hold trap: techniques for reducing foot injury and increasing selectivity. Pp. 1560–1578, *In* F. A. Chapman and D. Pursley, Eds. Worldwide Furbearer Conference Proceedings, Vol. III.

Novak, M. 1981. The foot-snare and the leg-hold traps: a comparison. Pp. 1671–1685, *In* J. A. Chapman and D. Pursley Eds. Worldwide Furbearer Conference Proceedings, Vol. III.

Strickland, M. A., and C. W. Douglas. 1981. The status of fisher in North America and its management in southern Ontario. Pp. 1443–1458, *In* J. A. Chapman and D. Pursley, Eds. Worldwide Furbearer Conference Proceedings, Vol. II.

Other Readings

Lautenschlager, R. S., and R. Terry Bowyer. 1985. Wildlife management by referendum: when professionals fail to communicate. Wildl. Soc. Bull. 13:546–570.

Anonymous. 1981. Report of the Federal Provincial Committee for Humane Trapping—a committee of the Federal-Provincial Wildlife Conference of Canada.

Chapman, J. A. and D. Pursley (eds.) 1981. Worldwide Furbearer Conference Proceedings, Vol. III-Session 11. (pp. 1553–1687).

Novak, M., J. A. Baker, M. E. Obbard, and B. Malloch (eds.) 1987. Wild furbearer management and conservation in North America. Ont. Min. Nat. Resour., Toronto. 1150 pp.

VIII ENDANGERED SPECIES—Some Management Strategies

Almost every day on television, or in the press, we are told about a spotted or striped cat, a white or black rhino, a seal, a whale, or even a salamander that is reported to be threatened or endangered. We are constantly asked to support organizations whose job it is to conserve or protect animals and sometimes plants from extinction. The message is often dramatic, and we are led to believe that the extinction of mammals and birds is happening hourly, daily, or weekly and that the rate of extinction is increasing rapidly. If the only contact we have with our wildlife is through the popular media, we may get the impression that the pending extinction of animals in our time is the most important wildlife issue there is. And this is the impression we are supposed to get even if the truth has been exaggerated somewhat. At any rate, we certainly know today that the endangered species issue is paramount in the minds of many and that something is being done about it both nationally and internationally. The authors agree that the issue is real but disagree with some of the management approaches that have been taken. For example, there has been a tendency to concentrate scarce resources on a few endangered species rather than examine the issue of threatened ecosystems or communities and hedge against extinction by protecting complexes rather than individuals. But just what is an endangered species? Perhaps we should briefly review something about extinction and then ask ourselves the question once again.

Fossil records tell us of literally thousands of extinct species of quadrupeds and fishes. In fact, there are probably many times more extinct species than living ones. Bird remains, fragile as they are, are not preserved well over periods of time, and yet in 1952 some 787 extinct species were already known from their fossil records. Hundreds of species of mammals have lived and become extinct over the past ± 150 million years, and there are thousands of species of amphibians, reptiles, fishes, and invertebrates, all of which first

199

preceded and then coexisted with birds and mammals, that are also extinct. Endangerment and extinction are certainly not new, although the circumstances surrounding them may be. Quaternary geologists and paleozoologists are gradually joining together the patterns of mammalian distribution dating from about 70,000 to 10,000 B.P. (before 1950). At times in the past, whole populations died simultaneously, and species seem to have been snuffed out like extinguished candles. With the stage swept bare, it appears that new participants made the scene in a brand new play of evolutionary history. New species presided on the land masses and in the waters of the earth again. Millions of years intervened before the newer cast of players would exit, but exit they did. To be sure, some have survived that shared the earth's habitats from ages past, particularly with quaternary species. Harrington (1977) suggests that mountain goats lived in British Columbia 70,000–23,000 years ago with the now extinct muskox (*Symbos cavifrons*), the ground sloth (*Megalonyx* sp.) mastodons, and mammoths. But why have so many species of wildlife been so abundant and then suddenly become extinct? This question has been a lively one for decades.

Uniformitarian geological theory as espoused by Hutton and Lyell in the eighteenth and nineteenth centuries has been accepted by most scientists up to the present. Cataclysmic theories developed to explain the most abrupt changes in flora and fauna in the fossil record have been shunned in most professional circles. In recent years, however, approaches involving a combination of the theory of uniformity and of the acceptance of catastrophic events have been gaining in credibility. This is because of findings that there have been at least four mass extinctions in the geologic past. Newell (1963) reviewed the theories dealing with changes in atmospheric oxygen, disease, cosmic radiation, and other factors and argued that sea level changes were probably at the root of the mystery. More recently, meteorite impact or volcanic activity has been suggested as the causative factor for the catastrophic theory with some convincing corroborative findings from the geologic record. Whatever the cause of the major changes, beginning with the earliest dated Cretaceous-Tertiary occurrence, extinction has happened on a grand scale a number of times in the past.

In more recent geological and ancient historical periods, we have a few documented causes for species extinction along with several reasonable theories to explain the loss of others. All of these conditions may also have occurred in the past, and most will probably recur. The original distribution of marsupials in the Americas suggests that climatic changes and the resulting alterations of habitat might have been factors in both distributional change and species decline. Overspecialization could have caused the demise of the Irish elk (*Magalacerus giganteus*). A combination of commercial and subsistence harvesting of birds and the gathering of eggs for human food probably eliminated the great auk (*Pinguinus impennus*), and perhaps genetic impoverishment was responsible for the decline and loss of other species, for as O'Brien et al. (1982) note: .

> It is tempting to speculate that similar circumstances (to cheetah) which have produced monomorphism followed by niche perturbation might explain extinction of successful species in the past.

It seems to us less likely, given the apparent low density human populations in the days of early man, that subsistence hunting could have eliminated many species as suggested by Martin (1971, 1973), but undoubtedly local populations of highly gregarious, large mammals and a few entire species were severely reduced, contributing to eventual extinctions. By far the greatest number of local—or total—species extinctions in historical times have been of animals existing in relatively low numbers in restricted range areas. For example, the giant sea mink (*Mustela macrodon*) occurred in low density, only along the New England and Bay of Fundy coasts; in the case of the localized subspecific population of Newfoundland wolf (*Canis lupus beothucus*), the animal was restricted to, and occurred in, low numbers on the island of Newfoundland only. But in other cases species existing in large numbers over extensive range areas also have declined and disappeared in historic times. The best-known such North American example is that of the gregarious, migratory passenger pigeon (*Ectopistes migratorius*), which apparently achieved incredibly high populations; 136 million birds breeding within 2200 sq. kilometers (Schorger 1937 in Welty 1962) and 2000 million birds in a flock (quoted from Alexander Wilson in Welty 1962). Passenger pigeons were highly vulnerable to commercial harvesting in their roosting trees and were slaughtered by the thousands. Their roosting and nesting habitats, which were traditional and critical for the species, were also destroyed!

Today humans and wildlife continue to vie for food and space, for land and water areas. These conflicts and the action resulting from them, in addition to the natural factors we have alluded to, form the bases of our concern for animals we consider to be endangered. There is no doubt that increasing human populations of the world are pressuring many species and heightening the intensity of change far beyond what would be the natural evolutionary trends occurring without man's presence. Human population size is clearly the common denominator at the core of our man-beast competitive problems. Our food needs allow for elimination of wild habitat through clearing and cultivation.Already several species, including Atwater's prairie chicken (*Tympanuchus cupido attswateri*), the kit fox (*Vulpes macrotis*), and the black-footed ferret (*Mustela nigripes*), have been threatened or lost in North

America largely because we took their lands or destroyed their prey base to make room for grazing our domestic stock and raising crops.

Commercial harvesting is still a factor as well. The blue whale (*Balaenopterus musculus*), for example, is a mammal with a low reproductive rate, and it has declined over years of poorly regulated commercial harvesting. Beddington and May (1982) have considered some of the ecological complexities we must cope with in relation to krill harvests and harvest of both toothed carnivores (*Odontoceti*) and krill feeders (*Mysticeti*). Since we, as well as the other mammals, are ultimately dependent upon the lower trophic levels of terrestrial and marine ecosystems, all wildlife managers should be aware of the implications of commercial harvest at these trophic levels. Animals must not be managed as individual species apart from the remainder of their habitat. Competitive release of related species and elimination of dependent species are two possible ecological consequences of such narrow action.

The influence of biocides is another factor that must be considered when we reflect on the effects of human action upon wild species. The peregrine falcon, a bird of prey in generally low numbers under the best of conditions, suffered considerably after World War II due to our use of pesticides. Many other species of birds of prey have also been harmed, including the bald eagle and the osprey, but fortunately these particular birds are rebounding vigorously today.

Oil pollution in the ocean has brought death to thousands of sea birds and has the potential to create a disaster, as was evidenced in Prince William Sound and the Persian Gulf. Such events could drop populations of some species to dangerously low levels because of their highly social breeding behavior. So far the losses have been generally sporadic in relation to major spills, but the presence of oil is a continuous problem in the North Atlantic and Arctic and causes considerable annual mortality in ducks and alcids. It has become a major cause of death that is clearly additive in the total mortality picture.

The separation of populations into isolated units with low numbers of animals may result in reduced breeding success and gradual declines, as suggested by O'Brien et al. (1982). In relation to the low levels of genetic variation reported from two geographically isolated populations of cheetah (*Acinonyx jubatus jubatus*), O'Brien notes:

> The extreme monomorphism may be a consequence of a demographic contraction of the cheetah (a population bottleneck) in association with a reduced rate of increase in the recent natural history of this endangered species.

All of these situations, as well as the rapid decline in local habitats because of development, have as their root cause the increase in human population.

As long as humans with their demands for energy, food, and comfort increase, the struggle to prevent the losses of populations and species will be a growing problem with which wildlife professionals will become increasingly involved. It seems inevitable that the rate of decline for some species will accelerate in future years in spite of the combined efforts of individuals, agencies, and governments as we increasingly compete with wildlife for food and space.

With all of the changes wrought by man and his activities impacting hundreds of species in dozens of ecosystems, the problems of determining just which animals are threatened or endangered and which are not—by any standards—is difficult indeed. The tolerance levels of each species relate to its social behavior, feeding, spatial requirements, and a host of other factors. With some wide ranging species such as the tiger (*Panthera tigris*), known space, cover, and food requirements clearly dictate the survival abilities of certain of its subspecies in the face of human population expansion and development. With other animals, the survival abilities relative to human disturbance are not so clearly defined. There has been considerable controversy in the past years over the status of the leopard (*Panthera pardus*). What does seem to be clear is that status reports, regardless of how they are obtained, often are not enough upon which to base final decisions. Nevertheless, in this case it is better for managers to err on the side of conservatism than to continue to exploit populations in the absence of adequate data bases and risk mistakes that are detrimental to the species.

It is also true in today's rapidly changing world that what is threatened or endangered at one time could become a pest at another time, in another place. The ability of some predators such as wolves to respond to protection and an adequate food supply is just such an example. On the other hand, an animal that is seemingly doing well might, under pressure of human harvest or some other human induced factor, begin to slide downward rapidly. Thus definitions must be broad enough and management efficient enough to encompass the changes resulting from an animal's response to range or population disturbance.

Perhaps some of the more pragmatic among us might ask "Why bother?" Why, indeed, bother trying to save what in the long run may compete with us more directly? And why try to save an animal when we know it will cost us a great deal of money, time, and effort with often little success? Others among us liken the endangered species problem to motherhood and apple pie; everyone should want to save the endangered from extinction. We agree, and offer several lines of reasoning to justify this view.

Hornaday (1914) held to an animal rights line in his view of this question.

> The murder of wild-animal species consists in taking from it that which man with all his cunning can never give back-its God-given place in the ranks of

living things. Where is man's boasted intelligence, or his sense of proportion, that every man does not see the monstrous moral obliquity involved in the destruction of a species?

Others in past years have used economics to justify their positions, as Williams (1917) wrote in defense of bird life in South Carolina:

> It is an undisputed fact that the prosperity of the State and nation depends on successful agriculture. Therefore, whatever assists in the production of crops has a money value in proportion to the degree of assistance rendered. The result of the study of the relation of birds to agriculture made by government experts shows that birds are among the farmer's best friends. Mr. Henry W. Henshaw, Chief of the Bureau of Biological Survey, is authority for this statement: "So great is their value from a practical standpoint as to lead to the belief that were it not for birds successful agriculture would be impossible". . . . If the birds' work in nature be of so much importance, bird conservation should become a part of the constructive work of the State, and any agency or condition which tends to reduce the bird population below the limits necessary to hold in check the countless hordes of injurious insects, should be considered inimical to the best interests of the whole people.

Still others have felt a strong moral obligation and tried to develop a conservation ethic of sorts to help us do the best we can by other creatures. Leopold (1949), for instance, wrote:

> We all strive for safety, prosperity, comfort, long life, and dullness. The deer strives with his supple legs, the cowman with traps and poison, the statesman with pen, the most of us with machines, votes and dollars, but it all comes to the same thing: peace in our time, a measure of success in this is all well enough, and perhaps is a requisite to objective thinking, but too much safety seems to yield only danger in the long run. Perhaps this is behind Thoreau's dictum: In wildness is the salvation of the world. Perhaps this is the hidden meaning in the howl of the wolf, long known among mountains, but seldom perceived among men.

We have come a long way since these people wrote in defense of their beliefs. Now we have a dozen organizations to protect wildlife and save the endangered when in the past there was one; a hundred books where there were a dozen. Now we have devised more precise ways of assessing values of wild things, and there are also more professionals to work on their behalf. But we have less land for the animals, too, just as there are more polluted areas, more examples of human competition within natural systems, and millions more people. The authors believe, however, that all of us do have a responsibility to help save the threatened and endangered. For some species, it will be possible in our time, while for others we may only be able to delay the inevitable. For a few, perhaps, society may unfortunately deem the costs too great even now. In recognition that the best strategy for slowing the human-induced extinction rate is to protect critical habitats, there is a move toward identifying and saving blocks of representative types. The Canadian Wildlife Service has established short and long grass prairie reserves among other ecosystem types while the U.S. Fish and Wildlife Service is seriously examining techniques for assessing and identifying high priority habitats.

The present movement to save wildlife has, among its supporters, groups from the entire spectrum of natural history interests. The Survival Service Commission of IUCN, the International Fund for Animal Welfare, the Humane Society of the United States, the World Wildlife Fund, the Society for Animal Rights, the Audubon Society, governments, Greenpeace, sportsmen, and industrial voices are all interested in preventing extinction. The organizations, agencies and individuals concerned have different justifications and motives; their degree of emotional involvement varies and their approaches and techniques differ markedly. It is also true that it is the nonprofessional who is gradually becoming the one influencing the public and public policy (through government) to the greatest degree. This is true partly because the greatest number of professional ecologists are employees of either governments or international agencies and in positions where they are not entirely free to express their opinions or discuss their study results. Professional ecologists and wildlifers also tend to report their findings in professional publications to solidify and enhance their positions within the organization they work for and to establish themselves among their peers. It is probably also true that most ecologists and wildlifers are not as adept at communicating as are writers, artists, showpeople, and advertising or other media people involved in the struggle to prevent sport or commercial harvesting of a wild animal. Many nonprofessionals now hold positions of influence with one or more of the agencies or organizations dealing with threatened or endangered species, and their views are not necessarily the soundest to enhance the future status of a species.

The Convention on International Trade in Endangered Species

Perhaps the most effective approach to date in aid of endangered species has been CITES, aimed at the market place. The first draft of a treaty was produced under the aegis of the IUCN in the mid-1960's. Between 1970 and 1972 a number of governments, including the United States and Kenya, and non-governmental organizations (NGO's) including the IUCN, the World Wildlife Fund, the National Audubon Society, and the New York Zoological Society produced several draft iterations. Then in 1973, the Plenipotentiary

Conference (a meeting of delegates imbued with full authority to conclude a treaty controlling international trade in wild animals and plants) was held in Washington D.C. The conference produced a treaty known as the Convention on International Trade in Endangered Species of Wild Fauna and Flora (CITES). Among the more significant provisions of this treaty are the following:

a. A presumption against trade in and a presumption in favor of protecting animals unless it could be shown that trade would not harm animal populations
b. Protection for certain species, sub-species, and populations
c. A requirement that species be maintained throughout their range at a level consistent with their role in the ecosystems in which they occur
d. A requirement that before trade is allowed, a scientific authority in the country of export make a finding that the export will not be detrimental to the survival of the species
e. Provision that the burden of proof for findings resides with those who would allow export.

In addition to these provisions, appendices listing endangered and potentially endangered species considered at the convention were adopted by consensus of the participating nations.

Appendix I species are those considered to be rare or endangered for which trade will not be permitted for primarily commercial purposes. Import permits from the receiving country are required as well as permits from the exporting country when one of these animals is involved.

Appendix II species could become rare or endangered if trade is not regulated. Permits are required from the country of export for such animals when importing to signatory nations.

Appendix III species are not endangered but may be considered in regulatory management where they exist. For several countries, export permits must be obtained prior to importation (CITES, Control List No. 5, 1981).

For participating nations, the convention (treaty) came into force in 1975. In effect, the agreement was imposed on many nonparticipants as well, since nations that did not issue export permits were prevented from shipping animals or their parts into member nations requiring such permits. In that the convention essentially eliminated markets through control of trade, the treaty was also imposed upon nonparticipating countries that sought to profit. Today, there are about one hundred member jurisdictions and it seems likely the number will continue to increase. In meetings held since 1973, the original treaty has been amended to strengthen the effect of the agreement. In particular, the Berne agreement added species to Appendix II that might be harvested more heavily because of trade restrictions on other species listed in Appendix I. This allowed more intensive monitoring of wildcat and lynx as a result of restrictions on the trading of leopard and other tropical cats.

In Canada and the United States, jurisdictional responsibility for nonmigratory birds and all mammals, reptiles, amphibians, flora, and fish within their boundaries lies with provinces and states. The control of export and import out of, and into, these countries, however, is a federal responsibility. An international treaty is the supreme law of the land in the U.S. Since export is initiated in the jurisdictions of the animal's origin, considerable cooperation has developed between federal and state or provincial jurisdictions in implementing CITES regulations in North America. Scientific authorities, which include representation from both federal and state or provincial agencies, keep abreast of all aspects of the status of endangered species and advise the relevant CITES administrators. Similarly, management authorities advise on minimum requirements for acceptable species management, while others administer the regulation of trade through permit.

The existence of CITES should offer an avenue for increased cooperation between federal and state or provincial agencies. It has already been responsible for improved monitoring of populations and has stimulated research, particularly on wild cats, in North America. With 800 or more species of animals and plants already considered under CITES and with the interagency and the "bicameral" approaches required for effective administration in North America, the future will bring problems. There are new and growing bureaucracies in each participating country involved with CITES. Some member nations wish to use the present treaty as a basis for an international environmental agreement that conceivably would attempt to bring at least uniformity of approach to environmental concerns such as habitat destruction. In Canada, the patriation of the Constitution in 1982 has reopened rather extensive considerations of present federal-provincial relations and responsibilities. With the exception of migratory birds, as far as wildlife is concerned it seems likely that provincial jurisdiction and responsibility could be strengthened. If the effects of federal agreements or legislation reduce the ability of a responsible jurisdiction to manage a species, conflict can result regardless of supremacy clauses.

Since 1975, the increasing effects of CITES have been to slow to a trickle the trade in most species considered to be endangered or threatened. Among the animals most affected and presumably benefitted by CITES are elephant (*Elaphus maximus* and *Loxodonta africana*), African rhinoceros (*Rhinocerptidae*, both black and white), leopard, tiger, and cheetah (CITES, Control list No. 5 1981. McMahan 1982). Johnson (1979), however, cautions that there is no proof that involvement with CITES has improved the status of any species. He feels that more time is needed before judgements of its effectiveness can be made. In 1989 CITES imposed a total ban on ivory trade in an effort to stem the rapid decline in African elephants. In doing so, countries such as Zimbabwe, that were increasing their elephant population while controlling illegal harvesting and realizing benefits from managed legal harvests, were penalized. Whether the ban will reduce illegal killing in other East African countries, such as Kenya, and stem the ivory flow to the carvers and artisans of the East, remains an open question. The effects of the ban will have to be closely monitored to be certain it is not counter productive but the initial impact in those countries with previously heavy poaching losses has been a significant reduction in poaching as ivory prices plummeted.

In the United States the secretary of the Department of the Interior is the management authority for CITES with operational responsibilities delegated to the USFWS. The Endangered Species Scientific Authority (ESSA) advises the management authority on scientific matters of the convention. Other important U.S. legislation, including the Endangered Species Act (1973) and its amendments, are listed in Appendix 1. The Endangered Species Committee is the listing body for all wildlife under U.S. legislation.

The Canadian Wildlife Service is the management authority and operational body for CITES. Within Canada's boundaries the Committee on the Status of Endangered Wildlife in Canada (COSEWIC) has a primary responsibility through its committees of assigning status (rare, threatened, endangered, extirpated, or not categorized) to all wildlife, including plants.

Strategies for Wildlife Managers

There have been management success stories in the past and there are some now. Among the species once threatened in North America, the wood bison (*Bison bison athabascae*) and the whooping crane (*Grus americana*) have been brought back from the edge of extinction, and dozens of other species have responded positively to management practices. It will take all the knowledge and ingenuity wildlife professionals can muster, plus strong political support, to stave off extinction for many animals from now on. In North America it seems likely that we will have reasonable short-term success. We are not yet extremely pressured by demands for lands inhabited by much of our wildlife, and we even have a good chance of protecting some habitat within intensive agricultural areas—at least for a while. We also have the benefit of an aroused public; we have legislation in place with additional enabling legislation ready; we have a body of professional people in established government agencies; and we have a number of well organized citizens' groups lobbying on behalf of wildlife. Nonetheless, even in the U.S., there are efforts to weaken the Endangered Species Act especially where economic interests are threatened. The situation is much more precarious elsewhere, particularly in Africa, South America and Southeast Asia. In these areas, and some others, the following strategies may be appropriate.

Protection through Area Preservation: Parks, Preserves and Buffer Zones

For some nonmigratory species that do not require an extensive home range and even for low numbers of more wide-ranging species, the concept of area protection is practical. In North America, the bison of Wood Buffalo Park illustrate a relatively wide-ranging, gregarious species succeeding in a protected area. Unfortunately, plains bison transplanted to the area in the 1920's brought brucellosis with them so that today the entire park population may have to be destroyed if Canada is to retain its status as a brucellosis free cattle trading nation. If the bison are destroyed, disease free stock will replace them eventually. But in this case, the land is available. What about the areas of the world where between 75 and 80 percent of all humans live and where the annual rate of population increase averages from 1.8–2.9 percent? In some countries, the human population is moving upward at a rate of 3.5 percent per year. What can be done?

In 1980, the IUCN published its World Conservation Strategy. Two of the three objectives of the WCS were (1) the maintenance of essential ecological processes and (2) the preservation of genetic diversity. While we admit that the publication of a strategy by an international body is, by itself, no solution, adoption by, or even agreement of, 503 member states, government agencies, international and national NGO's and affiliates signals a considerable degree of world support. Both of the objectives also relate directly to wildlife preservation because the absence of any species, or a reduction in a population we are concerned with, signals a reduction in genetic diversity and failure to maintain portions of ecological processes.

It may be, however, that undeveloped or underdeveloped nations do not wish to lose land to a national park or a legislated protected area of another type. The competition for land from various resource bases is strong, and development programs are not usually concerned with wildlife. Nor in many cases will the people using the land want to see a protected area established if it restricts their own use. In such circumstances, we must recognize that the protected area or park concept is specifically a Western one not always relevant to people of cultures different from ours. Indeed, the notion of protecting animals of specific value simply does not fit with the utilitarian concepts of many indigenous people. Furthermore, it makes still less sense to them to give costly protection to an animal that has little value, even as food. If 4 percent or more of the total land area of African countries is a goal for those interested in setting aside wildlife lands, perhaps the costs of establishing and maintaining them should be borne by the industrial nations of the world. It may even be necessary to consider compensation in land, goods, or currency for those people who are deprived through the establishment of a protected area.

Simien, in Ethiopia, is an excellent example of a national park that offers the viewer spectacular scenery, exhibits geological and ecological uniqueness, and serves to protect two of the world's rarest mammals, the Walia Ibex (*Capra ibex*) and the Simien fox (*Canis simensis*). Although a few people still resided inside park boundaries in 1981, a suitable resettlement appeared to be in view at that time. The conflict between people and park has been of considerable concern, but it has not yet been an insurmountable problem. Elsewhere, the problem has been far more serious.

Where international concerns are involved, the entire process of establishment, park protection, and maintenance in underdeveloped areas seems to fit best within the massive IUCN framework. Fragmenting programs and responsibilities among international agencies has long been a problem. Perhaps it is time to channel categorized approaches toward a single agency.

It would also be ideal if most parks had buffer zones around them. The notion that the boundary stops suddenly and any animal stepping across the line is dead is not always true, but in some areas there is real cause for concern. It is particularly serious where extensive migration of animals may take them outside of protected boundaries on a seasonal basis. Such movements occur from some of North America's western parks in the winter and from African parks during the rains. Nairobi National Park, for instance, is a very small area of high quality grass that draws savannah land species in large numbers during the dry season. Their numbers decrease with dispersal when forage is more readily available elsewhere at other times. In this case, buffer zones would certainly be inadequate, and even protected movement corridors would probably be less than adequate, even if possible. Parks such as the Luangwa in Zambia, where movements of many species are less extensive, lend themselves well to the buffer concept. In fact, "game management areas" around the portions of the Luangwa where most animal movement occurs serve as excellent buffers. It is not that animals are not harvested in the GMA's. They are, but the number taken by hunting parties is restricted. Illegal hunting also occurs, but ideally, regulations and enforcement keep the poaching at a low level. Dasmann (1981) discussed Olympic National Park as an example of a park with a buffer zone—the surrounding multiple-use national forest. The biosphere reserve concept of UNESCO's

Man and the Biosphere (MAB) program reflects this same concept, a protected area surrounded by a region in which the land and the ecosystem are essentially protected but where controlled economic development is allowed. In all cases where establishment of protected areas in underdeveloped countries is considered, wildlife managers should seek to implement measures to improve the living conditions of local people through extending services such as potable water or electricity, or through labor intensive development. Regardless of who pays, the park must be seen to benefit people living near it if we expect them to respect what it stands for.

Protection through Use: Utilization and the Marketplace

Conservation implies efficient and continuing use of existing supplies for the benefit of present and future generations. To Gifford Pinchot conservation meant "wise use." This connotation has been widely accepted in North America where preservation is but one of the management options included in conservation. Elsewhere in the world, and most particularly in underdeveloped countries, conservation is sill often synonymous with preservation. The dictionary definition of conserving—preserving, guarding or protecting—is the only one understood and accepted. Thus the approach of international agencies in Africa largely has been one of preservation rather than one of use. Conservation had been the international aid catchword, complete with its connotation of locking up the resource. More recently, natural resource conservation has started to assume its broader definition, even in the international aid arena.

We noted that the park or protection concept was essentially Western and not African in origin. Wherever possible, the African has coexisted with animals and used them since man became man in the heart of the continent. This was one of the areas where utilitarianism began and it is still present. The preservationist influence has been so strong, however, that in recent years the ability of African governments to use wildlife has often been paralyzed by fear of world censure—particularly because so much help was required from the Western world. Better to go along than risk losing a million dollars from the World Bank!

Without use, much wildlife is eventually doomed. The park of today may well be the management area of tomorrow. Remember, 80 percent of the world's people live in South America, Africa, and southern Asia; they are increasing at rates averaging over 2 percent per year. It seems unlikely that all protected areas can remain completely inviolate for long in the twenty-first century.

It is easy for us to say that use will help prevent wildlife species from becoming endangered or extinct. How will it though? Preservationists and hunters alike have argued against the concept, which they have often simplified to one of "kill in order to save." The heart of the problem relates to values. How does a society perceive a species from which it benefits? This question must be addressed to each of the several societies and publics within them, but it seems quite safe to say that whether the perceived value is utilitarian or aesthetic, the end result is similar; that is, each group wants to conserve the species. The difference lies in approach. The aesthetic approach would protect the species by any means possible, including the elimination of commercial exploitation (as with the harp seal), and the utilitarian approach would conserve the species by harvesting under specific regulations while otherwise protecting both the animal and its habitat. Since we can no longer depend upon natural animal population controls because man is altering the ecosystems which provide those controls, it may be that in an increasing number of situations a pragmatic approach involving use combined with an element of protection will become necessary. Indeed, the controlled-use approach may often be necessary to prevent uncontrolled use from creating further imbalances in the systems we are dealing with. For instance, if an illegal market for ivory persists, elephants will be harvested illegally, in an uncontrolled manner, with the largest tuskers being removed. If the elephant continues to be a problem as a garden marauder in areas of settlement, the guilty animals and others will be killed in self defense. A population of harp seals allowed to increase in the absence of major predation from man or other animals will eventually be controlled illegally by those elements of human society directly or indirectly competing with them for a marine food resource. Grey seals in the western North Atlantic have no significant natural predator affecting their numbers today; from a low population twenty years ago they have increased to become a pest species in the eyes of fishermen around the Gulf of St. Lawrence. They are now shot and wasted with impunity.

The failure of African governments and international agencies to provide the means whereby villages can benefit from wildlife has often led to a situation where the poacher fills the control niche left vacant by those in authority. It may be that the poacher provides the service the regulatory management should have provided. In the Luangwa Valley of Zambia, Dodds and Patton (1968) recommended the "removal of several thousand elephant" while Naylor et al. (1973), acting on more complete population and range data, recommended a two-step reduction of 5,000 elephants. No official action was taken, however, and poachers approximately effected the recommended capital reduction over the next several years. From the standpoint of the elephants and their range, this illegal removal was probably not terribly detrimental; but the specific animals chosen would probably not have been the same ones taken under an controlled removal. The prime bulls, reflecting an element of the best genetic stock, were harvested more heavily by the poachers than other age and sex categories.

Because CITES should continue to operate as an effective control over much commercial poaching, the poachers' activities may no longer affect wildlife detrimentally, as has been the case with some of the cats. The opportunity is present once again to consider an innovative approach to both subsistence poaching and small-scale use.

There are several methods the manager can consider for utilization. We consider some of them, but each situation has its own set of conditions that will dictate, to a great extent, the direction taken.

1. Perhaps the most logical approach is to allow controlled harvest of animals, within cultural contexts, under a system that would provide direct benefits to the people themselves in food, cash, or their equivalent. The equivalent values must be seen to be directly related to the process if food and/or cash are not provided.

   There have been schemes using this type of procedure, but they have not been generally successful. One such was the Kenya Wildlife Management project conducted by FAO in the early 1970's. The scheme did not involve the people; it was conducted by a new and different body essentially outside the existing agencies of government, and the connection between harvesting and benefits was not clear. The benefits did not exist as far as most people of the district were concerned. There were other problems that led to the abandonment of the project, but we emphasize that the concept itself was good.

   To be successful, operations should be small and restricted in area. Whenever possible, they should also be implemented through systems of organization already in place such as the farmers' (peasants') associations in Ethiopia, and they should involve the people who are expected to benefit. In some instances, fresh meat could be a benefit, in others biltong (sun-dried strips of meat); or currency might be provided and managed for a group, an association, or a village. The approach can be altered to relate best to certain rare or endangered species and it will always vary with species problems. It has the potential to be one of the more workable approaches to managing all wildlife, including the threatened and endangered in many underdeveloped areas—if it is done properly.

2. The legalization of subsistence poaching might be considered in certain specific situations. It is unlikely that existing regulations would be rescinded to allow this, but if enforcement was relaxed in an area for

periods of time the results might not differ greatly. A similar concept might be considered in areas of underdeveloped countries where imposed regulations make traditional practices illegal and where regulatory management conflicts with use patterns firmly established in culture. Subsistence poaching, of course, differs from commercial poaching. The latter has usually been induced by user societies providing ready markets for what has often been in the past a noncommodity for indigenous people.

3. Not only do the rural people need to benefit from the animals they coexist with, but so also do the governments of underdeveloped countries. If the use of impala by villagers reduces the burden of the government in caring for its people, a larger public benefit is present. Governments, however, need more tangible benefits than this. Several underdeveloped countries are desperate for foreign currency. With a devalued currency of their own and inflation rising as productivity remains stagnant, foreign monies from the industrial nations are highly coveted.

To provide a source of export income, countries may develop a limited tourist industry as Zambia has. In Kenya's case, tourism is a highly developed industry based, in part, on wildlife resources. There are two general categories of wildlife-oriented tourism; one based on viewing and one on hunting. In the first case, development costs may be considerable and capital programs are required for lodges, transportation, viewing facilities, and maintenance. Costs may be relatively low in the case of the "walking safari" where cameras replace guns carried by visitors and the participants stay under canvas. Both types of tourism generate foreign currency; both increase the value of rare and endangered species and other wildlife in the eyes of the tourists and local people; and both depend upon legal protection of the animals. From sport or safari hunting, a great deal of foreign currency is made available to the host country in exchange for the lives of a few animals. Under adequate supervision, this use of animals, including some which are threatened, like the leopard, can elevate the value and encourage protection of the species harvested. Ecotourism is a growth industry on a worldwide basis and is beginning to have considerable impact on many poor countries from Latin America to Africa.

4. The rare and endangered may benefit from game ranching of one type or another. Although North American managers are gradually moving into this arena where lands are available (as in Texas and Alberta), extensive and intensive ranching (farming) is developing most rapidly in Africa. In Canada, the question of whether, and/or how to develop game ranching is being considered and cautious policies are gradually

being evolved. The Canadian Wildlife Federation's position, however, is that game ranching is inappropriate. Nevertheless, the farming of once wild animals is being practiced in most provinces under highly restrictive regulations aimed at preventing escapes, preventing disease, and preventing the marketing of native wildlife. Land owners in the Republic of South Africa often harvest wild herbivores as well as their cattle. The wild animals are not usually rare or endangered, and as long as they are providing economic return they are not likely to be. Blesbuck (*Damalisus dorcus*), oryx (*Oryx beisa*), and sometimes eland (*Taurotragus oryx*) are killed and marketed within the country and elsewhere. In Texas, both indigenous deer and exotic ungulates are offered by landowners to sportsmen in various sport hunting schemes. Although the ranching of wild ungulates on an extensive basis (conducted within state laws) is available on only a few western U.S. sites, there are hundreds of ranches in the Republic of South Africa where the harvest of wild ungulates occurs. In subarctic areas, reindeer have been an exploited captive resource for centuries, just as camels (*Camelus bactrianus* and *Camelus dromedarius*) have been elsewhere. The degree to which once-wild animals have come under the control of man has been detailed by Clutton-Brock (1982). For certain species, this control may become the means by which they are perpetuated in future years. The eland has been herded in the Ukraine since 1968 and along with oryx and buffalo (*Syncerus caffer*) is managed today just as cattle are at the Galana River Estate in Kenya. Crocodiles are farmed in the southern United States, Southeast Asia, and soon may be in Ethiopia. The list is long, but the important things for us to consider are that both domestication and extensive ranching may allow an animal to continue to exist when others of its kind are eliminated; and that the presence of a variety of wild ungulates under semi-controlled conditions on open range can allow for the continuation of ecosystem elements, such as leopards and coyotes, at the next trophic level. The ranching and farming of animals can benefit endangered predators, but more importantly, the direct role of the domesticated, or exploited captive, in the market place will help prevent those species from ever becoming threatened or endangered.

Protection of Captives: Species Survival Plans

Clutton-Brock (1982) has traced the origins of our current domesticated animals. For some groups the domestic animals we have are the only reflection left of the original source stock. Such is the case with the cow (*Bos taurus*);

its last progenitor, the aurochs or giant ox (*Bos primigenius*), was apparently killed off in Poland about 1627. In other instances, the domestic progenitors are still with us. Dogs presumably descended, one and all, from wolves and other canid stock some 12,000 or more years ago. Our own progenitors, watching a competitor for certain prey, apparently struck up a liaison with the wolf to aid them in the hunt. It was a successful liaison. Perhaps other successful ones will develop from experiments we have alluded to previously; but there is another, obvious approach—to keep an animal as a *wild* captive, and this is what zoos are all about. Only one of the purposes of the zoo is to make representative wild animals available for public viewing. In relation to rare and endangered species, zoos are performing a much more important role today.

According to the World Conservation Strategy of the IUCN, captive populations and propagation should be an integral part of the global programs to preserve endangered species. The American Association of Zoological Parks and Aquariums (AAZPA) recognizes four ways in which zoos can contribute to the WCS objective of "preservation of genetic diversity." They are

1. to serve as refugia for species that are destined for extinction in the wild;
2. to provide sources of propagules for repopulation of natural habitat;
3. to reinforce natural populations which may be so small and fragmented that they are not viable genetically or demographically;
4. to maintain repositories of germ plasm in addition to or as an alternative to, populations of animals. (Foose 1983).

This role has evolved as a result of the Species Survival Plans (SSP) of the AAZPA. The original intent, however, was probably not completely altruistic in that for years zoos have been experiencing increasing difficulty in obtaining individuals of certain species from the wild. If not available, then raise them in captivity.

Foose also notes that the zoos can perform other significant roles "by conducting research that will improve wildlife management and by educating the public to support conservation."

The central theme of the SSP is to manage a captive, widely dispersed population through controlled breeding in order to maintain genetic diversity. Member organizations of the AAZPA alone house 47,000 mammals, 33,000 birds 23,500 reptiles and amphibians and about 159,000 fish in addition to invertebrates. As a result the selection of species to be managed and the establishment of spatial requirements for the minimum requisite number are significant problems. The AAZPA/SSP uses three basic criteria for deciding which species are to be selected: (1) A breeding nucleus of the species must be available for captive management. (2) Continued existence of the species in the wild must be imperiled as defined by IUCN, UCBP, USFWS, or reliable field reports. (3) There must be available an organized group of capture propagation professionals with sufficient support to ensure the program will reach captive preservation status. When too many species meet the basic criteria, the following are used to select candidate species: (1) the probability of successful captive management is high; (2) the degree of endangerment is relatively high; (3) the degree of rarity is relatively high. These latter criteria are not dissimilar to those suggested by Sparrowe and Wight (1975) for a system of assigning action priorities in the Endangered Species Program of USFWS or as practiced by Florida Game and Fresh Water Fish Commission in setting priorities for vertebrate conservation. The problems of logistics and timing are considerable, of course, particularly if zoos from around the world cooperate. The breeding of each species is directed by a species coordinator and a small propagation group chosen from the institutions housing members of the species in question. A typical master plan for a species such as the snow leopard (*Panthera uncia*) considers general strategies:

1. What the size of the population is presently, potentially, and optimally, in terms of numbers, ages and sexes.
2. How many institutions should accommodate the species.
3. Which animals should reproduce, how often, and with which mate.
4. Which animals should be maintained or removed from the population.
5. What basic standards of husbandry and considerations of sociobiology should be emphasized. (Foose 1982).

The master plan will also consider all aspects of demography, genetics, genetic diversity, carrying capacity, subpopulations, spatial and behavioral requirements, and other technical aspects.

Students are advised to obtain and study SSP's, such as those referred to here, to better understand the zoo approach and how it complements other aspects of endangered species management.

Of primary concern is the maintenance of adequate genetic diversity in the small remaining captive stocks. Although future genetic engineering developments may ease this problem, current management is designed "to preserve as much as possible of the heritable diversity that has evolved and exists in the wild gene pools" (Foose 1983). To achieve this, a strategy has developed which includes requiring an adequate number of founders, expanding the population as rapidly as possible from the founders to whatever carrying capacity has been determined, and then possibly subdividing the population. The founder question can be a significant problem for extremely rare species. Although as few as five to ten pairs can give the needed diversity if selected judiciously, the requirements are that the founders be unrelated, noninbred, and interfertile. In the case of the black-footed ferret, where only one extant population is known to exist, it may be impossible to meet these criteria. The prime objective then becomes to maximize the effective population size to minimize the loss of genetic diversity. The practicability of meeting this objective will vary dependent on captive holding capacity, founder sources, and opportunities for reintroduction, among other factors. Suffice it to say that the more individuals of a species with divergent backgrounds that can be incorporated into captive breeding programs, the greater the chance of ultimate success in species retention.

Obviously all animals that are threatened and/or endangered cannot be held in captivity in adequate numbers to allow this kind of population management. In an attempt to address part of this problem, zoo managers are trying to increase zoo capacities to provide more habitat. The overall approach should, however, guarantee the presence of wild representatives of several species for a considerable time period, perhaps several hundred years. The total number of zoos with representatives of any one species may well have to be restricted in future years. This may create a conflict between the zoo manager who wishes to show his viewers a wide variety of species, including representatives from the endangered list, and the pragmatic advocate of species survival plans.

Reintroduction

Where habitats remain but the animals are gone, reintroduction may be feasible. This depends on the absence or control of the original causative factors resulting in the demise of the species in question. For example, if animals are trapped to a level at which they cannot maintain their numbers, trapping must be controlled. If prey species are poisoned or otherwise eliminated, these activities must cease. It should also be obvious that a knowledge of social behavior, spatial requirements, and feeding habits assists the manager in deciding whether or not to reintroduce the species.

For peregrine falcons, the primary cause of their original decline (DDT use in North America) is no longer present; the habitat is, however, and captive breeding and release of stock from Cornell University and elsewhere have been effective. Other reintroductions depend upon wild-caught stock. Such a program is in effect in Newfoundland, where pine or American marten (*Martes americana*) are being taken from the only remaining population center at Little Grand Lake and moved into the two Newfoundland national parks. This is a reintroduction attempt, of course, but it may also turn out to be a salvage operation in that much of the presently populated habitat may be cut.

The peregrine and the marten are unique examples in that there is still available habitat and the animals are either free of the more important mortality factors, or totally protected, or both. Such situations are not likely to occur for many rare or endangered species, especially in Africa, Southeast Asia, and South America, where habitats are rapidly disappearing. Even if habitats are present, reintroductions can be failures. Woodland caribou were reintroduced into Maine and Nova Scotia in the 1960's and into Maine in the 1980's. All efforts failed, presumably because a mortality factor, the nematode *Parelaphostrongylus tenuis*, possibly not present during previous occupation by caribou, was present when reintroduction attempts took place.

Whatever strategies are employed in the wild, two conditions must prevail. One is that effective legislation must be in place to give adequate protection to the species in question, and an enforcement body must be present to effect that protection. A second is that for any endangered species measures, whether involved with protection or use, the wildlife resource base must be incorporated into economic and land-use planning.

Wildlife law is only now being effectively revised and enacted in underdeveloped countries, and many such actions now in effect were instituted by virtue of external (international) pressures. An example of a new body of legislation that may prove to be effective in protecting wildlife from overexploitation is present in Ethiopia. In 1981, the Food and Agriculture Organization of the United Nations assisted in drafting new laws for that country that protect endangered endemics while allowing controlled use of other species. Whether adequate enforcement staff can be employed to uphold the new regulations, only time will tell.

Recognition of wildlife in economic and land-use planning is necessary if any wildlife is to be effectively managed in underdeveloped countries in years to come. Without such acknowledgement, wildlife will continue to exist as a noncompetitive entity, eventually succumbing to the inevitable losses of habitat that will drive many species toward extinction. Wildlife cannot compete in the marketplace without controls, however, for that would soon decimate both populations and species.

Wildlife managers should understand that there are different ways to approach the endangered species problems and that certain strategies may work for certain species in some places but not for others. A balanced approach must be employed to consider the many alternatives, from use in the wild to captivity in zoos. What works for one species may not work for another because of the animals' varied biological requirements. Protection, it seems, may not be all that is necessary regardless of pressures from animal rights adherents, but it is just as true that use would do more harm than good for other animals, notwithstanding the strong utilitarian views held by some.

Perhaps one of the most important changes that needs to occur is for professional biologist-managers to assume influential positions in decision-making processes for endangered species. More than a strong emotional attachment is needed today to manage wild things, especially the endangered ones. Pragmatic decisions must be made daily on wildlife's behalf, and these decisions can only be made by knowledgeable professionals who exhibit a degree of realism. Perhaps a fence is required, as in Kruger or Etosha Park. Maybe meat protein is needed for human inhabitants and several species of antelopes might provide it, as is the case in the Central African Republic. Or perhaps people and wildlife, including an endangered species, are competing for land, as in Kenya. To the greatest extent possible, bureaucratic and political impediments must be surmounted or circumvented; emotionalism must take a back seat. It will take cool heads and professional skills to cope successfully with the frustrations ahead.

Bibliography

Beddington, J. R., and R. M. May. 1982. The harvesting of interacting species in a natural ecosystem. Sci. Am. 247(5):62–69.

Benson, D. A., and D. G. Dodds. 1980. Deer of Nova Scotia. Department of Lands and Forests, Nova Scotia. Revised ed. 92 pp.

Berglund, B. E., Hakansson and E. Lagerlund. 1976. Radiocarbon dated mammoth (*Mammuthus primigenius* Blamenbach) finds in South Sweden. Boreas 5:177–191.

Clutton-Brock, J. 1982. Domesticated animals from early times. University of Texas Press, Austin, TX. 208 pp.

Dasmann, R. F. 1981. Wildife biology. Second ed. John Wiley and Sons. New York, NY. 212 pp.

Dodds, D. G. 1976. Evolution of wildlife harvesting systems in Africa. Trans. Fed-Prov. Wildl. Conf. 40:106–113.

Dodds, D. G. 1983. Terrestrial mammals. Pp 509–550, *In* South, G. R., ed. Biogeography and Ecology of the Island of Newfoundland. Junk, The Hague.

Dodds, D. G. and D. R. Patton. 1968. Wildlife and land-use survey of the Luangwa Valley. Report to the Government of Zambia. FAO, No. Ta 2591. Rome. 175 pp.

Foose, T. J. 1982. *Panthera uncia*: genetic and demographic analysis and management. Int. Ped. Book of Snow Leopards 3:81–102.

Foose, T. J. 1983. The relevance of captive populations to the conservation of biotic diversity. *In* Schonewald-Cox, C. M., S. M. Chambers, B. MacBryde, and H. Thomas, eds. Genetics and Conservation. Benjamin/Cummings Publishing Company, Menlo Park, CA. 722 pp.

Grandy, J. W. 1982. Trial, error, and politics in international cat protection. Paper presented at the International Cat Symposium, Kingsville, Texas. (Abstracted *In* Cats of the World, 1986).

Gustafson, A. F., C. H. Geis, W. J. Hamilton Jr., and H. Ries. 1949. Conservation in the United States. Third ed., Comstock, Ithaca, NY. 534 pp.

Hamilton, P. H. 1986. Status of the leopard in sub-Saharan Africa with particular reference to Kenya. Pp. 447–458, *In* Cats of the World. S. D. Miller and D. D. Everett Ed. Proceedings, Second International Symposium, 1982, Leaser Kleberg Wildlife Research Institute, Kingsville, Texas and National Wildlife Federation, Washington.

Harrington, C. R. 1977. Wildlife in British Columbia during the Ice Age. B.C. Outdoors, Dec. 1977. 4 pp.

Hornaday, W. T. 1914. Wildlife conservation in theory and practice. Yale Univ. Press, New Haven, CT. 240 pp.

Johnson, M. 1979. Review of endangered species: policies and legislation. Wildl. Soc. Bull 7(2):79–93.

Leopold, A. 1949. A Sand County almanac: and sketches here and there. Oxford Univ. Press. NY. 226 pp.

Martin, P. S. 1971. Prehistoric overkill. Pp. 612–614, *In* Man's impact on environment. T. R. Detwyler, Ed. McGraw-Hill, New York, NY. 731 pp.

Martin, P. S. 1973. The discovery of America. Science 179:969–974.

McMahan, L. 1986. The international cat trade. Pp. 161–188, *In* Cats of the world. S. D. Miller and D. D. Everett Ed. Proceedings, Second International Symposium, 1982, Caeser Kleberg Wildlife Research Institute, Kingsville, Texas and National Wildlife Federation, Washington.

Millsap, B. A., J. A. Gore, D. E. Runde, and S. J. Cerulean. 1990. Setting priorities for the conservation of fish and wildlife species in Florida Wildl. Monogr. 111. 57 pp.

Naylor, J. N., G. C. Caughley, N. D. J. Abel, and O. Liberg. 1973. Game Management Habitat Manipulation, Luangwa Valley Conservation and Development Project. FAO. FO: DP/ZAM/68/510: Working Document No. 1.258 pp.

Newell, N. D. 1963. Crises in the history of life. Scientific American reprint, W. H. Freeman, San Francisco, CA. 16 pp.

Newton, I. 1979. Population ecology of raptors. Buteo Books. Vermillion, SD. 199 pp. plus 16 plates.

O'Brien, S. J., D. E. Wildt, D. Goldman, G. R. Merril, and M. Bush. 1982. The cheetah is depauperate in genetic variation. Paper resented at the International Cat Symposium, Kingsville, Texas.

Ratcliffe. 1973. Studies of the recent breeding success of the peregrine, *Falco peregrinus*. J. Reprod. Fert. Suppl. 19, 377–389.

Raup, D. M. and J. J. Sepkoski. 1982. Mass extinctions in the marine fossil records. Science 215:1501–1503.

Schorger, A. W. 1937. The great Wisconsin passenger pigeon nesting of 1871. Proc. Linnaean Soc. 48:1–26.

Seidensticker, J. 1986. Large carnivores and the consequence of habitat is-ularization: eology and conservation of tigers in Indonesia and Bang-ladesh. Pp. 1–41. *In* Cats of the World. S. D. Miller and D. D. Everett, Ed. Proceedings, Second International Symposium, 1982, Caeser Kle-berg Wildlife Research Institute, Kingsville, Texas and National Wild-life Federation, Washington.

Sparrowe, R. D., and H. M. Wight. 1975. Setting priorities for the endan-gered species program. N. Am. Wildl. Nat. Resour. Conf. 40:142–156.

Teer, J. G. 1968. Evolution of wildlife harvesting systems in Texas. Trans. Fed. Prov. Wildl. Conf. 40:114–121.

Welty, J. C. 1962. The life of birds. W. B. Saunders, Philadelphia, PA. 546 pp.

Wetmore, A. 1952. Recent additions to our knowledge of prehistoric birds. Proceedings of the Xth International Ornithological Congress, Upps-ala. Almqvist and Wiksells, Uppsala, Sweden.

Williams, B. 1917. The decrease of birds in South Carolina. *In* W. T. Hor-naday, (Trustee). The statement of the Permanent Wild Life Protection Fund. Vol. II. Published by the Fund, New York. 224 pp. plus bulletin section.

Recommended Readings

Foose, Thomas J. 1983. A species survival plan (SSP) for snow leopard *Panthera uncia*. Genetics and demographic analysis and management. Int. Ped. Book of Snow Leopards 3:81–102.

> An example of an SSP. The zoo approach.

Johnson, Mark. 1979. Review of endangered species: policies and legislation. Wildl. Soc. Bull 7(2):79–93.

> A clear and readable review for the United States.

Jones, R. F. 1990. Farewell to Africa. Audubon (September). 51–104.

> This Audubon special report graphically illustrates the changes oc-curring in the east Africa wildlife situation. Although listed here as a reading the article has relevance for Chapter 10 also.

Newton, I. 1979. Population ecology of raptors. Buteo Books, Vermillion, SD. 399 pp. plus 16 plates.

A good collation of literature with insight and interpretation from one of the world's leading authorities. The last six chapters are particularly relevant to the endangered species question.

Schonewold-Cox, C. M., S. M. Chambers, B. MacBryden, and L. Thomas, Ed. 1983. Genetics and conservation. Benjamin/Cummings Publishing Co., Inc., Menlo Park, CA. 722 pp.

A valuable reference updating the literature on the genetics of extinction. Highly recommended for students in wildlife.

IX ENVIRONMENTAL IMPACT ASSESSMENT—The New Dimension

Of all life forms, probably only man has totally eliminated natural systems in our environment while impacting others to the extent that plant and animal species have been reduced or destroyed. Goudie (1981) has traced the effect of man on his environment from the time our ancestors were hunters and gatherers and concludes that:

Primary impacts give rise to a myriad of successive repercussions throughout ecosystems which may be impracticable to trace and monitor. Quantitative cause-and-effect relationships can seldom be established.

Nevertheless, these primary impacts and their repercussions with cause-and-effect relationships are what a new breed of biologists and resource managers are trying to measure today with the environmental impact assessment (EIA). It is only too obvious that building an airport or highway will destroy, perhaps permanently, the portion of a natural system that is replaced by concrete and buildings. It is not so obvious what effects the same development may have on the flight patterns or resting behavior of gulls in the vicinity or what effects there may be on the movements of caribou if a highway intersects their migration routes. With many development projects, and often with existing industries, changes in the chemical nature of soils, water, or air are measurable long before the biota show signs of being affected. Ecologists should be able to quantify both the early and later changes and determine with reasonable accuracy what their influences may be.

In addition to the ecological portions of the environmental impact assessment, there are also social and economic aspects that must be studied. Possibly the wildlife manager will only be involved in one aspect of an EIA, but as the assessment, the resulting statement, the evaluation, and the review must consider the entire spectrum from the original project guidelines, today's wildlifers require a familiarity with all processes involved, including the socioeconomic ones.

The EIA in the USA—Background

We could say that the roots of the United States' environmental conscience leading to the government's intervention in environmental matters began with Thoreau, whose communion with nature at Walden led him to champion the cause of nature and absolute personal freedom. We might also trace these roots to Theodore Roosevelt or Aldo Leopold, but to try to do so is only to acknowledge the existence of a slumbering environmental conscience that was really not awakened until Rachel Carson wrote "The Book" (*Silent Spring*). Carson's work is of broad significance because it was written to be read; and it was read by millions of North Americans. With momentum from *Silent Spring*, the sixties became a decade of ecology in the United States, with names like McHarg, Hardin, Ehrlich, and Commoner becoming familiar to laymen and politicians as well. In 1969, the federal government passed the National Environmental Policy Act (NEPA), and by 1970 the Environmental Revolution was in full swing. Odell (1980) has said of this movement:

> So sweeping was this revolution that its adherents concerned themselves with almost all of society's and nature's activities—from the fate of the desert pupfish to that of an interstate highway, from soil erosion to sonic boom.

Odell also presents three goals of the movement as follows:

1. The safety and good health of individuals, including their psychological and physical well-being as affected by the natural environment.
2. The long-range survival and welfare of society, including the life-supporting environment on which these depend.
3. The achievement of a richer and fuller life, including desirable environmental characteristics.

There is little doubt that both public sentiment for the preservation of nature and public apprehensions concerning the future of human life were somewhat responsible for the interest exhibited in the 1970's by federal and state governments. The Environmental Revolution was primarily a grass roots movement spawned by the people. It was a broader approach to conservation than the great conservation movement for wildlife of the 1930's. Perhaps this was so because the problems of environmental degradation accelerated so swiftly following World War II and thus affected each citizen so much more directly. It was a movement that had a niche somewhere for almost every North American citizen.

The response of most governments was initially similar: pass legislation to protect the environment, but don't box government or private enterprise in to the extent that development would be unnecessarily impeded. Exceptions were continued expansion of the national parks system and the classification of wilderness areas. A significant aspect of most legislation passed was the environmental impact assessment. The National Environmental Policy Act, for instance, required all federal agencies to consult with each other and to employ systematic and interdisciplinary techniques in planning and decision making. For every recommendation or report on proposals for legislation or other federal actions significantly affecting the quality of the human environment, the act required a detailed statement (environmental impact statement or EIS) concerning

1. the environmental impact of the proposed action;
2. adverse environmental effects which cannot be avoided should the proposal be implemented;
3. alternatives to the proposed action;
4. the relationship between local short-term uses and . . . enhancement of long-term productivity;
5. any irreversible and irretrievable commitments of resources . . . involved . . . in the proposed action (U.S. Fish and Wildlife Service 1976).

In addition, the relevant Section 102 (C) reads:

Prior to making any detailed statement, the responsible Federal official shall consult with and obtain the comments of any agency which has jurisdiction by law or special expertise with respect to any environmental impact involved. Copies of such statement and the comments and views of the appropriate Federal, State, and local agencies, which are authorized to develop and enforce environmental standards, shall be made available to the President, the Council on Environmental Quality and the public as provided by section 552 of title 5 United State code, and shall accompany the proposal through the existing agency review process (Nelson 1973).

According to Zigman (1978), this federal legislation served as a foundation for similar legislation adopted by the states such as the California Environmental Quality Act (CEQA) of 1970 (amended 1972 and 1976) and the State Environmental Policy Act (SEPA) of 1972 in Washington. Some state legislation, however, serves a broader function in overall planning than the several state environmental acts. Florida's Environmental Land and Water Management Act (ELMS) passed in 1972 provides for state, regional, and local involvement in areas of critical state concern or in any development producing regional impacts.

With legislation in place, the EIA and its resulting statement had become, by 1975, a normal part of the development process accompanying the planning, construction, and operational phases of projects. Sometimes, the environmental assessment was carried out by in-house government agencies or combinations of agencies or departments. Often private consulting firms were called in by government either to project an image of impartiality or because civil service staff did not have the time to devote to such matters in light of their previously planned (and budgeted) responsibilities. For the most part, governments have now established specific agencies with responsibilities to monitor, coordinate, review, and sometimes direct the environmental assessment. With few exceptions, professional biologists, economists, and engineers in the government employ are closely involved with people undertaking the assessments, from beginning to end.

The EIA in Canada—Background

The shock waves from *Silent Spring* were also felt in Canada, and the defensive attitude of both industries and governments quickly became apparent. Carson and others prominent in the decade of ecology were often castigated in the press and within government circles in the early 1960's as being against progress, and the "environmentalist" label took on an almost antisocial connotation. Environmentalists were cast not as people concerned with environmental matters but as people out to stop development at any cost and, consequently, out to take dollars from the pockets of adults and bread from the mouths of children! Nevertheless, in Canada the 1960's did become a decade when the word "ecology" became a part of the average citizen's vocabulary. The Environmental Revolution smoldered first in the universities.

By the early seventies many an environmental, ecological, and anti-pollution organization was active and primarily involved young people. Unfortunately, perhaps, many such youth-led groups projected an image in common with some other "rights" movements of narrow minority interests or of student or university left-wing political ideologies. This made their positive environmental actions vulnerable to attack from conservative and centrist elements in society. These activist groups obtained little sympathy and little general public support. In the beginning, ecological "facts" were sometimes misleading or even dead wrong, and the environmentalists' credibility was often questioned. Attempts to amalgamate the many ecological action groups with the several more moderate resource institutes and associations in Canada were tried unsuccessfully, and it eventually fell to those few individuals in government agencies and universities that projected a moderate image to counsel the elected representatives toward reasonable, necessary action. As a result, the movement in Canada lagged somewhat behind the U.S., although the federal government had reorganized a number of departments to create the Department of the Environment in 1970.

But, by 1972, the pace had quickened and a federal cabinet decision on June 8 of that year directed that all proposed federal projects be screened to identify potential pollution effects. Then, on 20 December 1973, the minister of the environment was directed, again by cabinet decision, to establish in cooperation with other ministers a process to ensure that federal departments and agencies

1. Take environmental matters into account throughout the planning and implementation of new projects, programs and activities;
2. carry out an environmental assessment for all projects which may have adverse effect on the environment before commitments or irrevocable decisions are made; projects which have significant effects have to be submitted to the Federal Environmental assessments in planning, decision-making and implementation (FEARO 1978).

The decision further established definitions, responsibilities and procedures which had recently undergone a policy review, and on 11 July 1984 new guidelines for environmental assessment and review were published by the federal government (P.C. 1984–2132) as an order-in-council.

1. Federal projects requiring assessment are those projects initiated by federal departments or agencies, those for which federal funds are committed, and those involving federal property. Thus, under complicated general development agreements between the federal government and provinces and within cost-shared programs such as those considered under DREE (the Department of Regional Economic Expansion) and other federal agencies, most large development projects in Canada are subject to review and assessment.
2. Proprietary corporations and regulatory agencies are directed to participate in the process as long as it is corporate policy to do so and there is no legal impediment or no duplication of effort involved. The Canadian National Railway and the Canadian National Museum, as examples, would undertake a review only if it were corporate policy to apply the FEARO process. Although exemption seems to be a possibility, it is unlikely that these organizations would avoid an environmental review.
3. It is the responsibility of the initiating department in a public review

to ensure that the proponent and its own staff meet the responsibilities of the review process.

4. The public review is conducted by an environmental assessment panel appointed by the minister. Panel members are outside the political realm and generally experts on the anticipated technical, environmental, and social areas to be affected by the proposal under review. Departments and agencies are responsible for ensuring "in co-operation with other bodies concerned with the proposal, that any decision made by the appropriate Ministers as a result of the conclusions and recommendations ruled by Panel" are incorporated into the proposal.

The initiating department assesses each proposal to determine whether the review process outlined above is actually carried out. Among the possibilities are the following:

1. No adverse environmental impacts are expected and the proposal automatically proceeds.
2. It is a type of proposal that would produce significant adverse environmental effects and the proposal is automatically referred to the minister for public review by a panel.
3. The potentially adverse environmental effects that may be caused by the proposal are insignificant or mitigable with known technology, in which case the proposal may proceed or proceed with the mitigation.
4. The potentially adverse environmental effects that may be caused by the proposal are unknown, in which case the proposal shall either require further study and subsequent rescreening or reassessment or be referred to the minister for public review by a panel.
5. The potentially adverse environmental effects that may be caused by the proposal are significant, as determined in accordance with criteria developed by FEARO in cooperation with the initiating department, in which case the proposal shall be referred to the minister for public review by a panel.
6. The potentially adverse environmental effects that may be caused by the proposal are unacceptable, in which case the proposal shall either be modified and subsequently rescreened, reassessed, or abandoned.
7. If public concern about the proposal is such that a public review is desirable, the initiating department shall refer the proposal to the minister for public review by a panel.

The order-in-council complements regulatory requirements of several federal acts such as the Government Organization Act (1979) of which it is a part; Fisheries Act; Clean Air Act; Canada Water Act; Migratory Birds Convention Act; the Northern Inland Waters Act, and others.

Many provinces were developing their own environmental guidelines at the same time as the federal government. Government sponsored planning and discussions relevant to environmental legislation and organization had already begun in Nova Scotia in 1970, and in 1972 resulted in legislation which was proclaimed in 1973 (amended 1977). A new Act Respecting Environmental Assessment was drafted in 1988 with Regulations passed in 1989. By 1989, all Canadian provinces had legislation in place under which environmental assessments might be conducted and several had drafted "conservation strategies." Indeed, all Canadian provinces have also established Environmental Round Tables on environmental policy. At the Federal level, an Environmental Round Table also exists with representation from each province. Both elected members and representatives from the private sector serve on these advisory bodies. Bill C-78, the Canadian Environmental Assessment Act would overhaul the Canadian environmental assessment process. This bill which is currently being reviewed by a special commons committee will come up before the House possibly for final reading about the time of publication of this book. The intent of the bill is to strengthen environmental assessment procedures and make them law instead of guidelines which is the basis of the current FEARO process.

Some Approaches to the EIA

Elements of environmental analysis appeared in several early land-use planning exercises across North America. One method developed in Ontario by G. A. Hills is detailed in his 1961 text, *Ecological Basis for Land Use Planning*. The Hills' technique depends upon the classification of land units into physiographical land types, classes, and site types. It eventually results in landscape units with capability, suitability, and feasibility ratings for wildlife, recreation, and other resources (Figure 9.1). The approach was helpful to those involved in planning the nationwide Canada Land Inventory that classifies Canadian lands with a one (highest) to five (lowest) capability rating for agriculture, forest production, wildlife, and recreation. Hills' method was one of the first to recognize the importance of ecological factors as determinants in land-use considerations; however, neither use impacts nor long term effects were considered. Ecological entities were not considered as the dynamic, changing elements they really are in natural systems.

Another planning device used considerably in the United States is the technique of determining "environmental corridors" based upon the occurrence of identifiable landscape patterns (Figure 9.2). This method was worked

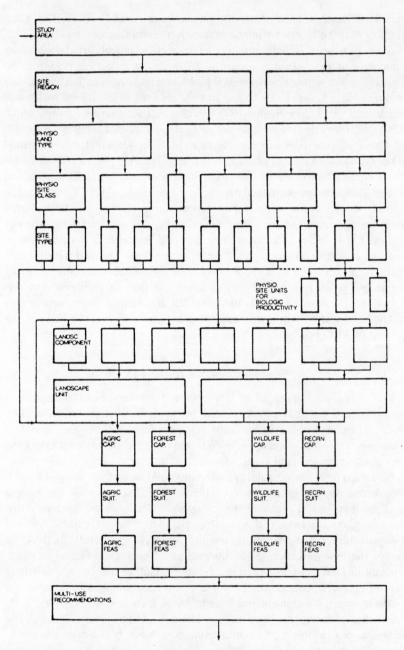

Figure 9.1   Diagram of method. G. Angus Hills. (Parks Canada, 1973)

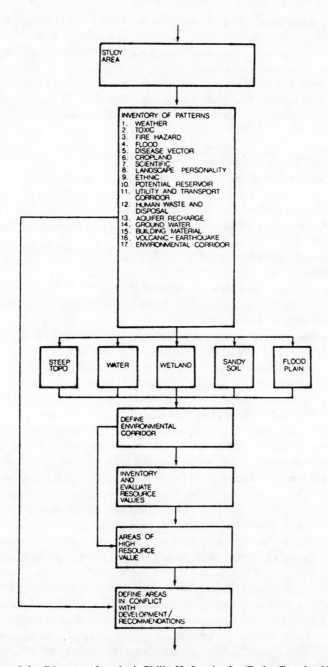

Figure 9.2   Diagram of method. Philip H. Lewis, Jr. (Parks Canada, 1973)

out by the architect, Philip H. Lewis, and its primary objective was to identify, preserve, protect, and enhance the most outstanding "natural values of
land units" and see that man-made values were developed in harmony with
the quality resources recognized.

Like Lewis, Ian McHarg is a visionary landscape architect who has been
involved with regional land planning for much of his life. McHarg's approach
involves an eight step method which may be further subdivided. The main
elements are

1. an environmental inventory
2. determination of the dominant prospective uses for each land unit
3. an assessment of land-use values
4. a determination of the suitability of land units for dominant uses
5. a determination of the compatibility of various land uses
6. an economic inventory
7. establishment of criteria for visibility
8. establishment of criteria for form and design
   (Abbreviated from Parks Canada, 1973)

The method is based upon the concept that any land area is valued as the
sum of its historical, physical, and biological processes which are all dynamic
and constitute social values. The method recognizes that each value has an
intrinsic suitability for a particular land use and that certain areas lend themselves to multiple, coexisting uses. Figure 9.3 diagrams the process which
is thoroughly detailed and articulated in *Design with Nature*, a book that has
influenced North American planning greatly since its publication in 1969.

Beginning with the seventies decade, the need to develop procedures to
measure the actual impacts or effects of a particular change in land use, or
of projects that would change entire systems, became imperative; legislation
was being implemented throughout the continent requiring that environmental
assessments be made. The earlier land-use inventories and planning approaches were valuable, but they did not meet the specific demands required
by the biological impact analysis, nor did they always involve socioeconomic
factors. The problems now were how to measure the biological, social, and
economic bases, determine their values, assess the effects of the known
measured changes with proposed developments, and determine mitigation
procedures, costs, and benefits. All of these problems have not been completely solved. New methodologies are regularly being developed as the need
for more precise measurements increases. The entire process of environmental
assessment is one of change, and because of the dynamic aspects of natural
systems, changing social values, and rapidly altering economies, the processes

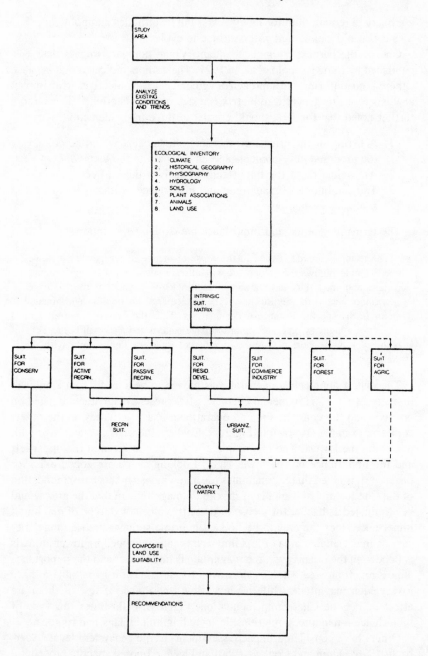

Figure 9.3   Diagram of method. Ian McHarg. (Parks Canada, 1973)

are likely to remain fluid for many years. Public attitudes and political priorities are also dynamic and will continue to evolve.

One of the earliest attempts to quantify and compare impact data was published by Luna Leopold et al. in 1971. The authors indicated that because "there is no uniformity in approach or agreement upon objectives in an impact analysis . . . this generalized matrix is a step in that direction." The authors further noted that the EIA should consist of three basic elements:

1. A listing of the effects on the environment that would be caused by the proposed development, and an estimate of the *magnitude* of each
2. An evaluation of the importance of each of these effects
3. The combining of magnitude and importance estimates in terms of a summary evaluation

The terms magnitude and importance are explained as follows:

The term *magnitude* is used in the sense of degree, extensiveness or scale. For example highway development will alter or affect the existing drainage pattern and may thus have a large magnitude of impact on the drainage. . . . importance *is* the significance of the particular action on the environmental factor in the specific instance under analysis. Thus the overall importance of impact of a highway on a particular drainage pattern may be small because the highway is very short or because it will not interfere significantly with the drainage.

The matrix approach, in general, has proven to be a useful tool employed in many EIA's. Environmental characteristics present in an area are listed on one axis and the construction and operational phase activities on the other. A matrix example is shown in Figure 9.4, where the scale is one to five with one being the lowest. The magnitude of the action is given at the upper left and the importance on the lower right. Looking at the horizontal axis, for instance, it is noted that for ungulates (deer and moose in this case) inundation of the Cheticamp Lake area is of maximum magnitude in that the area would be eliminated as habitat for moose or deer. It is also noted to be of maximum importance since the area to be flooded is prime summer moose range. Because a much smaller area of less important range inhabited by fewer animals is flooded in the other cases, the magnitude is rated lower and the importance almost nil. If an area is totally destroyed for ungulates, it is possible to have a very high magnitude while having a low importance if few of them are affected. For the Cheticamp inundation, Figure 9.4 illustrates this type of importance—magnitude relationship including amphibians and reptiles.

Others have considered impact assessments at the ecosystem level (Auerbach, 1978; Odum and Cooley, 1980) and have proposed specific procedural

PROJECT ACTIVITIES / ENVIRONMENTAL ELEMENTS	PHYSICAL												BIOLOGICAL									
	INUNDATION				IMPOUND-MENT			STREAMS					TERRESTIAL						AQUATIC			
	LAND	MARSHES	LAKES	FREE FLOWING STREAMS	WATER LEVEL FLUCTUATIONS	GROUND WATER	WATER QUALITY	MEAN FLOWS	MINIMUM FLOWS	WATER QUALITY	SEDIMENT & EROSION	LENGTH AFFECTED	FOREST	WETLANDS	UNGULATES	BIRDS – UPLANDS & PASSERINE WATER FOWL & SHORE BIRDS	OTHER MAMMALS & BIRDS	UNIQUE SPECIES	SALMONIDS	AQUATIC VEGETATION	AMPHIBIANS & REPTILES	EELS
-CHETICAMP:																						
CONSTRUCTION															3/-1	1/-1	1/-1		5/-4			
INUNDATION TO MAX. LEVEL	5/-2	5/-5	5/-2	4/-2		4/+2	5/-5	5/-1		5/-3			4/-1	5/-4	5/-5	3/-2	4/-2	2/-1	4/-5	4/-5	5/-1	
DIVERSION OPERATIONS					4/-5			5/-1	5/-2	5/-2		5/-4							4/-4	5/-4	5/-3	
-INGONISH:																						
CONSTRUCTION																			2/-2			
INUNDATION TO MAX. LEVEL	1/-1	1/-3	1/-1	1/-1		3/+1	1/-1	3/-1		1/-2			1/-1	1/-1	1/0	1/-1	1/-1		1/-1	1/-5	1/0	
DIVERSION OPERATIONS					1/-2			2/-1	5/-2	3/-1		3/-4							1/-1	1/0	1/0	
-EAST INDIAN:																						
CONSTRUCTION															2/-1	1/-1	1/-1		4/-4			
INUNDATION TO MAX. LEVEL	1/-1	1/-1	3/-3	5/-4		5/+1	5/-4	5/-3		5/-3			5/-1	1/-1	2/-1	2/-1	2/-1		2/-2	3/-5	3/-1	
DIVERSION OPERATIONS					5/-5			4/-3	5/-3	4/-4		3/-3							4/-4	4/-3	3/-2	

Figure 9.4 Matrix developed to show environmental impacts of proposed hydroelectric development

approaches. Barske (1978) and Truett (1979) were concerned with mitigation of impacts on natural resource entities, primarily through improved planning and design. A large number of authors have been concerned with various other aspects of the EIA. These include Hirsch (baseline studies, 1980), Lucas (statistical aspects, 1976), and Stover (general procedure, 1972).

Although precise determination of the effects of development is seldom possible, changes in physical factors such as flow, depth, and often temperature as well as chemical and biological characteristics can sometimes be accurately calculated for aquatic systems. In some situations, modelling results may closely reflect reality when the input data are adequate or when field environments can be replicated under controlled conditions. This may sometimes be possible in the laboratory. Accuracy is severely reduced for terrestrial populations and habitats where more variables present complex control problems and where input data for models may be far less precise. The wildlife manager must become familiar with as many approaches to obtain measures of change or impact as possible. The significance of any change is really a measure of change in productivity within the ecosystem. If an ecosystem is irreversibly damaged or destroyed to the point that it will not self-correct, there is no question that the impact is significant. At this point, it becomes a matter of values, social losses, and trade-offs. Society may make the ultimate value judgement of what it considers to be important. For example, loss of the supporting ecosystem of the whooping crane may have greater value than a similar loss of California condor habitat.

The Process—from the Beginnings

The steps in the process from the first project proposal to the submission of an EIS with recommendations and subsequent reviews will vary depending upon whether the project is initiated by a federal agency within the U.S. or Canada or whether it is of provincial, state, or other origin. The legislation within which it is considered may also affect the steps in the process. Regardless of the steps involved, you, the biologist or manager, will become involved if the proposed project has what may be considered a significant impact on some environmental entity affecting wildlife. Leopold et al. (1971) have described the possible sequence of events as follows:

1. A statement of the major objective of the proposed project is made.
2. The technologic possibilities of achieving the objective are analyzed.
3. One or more actions are proposed for achieving the stated objective. The alternative plans that were considered as practicable ways of reaching the objective are spelled out in the proposal.

4. A report which details the characteristics and conditions of the existing environment prior to the proposed action is prepared. In some cases, this report may be incorporated as part of the engineering proposal.
5. The principal engineering proposals are finalized as a report or series of separate reports, one for each plan. The plans ordinarily have analyses of monetary benefits and costs.
6. The proposed plan of action, usually the engineering report, together with the report characterizing the present environment, sets the stage for evaluating the environmental impact of the proposal. If alternative ways of reaching the objective are proposed in 3, and if alternative engineering plans are detailed in the engineering report, separate environmental impact analyses must deal with each alternative. If only one proposal is made in the engineering report, it is still necessary to evaluate environmental impacts.
7. The text of the environmental impact report should be an assessment of the impacts of the separate actions which comprise the project upon various factors of the environment and thus provide justification for the determinations presented in 5. Each plan of action should be analyzed independently.
8. The Environmental Impact Statement should conclude with a summation and recommendations. This section should discuss the relative merits of the various proposed actions and alternative engineering plans and explain the rationale behind the final choice of action and the plan for achieving the stated objective.

Projects in Canada that are subject to the Federal Environment Assessment Review Office may require up to nine general steps if environmental impacts are significant.

1. Environmental screening by relevant government agencies
2. Initial environmental evaluation
3. Guidelines (from the independent Environmental Assessment Panel for which FEARO serves as a secretariat); panel members appointed from outside government by the appropriate minister, generally on the recommendation of the executive director of FEARO
4. The environmental impact assessment by the proponent
5. The environmental impact statement
6. The public review process
7. Panel recommendations
8. Submission to minister
9. Cabinet discussion

The entire process, from conception to the decision to begin or cancel, may be short-cut if either the screening process or the initial evaluation indicates there are no significant effects. If there are, the in-house process is lengthened as depicted in Figure 9.5. As early as possible following conception of the project, the screening process is initiated by the departments or agencies involved. Referring to Figure 9.5 again, you will note that any of three decisions may be reached from the screening process, two of which can lead to the provision of guidelines, an assessment, and its resulting statement.

Nowadays, both public (government sponsored) and private enterprise developments must wait for a process to be carried out that is similar to those noted here; however, because political commitments or investment decisions have already been made, the project contemplated may be a fait accompli. Nonetheless, those involved with an EIA should take their work seriously, for the possibilities of mitigation through alternative design or development are still present. In past years, there have been examples, such as the hydroelectric development at Wreck Cove in Nova Scotia, where project construction was well underway before the environmental process was even started. In these cases, the proponent of the project may have spent very little on the environmental assessment processes, or if pressured by the public, spent a great deal more than necessary! Mitigation recommendations were seldom implemented to any extent unless regulations required them. Then the regulations would have been recognized and some action taken even without the EIA. The current processes regularly under review now help to prevent this from occurring.

The Assessment Proposal

Usually consulting companies are invited to submit an EIA proposal which includes a general budget and breakdown of costs. The invitation comes from the proponent—the company or political jurisdiction undertaking the project having potential environmental effects. An invitation may be very detailed or it may only indicate that a project of a given magnitude is being considered in a particular location and provide spare details. Detailed invitations are the norm however, because everyone in any particular state, province, or country in North America now operates within the same or similar regulations. If the invitation is not detailed, it is possible that a decision has already been made as to what consulting firm will be conducting the EIA.

Usually the invitation will include information on the proposed project design, its construction, and its operation (plus alternatives, if any); the time frame involved; the kinds of environmental baseline data required; an outline of environmental impacts relating to each environmental data base; outlines for mitigation; and recommendations for both construction and operational phases of the project. The nature of the project will dictate the content and to some extent the approach used. Guidelines for the EIS in Canada are usually available to the proponent at an early date after a panel review has been initiated and can be used by those bidding on the EIA study or portions of it. These guidelines are very complete and will probably cover all necessary environmental entities, as they are prepared by professionals serving on an assessment panel for the specific project.

If you have been supplied with detailed information, your proposal should generally follow the outline and approach provided. If you know that the information you have is incomplete, you are responsible for securing whatever clarification your professional judgement deems necessary.

The proposal you may be asked to draft should reflect activities related to each of the environmental data bases noted on the invitation or guidelines, as well as activities pertaining to impact determination for each ecosystem or data base under each construction and operational alterative. The consequences (to an ecosystem and/or species) of the impact with and without mitigation are also significant and must be recognized in the proposal. Note that you should provide mitigation recommendations and cost estimates for implementing them. Also include community effects, benefits, and costs. These are socioeconomic concerns important in all projects.

In addition, the proposal should indicate the time frame you expect to follow, the approach you will take in completing the work (the management, administration, and coordination), a budget for each phase and each professional entity, methodologies to be employed, and a list of team members detailing their expertise and showing how their special abilities relate specifically to the project. If the proposal is well conceived and if the design of the EIA study remains essentially unchanged, the proposal can serve as a reasonable outline for the EIS. This is the way it should work out unless the unexpected occurs on a grand scale!

The Environmental Impact Statement

Few reports purportedly of a scientific or professional nature have been criticized and even ridiculed as much as many of the environmental impact statements prior to the late 1970s. But, until the EIS came around, few reports were available for criticism. In-house government reports were discussed in the offices involved, and usually problems were ironed out before senior people saw them; or perhaps the seniors were not even able to digest the reports fully enough for a critical analysis. Government reports that were

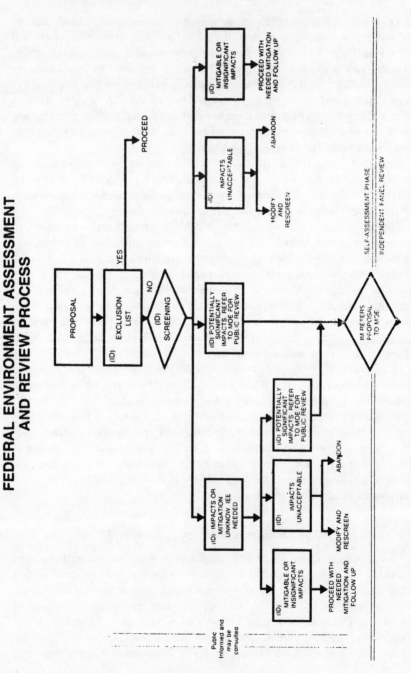

Figure 9.5   Schematic diagram of the Canadian federal environmental assessment and review process

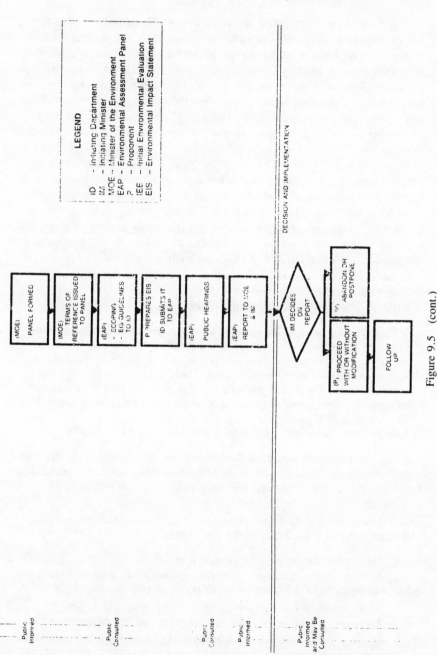

Figure 9.5 (cont.)

prepared for others were tidied up before release. Some poor ones escaped, but by and large they were capable of withstanding the ordinary critical review. Of the millions of other reports available to the public, most were of limited interest, used by limited groups. With the EIS, we had a different situation. Here was a report prepared for a proponent who might not always be capable of dissecting it thoroughly; but the public and a large body of professionals from both sides of an issue were able to read it and pick it apart. This happened often in spite of reviews and rewrites of early confidential drafts.

According to the commonest complaints, many impact statements are too big, too complex, too descriptive rather than analytical, and generalize on too many environmental concerns without pinpointing and developing the most important ones. Many times the EIS is stuffed with irrelevant data and generalized statements of no use to anybody. Don't pad your EIS. Remember that you have a proposal which can serve as an outline. If you find items in the proposal to be inapplicable, then say so. Remember to justify any changes you make, and put general data packages in an appendix or make them available on request. Don't put your EIS in between expensive covers. Here is what the FEARO has to say about the EIS.

> It describes the project, its location, the need for it and any alternative methods of achieving the project other than the one proposed. The EIS also describes the area's existing environment and current patterns of resource use, social factors such as population characteristics, community life style and the economic base of the area. It provides a detailed description of the potential effect of the proposal on the area's environment and identifies the measures the proponent intends to take to reduce those impacts. Any impacts that might remain after these mitigating measures have been taken must also be identified (FEARO 1979).

If the proponent has not yet indicated plans for mitigation, such measures should appear in the proposal as recommendations. Similarly, remaining impacts should be identified and their suggested mitigation procedures written in as well.

In the Leopold et al. (1971) approach to the EIS there are four basic items. The authors listed these items, in part, as follows:

1. A complete analysis of the proposed action
2. An informative description of the environment to be involved, including a careful consideration of the boundaries of a project . . .
3. A discussion of the pertinent details of the proposed action
4. An assessment of the probable impacts of the variety of specific aspects of the proposed action upon the variety of existing environmental elements and factors

In enlarging on these items, the authors note that point 1. the analysis, should also be a justification "which considers the full range of values to be derived, not simply the usual cost-benefit analysis." Concerning point 2, the authors indicate that special emphasis should be placed "on those rare or unique aspects, both good and bad, that might not be common to other similar areas. . . . The description should include all the factors which together make up the ecosystem of the area. . . . " And in considering point 3, the authors signal that details of the proposed action " . . . should include discussion of possible alternative engineering methods or approaches to accomplish the proposed development." Their point 4 is an explanation of the Leopold matrix and its use.

So follow the outline of the proposal. Add and subtract the newly relevant and irrelevant, justify your statements, and use a good guide such as FEARO's approach. If you write clearly and simply, reducing jargon and complex theory as much as possible, and if your statistical handling of data is appropriate and thorough, your EIS should be acceptable.

Assessment Problems

Later in this chapter we will look at problems in the assessment process from several viewpoints that may be in conflict with one another. First, we will have a brief look at a few common problems the environmental assessment team has to face.

Perhaps the most difficult is one you may not become directly aware of until sometime after you enter professional ranks. That is the overall management of the assessment project. Management is less difficult if the successful bidder put together a proposal with no need to contract for expertise outside the company. Within a single company, employees can work as a team and agree on time frames, minimum data bases, methodologies, costs, deadlines, and meeting schedules. With a stable team, it becomes a simple matter to prevent over expenditure. However, all budget processes must include a margin for increasing costs, necessities like editing and printing, and extra meetings with people outside the company. In addition, you must be ready for unexpected problems in the field, even when personnel are familiar with the terrain, waters, and ecosystems involved. The biologist never knows in advance all of the problems he may find or all the organisms he must study with extra time in the field, in the lab, or on the computer. Good management is able to account for such situations yet still meet deadlines with a sound product at an acceptable cost.

Cooperation is part of the management picture, something each team member should be concerned with. Much of the background and most of the data base are often obtained from existing information already in government agency files, in the files of university researchers, or in publications or files elsewhere. Publications are no problem; the data are available. But getting data from a wildlife biologist working for the state of Washington, or the province of Nova Scotia, is another problem. Freedom of information legislation, if present, may be relevant in such cases. Nevertheless, a biologist seeking information from another person in government usually depends on him to provide all the necessary data. However, the government biologist might not be willing or able to do so. Neither is it always easy to extract data from university research people. Sometimes it is impossible, and the assessment team may have to duplicate a great deal of work. The authors have been in both positions; we have had to ask others for data, and sometimes data interpretation, and we have had consultants request unpublished information. In the first instance, familiarity with an agency and personal contacts have helped. In the second instance, we admit that we often are unwilling to cooperate fully with a stranger who is unfamiliar with the area or the subject, and who works for a company from another jurisdiction 2000 miles away. Like others in these circumstances, we often wish to protect data for personal use. Schindler (1978) has argued from a government employee's point of view as follows:

> I am often interviewed by someone from a university or consulting firm who is hoping to obtain insight into a particular impact. Almost without exception these are people with bachelor's degrees. Also almost without exception, they were not totally capable of assimilating all of the complex information which I could put at their disposal. Upon questioning them more closely I found that they (or their firm) had been contracted by the government (my employer) to investigate a problem in which our department had several international experts. Even more ludicrous, the salaries paid to these undereducated individuals to interview government experts were higher than those paid to the experts themselves.

Even though all assessments subject to the federal EARP in Canada are now carried out by an independent panel of experts, it is still possible in many states and provinces to have such problems. Surely it is not the fault of the interviewing biologist that others become upset at his presence, but if a protocol similar to FEARO's is not in operation, the consulting firm should make the initial approaches and establish a cooperative climate for its people before the interviewer calls or makes personal contact. As has been recognized by the government of Canada, the problem is one of establishing a level of expertise in the overall process and determining a protocol to be followed. The project team is almost always short of time for portions of work deemed important to them. We have seldom found any field biologist to be really satisfied with his efforts, even though he, himself, may have helped establish his own budget and time allotment. *Something* always occurs to make more time and work desirable. Good planning reduces the extent of problems, but they are always present. That one last sampling season you really want is not available because deadlines must be met! The unexpected notwithstanding, field biologists must often cut the cloth to fit the available time and money. In doing so, they have to indicate to the project manager and (directly or indirectly as the process requires) to the proponent, the limitations of their data pack and the resultant data analyses. Except in rare circumstances, the EIS will not include original research and will seldom provide new findings in ecology. The short-term nature of the EIA usually demands that scientific precision be reduced in favor of good scientific judgement. This fault in the entire process goes against the grain of all of us, at one time or another. It is the basis for many attempts on the part of ecologists to find ways of improving EIS ecosystem data packages and their interpretation and analysis.

Different Viewpoints

Depending upon the roles they play by choice or necessity, people obviously view the EIA and the EIS in very different manners. We are indebted to Beanlands and Duinker (1983) for an examination of many attitudes and an excellent digest of process data which end on a relatively positive note. We here present extracts portraying viewpoints of the government administrator, the proponent, the consultant, and the research scientist.

The Administrator's Perspective

Government administrators tend to view environmental impact assessment as the fulfillment of required procedures set by policy or legislation. For these people, the main question is whether the assessment guidelines have been met. In most cases, the first priority is on running the administrative machinery with less regard for the details of the resulting studies. Although the agencies may retain outside experts for the preparation of guidelines, such terms of reference usually amount to lists of "things to do" rather than providing scientific direction or performance standards. It is only at the review stage that the administrators are faced with determining the scientific or technical substance of the assessment studies undertaken. At this time, outside experts may be brought in to give their opinion. In doing so, such experts almost invariably adopt a fairly rigorous interpretation of the guidelines—a perspective which may have helped at the beginning of the assessment but which can be very disruptive at the end.

The Proponent's Perspective

In industry, environmental impact assessment is tied directly to the project approvals and licenses. Because of the high public profile which is often adopted in review procedures, impact assessment is also important to industry from a public relations perspective. With project approval in mind, the proponent's main objective is to develop an acceptable IS. Proponents will 'do what has to be done' to get that document approved, but are understandably reluctant to consider anything beyond that as part of the impact assessment process. This IS focus may present problems when it comes to implementing impact assessment in a much broader time frame as implied by the inclusion of operation-phase monitoring. It seems that not all industrial proponents believe it is in their best interest to have the scientific quality of impact assessment studies improved. A certain degree of flexibility in study results can sometimes be used to advantage when debating potential impacts. On the other hand, there is ample evidence to indicate that industrial proponents in Canada have generally adopted a positive attitude toward environmental impact assessment. As stated on a number of occasions during the workshops by various industrial representatives, ''Any reasonable study will be funded.''

The Consultant's Perspective
In Canada, the task of conducting environmental impact assessment studies and preparing an IS most often falls to consultants in the employ of the proponents. They find themselves caught between the differing perspectives on the assessment process held by government agencies and proponents. The consultants' main role is to translate assessment guidelines, which are often generalized and vaguely worded, into a number of field or laboratory studies, or both. Basically, they try to establish a short-term applied research program. In so doing, they are normally directed by their clients to limit their efforts to a level which is necessary to get the project approved. However, they must also consider the possibility of project delay or refusal if the studies are found unacceptable to the reviewers. In effect, the consultants are expected to practice good science in a politically motivated system. In many respects, the role of the consultants in environmental impact assessment is the most difficult of all. They do not have the luxury of working according to their own fundamental objectives for the assessment process. They must develop a compromise between the approval required by the client and the scientific and technical standards which they would like to adopt to ensure acceptance within a process that is essentially a peer review.

The Research Scientist's Perspective
Research scientists in government and universities have not generally been attracted to environmental impact assessment. From their perspective, the overriding constraints of time and politics usually preclude the conduct of acceptable science in assessment studies. They are, however, often called upon to assist in the preparation of assessment guidelines. Since the guidelines are seldom written in a contractual format which would guarantee the conduct of acceptable work, their basic suspicion of impact assessment tends to be confirmed.

As well, government and university researchers and staff of resource management agencies are often called upon to review the results of impact assessment studies. In so doing, they wear their scientific hats and evaluate the studies according to standards of excellence which are rarely established at the outset. In effect, they undertake a peer review of the work in much the same way as they would evaluate an article submitted for journal publication. This amounts to implementing a quality control programme at the end of an assembly line with no feedback loop. It is frustrating to both the reviewers and authors of the documents.

We believe these statements include most of the concerns except those the general public may have. Because the EIS is often provided to interested groups within the public and as public hearings frequently occur in the process, we should also be aware of the public's concerns. There are a variety of public opinions, but in most cases, the portion of the public that is against the proposed project will be the one dealing most actively with the EIS. These people, or groups, may even provide their own experts to find whatever weaknesses they can in an EIS. Should the EIS suggest little in mitigation, or even in serious impact, the public may try to denigrate the work, if possible, as unscientific and erroneous. It is not uncommon in public hearings for people to attack the EIS, the consulting firm, and the proponent, together. Here is where good public relations at the outset on the part of the consulting group and the proponent can help lessen the conflicts in the public hearing processes. Keeping various elements of the public aware and knowledgeable can often be more helpful to everyone than keeping them in the dark. The public won't disappear!

Areas of Concern to the Wildlife Biologist

A good way to familiarize yourself with the EIA process is to study maps and land-use patterns of an area before a development project begins and then visit it when completed. The before-and-after look can be quite striking in the case of projects resulting in large scale impoundments or super highways and less so in specific restricted-site, industrial developments. It is difficult to assess the before and after when air pollution is involved or for large scale off-shore arctic developments. In these instances and some others, a review of the process steps, complete with the engineering, ecological, and socioeconomic data packages is helpful. Detailed study of several case histories will help give you a feel for the EIA.

For most environmental projects, the wildlife manager should be knowledgeable about eight information sets, which we have expanded on here.

1. Most states and provinces have legislation (guidelines) which indicates when an EIA is required and often outlines the general processes. The wildlife employee is advised to be just as familiar with this type of environmental legislation as he is with wildlife or other land-use and pollution legislation. Most particularly, government employees will need to understand the legislation involved, for they will be conducting their work and representing their agency under its regulations. Some jurisdictions also publish guidelines which expand on the process and indicate the general format required for their IS. Copies of this material should be within reach of all professional wildlife workers.

2. The reasons for the proposed project and the proponent's position must be clearly understood. Justifications for the proposed development may not satisfy you as an individual, but whether they do or not, a clear understanding of why the project is being undertaken is necessary because you may be balancing certain wildlife habitat losses with the benefits and needs indicated by the proponent, the initiator, or both. Often the proponent's position is a defensive one. The more clearly you understand why a defensive posture exists, the easier it will be for you to state the positions dictated by your results. You are not likely to change a proponent's attitude, but you can help avoid confrontation by the approach you take, both orally and in writing.

3. An understanding of the project is necessary. This is where your ability to absorb engineering, construction, and operational details comes in. You must learn to understand the language of civil and hydrological engineers, petroleum geologists, resource economists, foresters, and others. The wise wildlifer has already prepared himself for this role by carefully planning his university course background. If this wasn't the case, then he must learn on his own. If you don't understand the portrayal of various sets of data, ask questions. Don't stay in the dark, or your inability to interpret will surely show in your writing of the IS.

4. The ecological aspects must be clear enough to you so that you can articulate them for others, ecologists or non-ecologists. Remember that your work is to influence engineers, politicians, and the public. Still, you must work with enough detail, accuracy, and statistical thoroughness to please yourself and other professionals. If you, yourself, are satisfied, your fellow biologists will usually be reasonably well pleased. Ghiselin (1980) provides considerable guidance for the wildlifer here and for impact assessments generally. We suggest that you read his section in the *Wildlife Society Techniques Manual*.

5. Social and economic concerns should also be understood by the wildlife

biologist. It is important to know how many families will have their life-styles altered detrimentally in the development area and how many will have theirs improved, both on site and away. Is the project labor intensive? Is the operational phase after construction labor intensive? What are the attitudes of the people, and what are the costs to the taxpayer? You should have some grasp of these and other socioeconomic considerations but need not become involved in a people versus wildlife issue. If you know what the public pulse is, and why, you can deal more effectively with conflicts as they arise.

6. Clearly understand the project's impacts for the present and for the future. The impacts from alternative construction and operating models have also to be thoroughly understood. Your report may influence the selection of alternatives; you need a thorough understanding of the ecological impact of all present and potential phases. Your data will not usually allow you to be exact, particularly if you are dealing with a terrestrial system. This is all the more reason for you to know and understand the differences between alternatives, even if you are inexact as to the degree. Subjective opinions based on guesses are not good, but subjective opinions from a professional knowledgeable in the field are respected.

7. The wildlife professional is the one who can recommend and defend actions to alleviate or reduce the magnitude of impacts. Mitigation is sometimes not possible, but where it is—within cost parameters—it may be the only positive note in an otherwise dreary tale for the environment and for wildlife. This means that you may have to think beyond the project. If a wetland or stream is to be dredged, maybe a tributary can be dammed to continue the area's waterfowl and muskrat production. Or mitigation may mean setting out food plants, stocking fish, providing nest sites, altering maximum drawdowns, realigning a pipeline route slightly, providing road or pipeline crossings for animals, or any of a host of other activities appropriate to the type of project you are dealing with.

8. Finally, understand both the costs and benefits. There are apt to be some cost-benefit analyses conducted using different inputs relative to revenue and expenditure. Be sure to understand these statements, for they are probably crucial in decision making prior to and during construction. Your own cost-benefit concern about ecosystem impact might be enough to deny continuation of the project when added to the specific economic analyses available. Decisions will usually be made on a political basis with economic justification, of course, but if there is resistance to the project from a segment of the public, your

recommendations can help substantiate one or the other position and may be the strongest factor in a decision.

Wildlife professionals are more likely to hear of and understand the sentiments of the nonprofessional public. The opinions of the opponents to the project must not influence you, but knowing them may help create bias on your part if you are not careful. Working alone with your fellow professionals, completely apart from the pressures of all interested parties, you would be much happier than you are likely to be in a realistic situation where both the press and the public try to give you direction. The professional wildlife worker plays it straight and keeps his opinions to himself even in private.

The Future of the EIA in North America

The EIS is here to stay; that seems certain. It should be clear that environmental legislation probably cannot protect wildlife or natural systems from the pace of development. What has occurred since the late 1960s is the evolution of a general process which admits that environmental concerns exist. To be sure, in many cases, the worst possible impacts have been avoided and in others alternative procedures or mitigation activities have partly replaced what was lost. Even in these latter instances, the ecological changes have usually been considerable. There are a few places where development has been stopped or delayed because of impact studies, but there are probably many more cases in which a vocal public has caused the government to put a moratorium on an activity that it deemed either to violate the integrity of natural systems or to threaten human health, or both. Nevertheless, the EIA will endure. It is sometimes a valuable tool to politicians. The process also creates employment. It has added to the short-term costs of government and industry. It may be responsible for some increases in taxes as well as higher costs on consumer items. Still, as decisions to conduct impact assessments are gradually moved from political decision making processes as legislation makes them mandatory, the benefits to wildlife and habitats will increase. The EIA will become a major tool in building the road toward sustainable development.

Whereas impact assessments have the potential to provide environmental data for decision making in developments where risk factors can be determined with some confidence, they may be less helpful in situations where human error or non compliance may occur, as exemplified by the disastrous oil spill of 1989 in Prince William Sound, Alaska.

The upper Bay of Fundy is an example of a development where risks are well defined and where mitigation should be applied at the time of development. A Bay of Fundy site may become a giant project to elicit energy from the world's highest tides. Consideration of the use of Fundy's tides began soon after French tidal power projects were successful and over the past 20 years interest has increased. Today, a growing data bank of biological and physical information is being developed in studies from several universities and government agencies, primarily in the Atlantic region. One data set includes the approximately 1.4 million shorebirds that use the extensive tidal mudflats as staging areas prior to their non-stop, transoceanic flights to South America. Two areas, Shepody Bay (Mary's Point) and Minas Basin (Evangeline Beach) have already been included as Ramsar Convention sites and are a part of the Western Hemisphere Shorebird Reserve Network (WHSRN). The WHSRN is a private support group with participation from 5 federal and about 63 state or provincial governments in the Western Hemisphere. The presence of the shorebird network and the Ramsar sites in the Fundy region, along with a myriad of fishery and marine mammal interests, should help ensure a sound environmental impact assessment through the Canadian Federal process, should the project approach reality.

The EIA Elsewhere

Although some form of environmental impact assessment can now be found in many countries, it might be useful to look at examples from Africa. What follows is not therefore a comprehensive treatment on a world-wide basis, a task too formidable for a book with a North American emphasis.

Attempts to improve the lot of indigenous people through large-scale developments have often been unsuccessful. The condition of people after the project became operational was no better than it was before. Until recently, these development projects have proceeded without environmental assessments. In some cases, special studies were conducted by sociologists, demographers, or anthropologists. The wildlife people usually ended up on a search and rescue type of salvage operation, as in the Kariba hydro impoundment in Zambia. Today the EIA is sometimes, but not always present. It seems unlikely, however, that a development that is touted as a major source of employment or which might help thousands to irrigate their lands will be held up because of possible impacts or ecological boomerangs like disease or even starvation. This is especially true if these conditions are not envisioned or are predicted but not articulated.

Consideration of the great land improvement programs of the Third World are beyond the scope of this text. We note only that initial impact statements and some intensive studies have been produced for some of them. Their effectiveness will probably depend as much on the existing wildlife lobby as on the accuracy and completeness of the statements themselves. If serious impacts are detrimental to human populations and also the wildlife, then wildlife may occasionally obtain a reprieve. Policy and the resultant management of wildlife are still unsettled throughout much of the world today. Until the utilization-preservation issue is settled and until wildlife resources are a part of planning data, we can expect a variety of responses from governments to impact assessments. Baseline studies such as those of Manning and Moss (1976) may be considered in development plans for the Bangweulu area of Zambia, or they may be buried. It seems unlikely that further impact studies will ensue.

As one might expect, the situation is considerably different in the Republic of South Africa, where the Environmental Conservation Act was passed in 1982 (Government Gazett, Vol. 205, No. 8291, Cape Town). According to J. L. Benade, director general of the Department of Environment Affairs (Pers. Comm.), "this Act provides, among other things, for the establishment of a Council for the Environment. A function of this Council is to advise the Ministry of Environment Affairs and Fisheries on the co-ordination of all actions directed at, or liable to have an influence on, any matter affecting the conservation and utilization of the environment. It is anticipated that the Council will examine the feasibility of mandatory EIA through its technical committees." Here as in North America we see the beginnings of a process. It may not provide panaceas for wildlife-development conflicts, but at the very least it will reflect an awareness that conflicts exist. The Republic of South Africa is well advanced in environmental affairs, and many EIA's have been conducted even without legislation. There is an Environmental Planning Professions Interdisciplinary Committee (since 1947), which has drafted a set of guidelines to assist developers in effectively taking environmental aspects into account. Within government itself, policy has been articulated by the 1980 "White Paper; National Policy Regarding Environmental Conservation." As in other matters relating to wildlife resources, there is much the Republic of South Africa has already in place that could benefit newly independent Third World countries, especially in Africa, if there were no political barriers.

In Europe, the EEC has resulted in greater standardization of environmental assessment procedures. The EEC's Multi-year Political Plan for the Environment (1982/85) set the stage for member countries to address environmental concerns and develop comparable mechanisms for assessment. Individual EEC countries have revised their national regulations to meet community standards.

Gradually we are seeing a world-wide acceptance of the principle that we can no longer afford to insult the planet's air, water, and soil as we have in the past. For instance, in 1987 the United Nations' "World Commission on Environment and Development (1983)" produced a final report, *Our Common Future*, more popularly known as the "Bruntland Report" after its Norwegian chairperson. The recommendations there have stimulated action to establish environmentally-sound-economy structures and processes in several countries, world-wide. But we must not be complacent. We are only beginning, and while the environmental impact assessment process may be slowing the rate and the degree of environmental insults, we have a heritage of abuse dating from the early years of the Industrial Revolution. Considerable remedial response is necessary before substantive improvement in environmental conditions will be seen.

Bibliography

Auerbach, S. I. 1978. Current perceptions and applicability of ecosystem analysis to impact assessment. Ohio J. Sci. 78:163–74.

Barske, P. 1978. Environmental concerns in planning and development at the local level. *In* S. Bendix and H. R. Graham, eds. Environmental assessment, approaching maturity. Ann Arbor Science Publishers Inc., Ann Arbor, MI. 288 pp.

Beanlands, G., and P. Duinker. 1983. An ecological framework for environmental impact assessment in Canada. Institute for Resource and Environmental Studies, Dalhousie Univ., Halifax, NS. 132 pp.

Benade, J. L., Director-general Department of Environment Affairs. Private Bag X313, Pretoria, RSA.0001. Letter to the authors. January 27, 1983.

Burchell, R. W. and D. Listokin. 1975. The environmental impact handbook. Center for Urban Policy Research, Rutgers University, New Brunswick, NJ. 234 pp + index.

Carson, R. 1962. Silent spring. Houghton-Mifflin. Boston, MA. 304 pp.

Department of Water Affairs, Forestry and Environmental Conservation. 1980. National policy regarding environmental conservation. W. P. O. 1980. Republic of South Africa. 13 pp.

FEARO. 1978. Federal environmental assessment and review process. Federal Activities Branch, Environmental Protection Service and Federal Environmental Assessment Review Office, Ottawa.

FEARO. 1979. Revised guide to the federal environmental assessment and review process. Supply and Services, Canada, Ottawa. 12 pp.

FEARO. 1988. 1988 Summary of current practice. William. J. Couch, Ed. Canadian Council of Resource and Environment Ministers. Federal Environmental Assessment Review Office. Ottawa. 55 pp.

Ghiselin, J. 1980. Preparing and evaluating environmental assessments and related documents. Chapter 25 *In* Wildlife management techniques manual. S. D. Schemnitz, ed. The Wildl. Soc., Washington, DC. 686 pp.

Goudie, A. 1981. The human impact. Man's role in environmental change. The MIT Press Cambridge, MA. 316 pp.

Government Gazette 205 (8291). 1982. Environment Conservation Act. Capetown, Republic of South Africa. 15 pp.

Heiser, D. W. 1978. Implementing the environmental policy—Where we've been and where we're gong. *In* S. Bendix, and H. R. Graham, eds. Environmental assessment, approaching maturity. Ann Arbor Science Publishers Inc., Ann Arbor, MI. 288 pp.

Hills, G. A. 1961. The ecological basis for land-use planning. Ontario Ministry of Natural Resources, Research report No. 46, *In* Parks Canada, 1973. Environmental analysis. A review of selected techniques. Planning Studies Section, Planning Division. National Parks Branch, Parks Canada, Ottawa. 144 pp.

Hirsch, A. 1980. The baseline study as a tool in environmental impact assessment. *In* A compendium of selected papers on ecology and environmental impact assessment. Institute for Resource and Environmental Studies, Dalhousie Univ., Halifax, NS. 99 pp.

Leopold, L. B., F. E. Clarke, B. B. Hanshaw, and J. R. Balsley. 1971. A procedure for evaluating environmental impact. U.S. Dept. Int. Geol. Surv. Circ. 645. 13 pp.

Lucas, H. L. 1976. Some statistical aspects of assessing environmental impact. Proc. Workshop on the biological significance of environmental impacts. R. K. Sharma, J. D. Buffington, and J. T. McFadden, eds. Nuclear Regulatory Commission, Washington, DC.

Manning, I. P. A., and P. F. N. de V. Moss. 1976. Appendix C. Environmental studies. Report on ecology. Report on feasibility of producing hydroelectric power on the Luapula river. Watermeyer, Legge, Piesold, and Uhlman (Lusaka) in assoc. with Merz and McLelaln (Lusaka).

McHarg. I. 1969. Design with nature. The Falcon Press, Philadelphia, PA. *In* Parks, Canada, 1973. Environmental analysis. A review of selected techniques. Planning Studies Section, Planning Division. National Parks Branch, Parks Canada, Ottawa. 144 pp.

Milledge, A., and E. G. Gallop. 1978. Environmental assessment: the Florida perspective. *In* S. Bendix and H. G. Graham, eds. Environmental assessment, approaching maturity. Ann Arbor Science Publishers Inc. Ann Arbor, MI. 288 pp.

Munn, R. E., ed. 1975. Environmental impact assessment: Principles and procedures. SCOPE Rep. No. 5, Toronto, Canada. 160 pp.

Nelson, J. G. 1973. Some background thoughts on environmental impact statements. Park News 9(2):34–44.

Odell, R. 1980. Environmental awakening. Ballinger, Cambridge, MA. 330 pp.

Odum, E. P., and J. L. Cooley. 1980. Ecosystem profile analysis and performance curves as tools for assessing environmental impact. Pp. 94–102, *In* Symposium Proceedings, biological evaluation of environmental impacts, FWS/OBS-80–26, Council on Environmental Quality. Washington, DC.

Parks Canada. 1973. Environmental analysis. A review of selected techniques. Planning Studies Section, Planning Division. National Parks Branch, Parks Canada. Ottawa. 144 pp.

Schindler, D. W. 1978. Unpublished remarks presented at wildlife meeting, Can. Soc. Zool. University of Western Ontario, London. 11 pp. mimeo.

Stover, L. V. 1972. Environmental impact assessment: a procedure. *In* Environmental analysis, a review of selected techniques. Parks Canada, Document 1042OUC, June 1973, 145 pp.

Truett, J. C. 1979. Pre-impact process analysis: design for mitigation. Pp. 355–360, *In* Mitigation symposium: A national workshop on mitigating losses of fish and wildlife habitats. Gen. Tech. Rep. RU-65, Rocky Mountain For. Range Exp. Sta., Fort Collins, Co.

U.S. Fish and Wildlife Service. 1976. Final environmental statement. Operation of the national wildlife refuge system. U.S. Fish Wild. Serv. Dep. Int. Washington, DC.

World Commission on Environment and Development. 1987. Our common future. Oxford University Press, Oxford and New York.

Zigman, P. E. 1978. The California Environmental Quality Act and its implementation. *In* S. Bendix and H. G. Graham, eds. Environmental assessment, approaching maturity. Ann Arbor Science Publisher Inc. Ann Arbor, MI. 288 pp.

Recommended Readings

Beanlands, G., and P. Duinker. 1983. An ecological framework for environmental impact assessment in Canada. Institute for Resource and Environmental Studies, Dalhousie Univ., Halifax, NS. 132 pp.

An invaluable review of ecological problems and processes applicable to wildlife workers everywhere. The examples are Canadian.

Bendix, S., and H. Graham, eds. 1978. Environmental assessment, approaching maturity. Ann Arbor Science Publisher Inc., Ann Arbor, MI. 228 pp.

Ghiselin, J. 1980. Preparing and evaluating environmental assessments and related documents. Chapter 25 *In* Wildlife management techniques manual. S. D. Schemnitz, ed. The Wildl. Soc., Washington, DC. 686 pp.

A balanced consideration of most wildlife aspects in relation to environmental impact.

X WILDLIFE INTERNATIONAL—Aid Policies, Problems, and Management

Most people visiting the United Nations plaza in New York City are unaware of the massive complexity of the United Nations Development Program (UNDP) (Figure 10.1). The political arm of the UN dwarfs the development arm, both in budget and in the number of people involved, yet the programs approved and monitored through the UNDP reach every facet of progress in our underdeveloped world. There are three UN "family" agencies that may be involved with wildlife or related concerns: the Food and Agriculture Organization of the United Nations (FAO) in Rome; the United Nations Educational Scientific and Cultural Organization (UNESCO) in Paris; and the United Nations Environmental Program (UNEP) in Nairobi.

FAO involvement in wildlife can take several forms. Assistance from personnel in Rome includes reviewing and drafting wildlife legislation. FAO's work can involve reviews of wildlife policy, administration, and management through FAO's wildlife and parks office, whose staff sometimes drafts operational plans. Wildlife representatives from FAO customarily become involved in overall country programming through UNDP. Projects in progress may also be reviewed by an FAO or UNDP representative, and short studies leading to development programs are often carried out over a period of several weeks. Larger projects established through FAO are a part of the UNDP country's program for the jurisdiction in which the project is located. Such projects are usually management oriented and are seldom specific to the wildlife resource alone. They most often involve tourism, agriculture, or even several resource bases. In other instances, FAO provides wildlife or park advisors who work very closely with the governments of underdeveloped countries and who may work directly with wildlife and local staff in the field. FAO also provides instructors for universities or technical schools such as the African College of Wildlife Management in Tanzania.

261

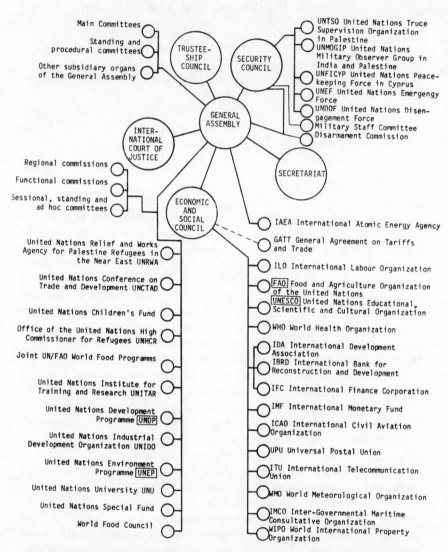

Figure 10.1 An abbreviated organizational chart of the United Nations system. The units which may be involved with wildlife are boxed. Overall administration of wildlife oriented development programs is a responsibility. The interlocking nature of funding and ancillary support and cooperation tends to make the autonomous agencies such as FAO, responsible organizations not only to UNDP but to other countries both developed and underdeveloped

(Courtesy, C.J. Lankester, UNDP, New York, Chart dated December 1979.)

The primary wildlife concern for UNESCO is the biosphere reserve network, which is directed toward the preservation of ecosystems. It protects their resident and seasonal wildlife populations while still encouraging economic development, as explained by Dasmann (1981). In some cases, a UNESCO scientific advisor may become involved in wildlife or parks development through his advice to the ministries involved, or through personal contact with UNDP projects or experts on the ground. UNESCO also responds to requests from underdeveloped countries for short-term consultant studies similar to those done by FAO. The studies may be involved with land-use complexes, tourism, or national parks, which by their nature often involve wildlife in relation to the establishment of World Heritage sites.

The youngest (1972) of the three family groups with some wildlife conservation interest is UNEP. Its involvement with wildlife is not as direct as that of FAO and UNESCO, as UNEP concerns tend to be of a human-environmental nature, although it does have wildlife experts providing advice when asked. UNEP cooperates regularly with other agencies. It also assists the cause of wildlife conservation through the International Union for the Conservation of Nature (IUCN) in Gland, Switzerland.

The IUCN was established by UNESCO in 1942 and has become the international organization that regularly reports on the status of rare and endangered species. Its scientists (and nonscientists) play important roles in establishing national park policies throughout the world, and to many people in the developed world the IUCN is the agency that provides wildlife with an international image. The several commissions of the IUCN cover a broad area of interest pertaining to ecosystem survival, diversity, and the sustained use of natural resources. In 1951 the IUCN was, to a great extent, responsible for the establishment of the World Wildlife Fund. The IUCN is not a member of the UN family and depends to a considerable extent on public support throughout the world for its funding.

Some developed countries provide ''associate experts'' to international aid projects. These people are usually well trained but often lack the longer-term professional experience of those normally employed as experts by a UN family organization. They are obtained through bilateral aid and assigned, on agreement of the host country, to a particular project or special development problem. Many countries also support volunteer aid organizations such as the U.S. Peace Corps, the VSO (voluntary service overseas) in the United Kingdom, Canadian CUSO (Canadian University Service Overseas), and the UN volunteers from UNDP. People working for such agencies are usually recent university graduates or comparatively untrained or inexperienced professionals who offer their services to developing countries through their own countries' volunteer agencies. They also may be retired professionals who volunteer their considerable experience. On occasion, such people may be engaged in a park, wildlife or fish management project, or a special conservation program for two years or more.

Bilateral aid in wildlife management is particularly important on the international wildlife scene. Canada has the Canadian International Development Agency (CIDA), the U.S. has the Agency for International Development (AID), and other developed countries have their organizations specified by appropriate acronyms. Much expertise in wildlife and parks matters also comes from Great Britain, West Germany, the Netherlands, and France. The Scandinavian countries (especially Sweden), New Zealand, and Australia may also provide assistance. Not all underdeveloped countries are willing to accept aid from all developed jurisdictions. The matter of neocolonialism, or influence through economic control, is a concern with some host countries, as is political ideology. A particular jurisdiction might accept a national from an "unfriendly" country through a UN agency and yet not accept aid from that country. It should be understood that bilateral aid is not completely altruistic. One of the reasons that donor countries are willing to help the underdeveloped countries is that trade ties may be established allowing for the donor both future markets and the import of goods, including raw materials. The so-called north-south dialogue popular with many politicians today is a part of the desire to increase trade opportunities that represent potential future sales to the large and increasing populations of underdeveloped countries. The image donor countries have in the Third World is often so important to their governments that they tend to seek bilateral aid avenues with underdeveloped nations and often shun multilateral approaches, even through such programs may be available. Sharing the development limelight with other countries or with an international agency is not as desirable as taking full credit! Far more money is available and spent through bilateral aid than through UNDP.

The international development picture is complicated, in its politics, funding arrangements, management, and number and variety of projects. For example, in 1972 when one of the authors was on foreign assignment Zambia had 146 visiting experts on 43 UNDP or other UN agency projects alone, besides the bilateral aid programs and aid in research through universities outside the country. Wildlife, fisheries, and parks were only a small component of this overall aid picture. The number of projects and experts only tells a part of the story, for the projects have counterpart experts as well as associate experts, technical and clerical help, and one or more guiding management committees. Usually a wildlife or park development operation is initiated by UNDP after a host country understands it has a specific problem or when it wishes to provide assistance to one of its endangered or undeveloped resource potentials. International aid offices are contacted locally, and a consultant or a group of consultants eventually reviews the situation. Recommendations favorable to both the host country and the counterpart agency (usually a wildlife, parks, tourism, or game department, authority, or ministry) go to the UN family agency sponsoring the review and to the regional UNDP office. Perhaps further reviews will take place, but if the host country and the UN agency approve, a project document (called a plan of operation) is eventually drafted and considered by the regional resident representative of UNDP (an ambassadorial status position). Others in the regional office, senior people in the UN agency, interagency groups, and the UNDP office in New York also review the plan. If the wildlife project is implemented, it may call for certain experts for specific periods, counterparts, associate experts, buildings, equipment, cooperative research, and management assistance. A number of designated inputs from the UN, other organizations, and agencies in the host country itself may also be specified in the plan of operation.

Competition is sometimes keen between UN agencies and bilateral aid offices in underdeveloped countries. On occasion both a UN agency and a bilateral aid representative will compete to establish the same project. This may well confuse the host country officials who represent a potential counterpart agency or a planning ministry in government. In 1974, a senior UNDP official asked why the Canadians (CIDA) believed they could do a better job than FAO with a range-wildlife program. Both were involved in the same potential project, but each had its own approach. The same query was repeated by people in the Ministry of Finance and Planning, including visiting expert advisors to the ministry. The Canadians won out, and the KREMU (Kenya Rangeland Ecological Monitoring Unit) project replaced the FAO project that was in progress and under review. In an earlier situation (1967), a Canadian CIDA representative ceased to be interested in a project in Zambia when it appeared that the operation was heading toward a multilateral approach. Sometimes competition even shows up among UN agencies themselves, and often one agency representative in the field will openly criticize the work of another, even in reports to senior officers. Such infighting and disagreement is discouraging to host country officials. Also discouraging are the lack of clear intent expressed by representatives of some donor agencies, and the conflicting advice that often is expressed by a myriad of donor experts.

Wildlife problems are often bypassed in Third World countries even if they seem crucial to a wildlife expert from the United States or Canada. In underdeveloped areas they are considered to be less important than agriculture, education, communication, trade, energy, and a host of other development needs, as they probably should be. When financial credit, starvation, and productivity are all serious socioeconomic and political concerns, wildlife must be directly related to those fundamentals if it is to be included in planning and development. One only needs to remember the developmental history of the North American continent to realize this was the basic pattern here as well.

The interagency meetings of UNDP and the country programming exercises prevent some conflict and turmoil in international aid, but there is still confusion. To complicate matters further, UNDP development projects may have experts from six or seven different countries communicating, with difficulty, in two or more languages. The counterpart personnel of the host country, several associate experts, and others acting as clerks and support personnel complete the project staff. There may also be fifty or more dues-paying member countries of a UN agency, each wanting a share of the trade input for development, and each wanting representation at the head office. Most are underdeveloped countries wanting to influence the manner in which aid should be directed and who should get it! The wildlife agencies and/or senior officials of underdeveloped countries have their problems. They are invariably understaffed, undertrained and underfunded. Politically, they are weaker than the professionals representing agriculture, forestry, finance, and many other government agencies. Usually land planning has proceeded without input from a wildlife agency (except recently in Kenya), and unfortunately for all, wildlife has suffered and will continue to suffer because of it. If this sounds familiar, it should. The wildlife biologist from Canada or the U.S. will find reflections of the same complex, professional microcosms in an underdeveloped country that he finds at home. Wildlife organizations everywhere are no better, or worse, than their personnel and their progress no greater than the political will of their masters. Whether it be permanent secretaries, their deputies, directors, and wardens in Zambia, or general managers, heads, and wardens in Ethiopia, administrators of wildlife policy face similar problems. There is a feeling of familiarity in the offices and field stations of wildlife agencies almost anywhere in the world.

In addition to the UN family, the IUCN, and bilateral aid, universities and nongovernment organizations (NGOs) may also be involved in cooperative wildlife research and management in underdeveloped countries. The African Wildlife (Leadership) Foundation, whose main office is in Washington D.C., has its African office in Nairobi. Among its efforts is a commitment to education; with FAO and other agencies, it helps support the African College of Wildlife Management at Mweka, Tanzania. Organizations such as the New York Zoological Society and the Frankfurt Zoological Society also support research, while the Serengeti Research Institute in Tanzania has produced some of the continent's finest ecological research.

Wildlife Policy and Management: Some Concerns in Africa

There have been hundreds of wildlife and general ecological experts in Africa in the past and there still are a great many, yet problems remain. Many problems are becoming even more acute. From the press and popular writings we tend to get a rather romantic picture of a magnificent wildlife resource being rapidly decimated through mismanagement, trophy hunting, and poaching. The word *endangered* is usually present somewhere in the narrative, and this is what we tend to key on. African wildlife is endangered; but is it?

Perhaps our starting point should be an understanding of what is happening to the land and the people of many African countries, for wildlife populations are responding naturally to both human population increase and the resultant land-use changes. Although there are thousands of local and regional complexes, a general view of Africa south of the Sahara (except the Republic of South Africa) is as follows:

Soon after World War II human populations began to increase because of improved medical and health facilities, disease control, and limited industrial and agricultural development. Population distribution also changed, and a rural-to-urban migration surfaced with large concentrations of people gathering around cities and towns to obtain employment and reap the "benefits" of Western life. Through a new communications explosion, most could now learn of the wonderful gadgetry available. Transistors in the bush, new paths or roads for bicycles and four-wheel drives, and increased contact with others outside the village or tribal unit made millions more aware and caused hundreds of thousands to have aspirations new to the people and their cultures. Population increases soon outstripped developments, and in many cases government policy was heading toward a cultural breakdown, which often included an altered lifestyle. Divided loyalties were not in favor with newly independent governments. The influence of the Christian church, tribal chiefs, and elders was often undercut to direct people toward a single, nationalistic objective: to build the economic resource base and infrastructure of the country, everyone's country. The old ways were often lost, and among them sometimes was a successful subsistence means of living. Dependency on governments increased; development, good or bad, was slow primarily because of a culturally induced inefficiency in production and management inherent in the people themselves.

Population growth continues to forge ahead of development, and efforts to move people back to the land are in progress in many areas. But as the land mass has neither increased in area nor improved in fertility, the competition for land also grows daily. As populations explode, land-use changes are occurring in an ad hoc manner, responding to apparent agricultural needs. Agricultural production schemes on large scale bases are not always economically successful, nor do they necessarily meet the needs for a majority of the human population. Regardless of the successes or failures, wild land is being lost, and wild animals compete with humans to a greater extent each day.

Wildlife must become a competitive source of economic benefit to both governments and local people if the resource is to survive. Nationally, countries need sources of foreign currency, so wildlife must provide an economic return through both consumptive and aesthetic (nonconsumptive) uses. The people must benefit locally from the existence and use of the resource. They must understand that the social and/or direct benefits received are obtained *because of* the wildlife resource. The inability to direct parts of the wildlife resource base into the market or national economy is a primary problem facing those responsible for the wildlife of Africa. Until wildlife pays its way it will not be recognized as a viable renewable resource to manage and will continue to be upstaged in government planning by other natural resource bases. This really means that when it comes to wildlife and people, it is people who must come first. It may be that wildlife can be used to help a people, and if so, wildlife will be maintained. If not, wildlife may be lost. This philosophy, difficult as it may be to implement, is also logical in view of the indigenous African's utilitarian attitude toward wildlife. Wildlife cannot compete in an open market economy, and its uses must be rigidly controlled.

Allied to this basic problem is the inadequate representation of the wildlife resource base in land-use planning and primary resource development. The potential to produce both protein and export income through utilization should be measured against capital and recurrent expenditures and the production levels employed by agricultural and other primary resource people. Utilization may include subsistence and safari hunting, game viewing, or cropping. In Kenya, the Range Ecological Monitoring Unit's planning has, for perhaps the first time in Africa, provided a wildlife resource with a data base that should allow it to be included as a partner in both land-use and economic planning. This may be a first step in doing something positive for a wildlife resource, but the program is restricted to Kenya, and to date it has not been entirely successful. Just north of Kenya, in Ethiopia, a great wildlife resource continues to suffer because it has not been shown to be economically viable and because it is not included as an important entity in government planning. This is the case in various degrees in many African countries south of the Sahara.

If all we know about wildlife in underdeveloped countries is what we see on television or read about in advertisements, we might think the greatest problem is that some species are considered endangered. Endangered species may well continue to exist long after much of Africa's wildlife resource is gone if the world concentrates only on rhinos and leopards! Endangered species do exist, and it is not illogical to attempt to save them. If the attention of the world is focused only on a few endangered animals, however, it will become increasingly difficult to provide support to those species that constitute the bulk of the resource base. It is even questionable, for some species, whether the Convention on International Trade in Endangered Species (CITES) and the resultant legislation or the annual IUCN publicity on endangered species is always entirely positive. Do legislating and publicizing save or destroy? Or both? Making an animal more valuable because of its rarity clearly creates markets, although they may be illegal, and poachers will attempt to fill those markets. Rhino horn is not declining in value, and the spotted cat market is bullish although often illegal and usually restricted. Profits are limited to fewer people because of new legislation and better enforcement, but the animals remain vulnerable and underground distribution continues. Perhaps another method might have been more successful. One alternative approach would include the rhinos and leopards in nonconsumptive use and management programs, with occasional consumptive use through trophy hunting, with the returns clearly shown to be used for the public's benefit. If the people actually realized benefits and understood their source, maybe they would help to maintain the resource. We will not have an opportunity to measure the value of this stratagem because many species are already sheltered and immune to most management except preservation.

There are a great many other problems. One involves staffing, training, and education. After independence, gradual Africanization of the civil service in many countries became a political necessity. Similar staffing by indigenous people occurred in other postcolonial countries in Asia. Obviously it was more desirable from consistency and continuity standpoints to staff wildlife posts in Zambia with Zambians and in Kenya with Kenyans. For thirty years after World War II, American, British, Canadian, German, and other nationals trained in animal ecology drifted into Africa and back out. They started projects in development, management, or research and then disappeared, leaving only reports behind. Impact studies and development schemes have invariably been directed by non-Africans. Training and fellowship components of projects have been of limited success. If an important government ministry needed someone with advanced training (beyond high school), a wildlife-trained Fellow might be lost to his own ministry by moving him to a more critical post. Others on wildlife projects would more often than not be lost at the close of a project. There are many other fields more attractive to young men and women than wildlife management. All professions were new opportunities at independence, and few young people even knew what being a wildlife professional might allow them to do! These problems, coupled with the lack of money to provide training and the difficulties sometimes brought about by major changes in government, as in Ethiopia since 1970, have resulted in wildlife agencies that are often not staffed with the necessary well-trained professionals. Frequently, a senior position is held by someone educated and trained in another discipline or by a graduate of a low to medium-grade diploma program like those provided in Chad (Garoua) or Tanzania (Mweka). With improved education and training for present and future staff members, the operation of many wildlife agencies will become more efficient in day-to-day work and more competitive in influencing policy within whatever framework may exist. Certainly this is another key to wildlife's future in Africa.

We could examine other problems: the need for an improved data base; better monitoring; improved interagency cooperation; the role of energy and fuel requirements versus forest cover and wildlife; the strengths and weaknesses of cropping and game farming or safari hunting. Still, three concerns are the most important in understanding basic wildlife policy and management problems in Africa today:

1. Wildlife is not usually a competitive source of economic benefit at either the national or local level.
2. Wildlife is usually inadequately represented in land-use planning and primary resource development schemes.
3. There are too few professionally trained wildlife administrators, managers, and research biologists.

The necessity for the wildlife resource to provide an economic incentive if it is to continue to exist has been stated repeatedly by professional wildlifers familiar with African conditions. The idea is not new, and to many African professionals it has been, and still is, obvious. Since progress has been slow, this challenge still awaits anyone who may have the opportunity to work with African wildlife. The present multiple resource, integrated management experiment in Zambia's Luangwa Valley (the Luangwa Integrated Resource Development Project), which is actively supported by President Kenneth

Kaunda, is an example of the kind of progressive wildlife approach that at least holds some promise for the future.

Wildlife Management: the Status in Central Europe and Elsewhere

Wildlife policy and management in Africa have evolved recently from colonial systems, but have been influenced by the veterinary services people because of the importance of tse-tse, rinderpest, and other diseases harbored in wildlife species that are transmitted to humans or domestic livestock. In contrast, the Central European system has been evolving for hundreds of years and reflects the primary right of the landowners to reduce game to possession. Bubenik (1976) has enumerated the key points of several systems in Central Europe as follows:

The concept of the central European hunting law before and after *World War II.*

1. The right to reduce the game into possessions belongs still to the landowner, if his land has the minimum acreage of *revier*. For using his right he must be an accredited hunter. This means that:

   a. He has to apply to attend a special educational course for accredited hunters, pass the examination and, in some countries, must be a mandatory member of the hunters' organization
      The applicant must prove that he has no criminal record. The certificate of accredited hunter is also his gun licence, and he can buy any hunting gun (in a communist-led country only a shotgun) without any certificate. In countries such as Czechoslovakia, Poland, Hungary or Yugoslavia, a special certificate for buying rifles and ammunition is necessary. In USSR it is very difficult to get such a permit.

   b. Education is theoretical and takes about 30 to 65 hours. The disciplines are: hunting and conservation laws (in communist countries also basic knowledge in Marxism-Leninism), biology, basic physiology and anatomy of game, game ecology, hunting and management operations, game diseases, feeding of game, keeping and using of hunting dogs, gun types, mechanisms and ballistics. Also included is mandatory training in shooting with gun and rifle. In some countries, at intervals of some years, mandatory shooting at a target is ordered. In Fennoscandia, nobody can buy a moose license unless he presents a new certificate from an official shooting station, proving that he has hit the necessary minimum score of a moving moose target. Generally, the applicant can pass the examination shortly after the course. In Czechoslovakia he must voluntarily serve one year as a helper in a *revier*, before he can apply for examination.

2. The *revier*-owner must have at least three years experience as an accredited hunter. In Czechoslovakia, he has to attend a special course for *revier*-manager and pass a new examination. The *revier*-owner is liable for damage caused by game on crop or forest.

3. A *revier* with small game, e.g. winged game, furbearers and roe deer, must be leased for six years; with large game, for nine years. The deposit of a one-year fee must be put into a special account in case the contract is cancelled during the time when feeding of game is necessary.

4. The game-feeding is mandatory. The hunters' organizations have the right to check and see if the game is being properly fed.

5. Inventory of game (not only census of numbers) is mandatory. In some countries it is done under official supervision. The "harvest or shooting" plan prescribes the number of game in both sexes and age, or the "social classes." About 50 percent of the planned kill is the class of fawns and calves. With few exceptions, no one sex is protected, but according to the structure of specific species, one or other sex could be more or less hunted.

6. The *revier*-owner is liable for not fulfilling the plan or for overshooting. In both cases this could be the reason for cancelling the contract: especially he could lose his certificate of accredited hunter.

7. Species belonging to trophy game have a mandatory yearly trophy show, to avoid overhunting of the best breeders.

8. The *revier*-owner or his deputy, and/or the members of the hunting society, have the right to kill dogs and cats preying, or being, in the *revier*.

9. The department of game and the hunters' organizations are stratified after the same pattern. On the top is the government department and the presidium of the hunters' organization. Then there are provincial, regional and district offices. Experienced hunters and accredited game managers can be elected representatives for game management with a rank similar to the stratification pattern of the department of game. These *jagermeisters* cooperate with the departments and are responsible for the game planning and management.

10. Very large *reviers* must employ gamekeepers. In some countries they are organized in labor unions.

11. There is a mandatory search for wounded animals.

12. By collective hunts on small game, the number of hunting dogs per distinct number of hunters is also prescribed to avoid losses. In Czechoslovakia, with about 130,000 hunters, there are 40,000 purebred hunting dogs.

13. The game belongs to the *revier*-owner. He can utilize or sell it. The trophy and viscera belong to the hunter as his hunting right.

14. The hunters' organizations have their own hunters' court. Any offence to the hunting law or hunting ethics must be handled independently from the judiciary procedure, before the hunters' court. If this court orders that the

certificate of an accredited hunter should be removed, nobody can reverse this decree and the offender is expelled from the hunters' fraternity. He automatically loses the right to possess hunting guns. The number of accredited hunters varies from country to country: between 1.0 up to 2.5 percent of the whole population, or about 2.5 to 5 percent of all citizens in the age allowed by law for hunting persons.

The *revier* system and the hunting regulations, as mentioned above, represent surely the most efficient game management. The most important points of this system are the mandatory courses, examinations and accreditation. These benefits were acknowledged just a few years ago by other countries with a licensing system such as Switzerland or Fennoscandia. Just recently, France also introduced the mandatory hunter's examination and the hunter's certificate in order to raise the hunters' morale and discipline and to ensure an adequate supply of game.

The *revier* system is the most economic for other reasons. The *revier*-owner has so many duties before the law that he must be year-long in the *revier*, to feed, make inventory, and to familiarize himself with the ecology and behavior of his game, so that he will be capable of shooting the prescribed number and social class of game. For this reason the open seasons are long enough, i.e., for small game about two or three months, for large game six to seven months.

One benefit to wildlife researchers should be quite clear under such a system. All necessary data are available to allow for intensive harvest management. We often depend upon the cooperation of interested sportsmen in North America, but hunter, researcher, and manager can operate as a unit under the European system. In much of Africa, however, almost all biological data are lost from safari, sport, and subsistence hunting operations. The only research materials available come from a few research and management projects that may cover short periods of time. We should recall that for hundreds of years the existence of animals on a European land holding has been tantamount to legal possession. Today, this type of possession continues in relation to both state and private land in Europe. How much simpler this makes regulatory management! The restricted use and disciplined approach in central Europe must be considered a success in relation to several species and their habitats even though intensive land use practices have reduced other species. Many still remain after hundreds of years of exploitation and perturbation. The intensive management common to the European system is explained further by Nagy and Benaze (1973), who indicate that game ranching, winter feeding, habitat management (plantings), game-damage control and payment, and the maintenance of salaried professional game keepers by hunters' associations are among the approaches used in Hungary. Nagy and

Benaze noted harvests by 1100 hunters on 500,000 ha (1,250,000 acres). Total harvest was 11,400 hare, 11,120 pheasant, 4,250 partridge, and 187 roe deer. Foreign hunters shooting for paid fees may kill up to 100 pheasants a day or, if they wish to pay more per bird, up to 200 a day! It is also interesting that these authors indicated there was " . . . little if any, anti-hunting or anti-hunter sentiment." They attributed this lack of "anti" sentiment to the fact that hunters are disciplined and "devoted to customs and traditions which tend to deemphasize the killing aspect of hunting." They described ritualization following the kill and emphasized that hunters are "devoted and successful game managers." But that was in 1973; since then there has been growing anti-hunting sentiment in much of Europe, some generated by animal right groups and some by those opposed to the elitist nature of the sport.

For Czechoslovakia, the intensive management of wildlife and land by hunting associations is reviewed by Newman (1979). He indicates the importance of determining population densities through censuses to aid in establishing quotas. As in Hungary, it is the hunter who is the important game manager, although professional game keepers are employed.

In [West] Germany, where most of the land available to hunting is privately owned (versus state ownership in Hungary and Czechoslovakia which is now changing), the revier system is in effect. About 0.4 percent of the population hunts, and game may be marketed. Foresters and hunters have a close relationship, and forest managers also serve as hunting managers. Most hunters (86 percent) belong to the German Hunter Society, and until recently were respected by the nonhunting public.

Although no one person and no public authority own the game in Norway, landowners have an exclusive right to hunt and trap on their own property. On much state owned land, hunting and trapping are open to all citizens on payment of a fee. On other classes of state land, however, the number of hunters may be restricted by the control of special licenses. Game management in Norway is conducted primarily through the approximately 450 Game Boards existing at the community level, as well as the state organized wildlife bodies in each of the 18 counties. Most research information on management is provided by the privately operated Norwegian Institute for Nature Research (NINA), which obtains much of its funding from the state and is administered by the directorate for Nature Management under the Ministry of Environment. Hunting associations are prominent, and obligatory exams must be taken by first-time hunters both in Norway and in Sweden, as has been the practice in Finland and Denmark for some time. Management activities are related to regulatory measures (harvest management), agricultural and forest damage control, depredation control, habitat management in the context of forestry and agriculture, translocation and total protection.

"In Finland matters pertaining to hunting fall under the jurisdiction of the Department of Fishing and Hunting in the Ministry of Agriculture and Forestry. The Department supervises and regulates hunting, game management and the marketing of game, handles any questions arising from damage inficted by game, and issues special hunting permits and regulations. The Ministry of Environment serves as the highest authority for those species protected under the Nature Protection Act. The authorities responsible for the enforcement of the Hunting Act are the police and game-wardens under the jurisdiction of the county governments, the Frontier Guard Establishment, the Customs, and National Board of Forestry.

The Hunters' Central Organization (Metsastajain Keskusjarjesto) was officially established in 1982 to look after the affairs of hunting. Run by the hunters themselves, its chief tasks are to distribute information, provide advice, and make the practical arrangements for game preservation. Earlier the comparable tasks were the responsibility of the Finnish Hunter's League (Suomen Netsastajaliitto-Finlands Jagarforbund r.y.), which was established in 1931 and which continues to act in a non-obligatory way as a link between hunting organizations in different parts of the country. Alongside it there operates, likewise on a voluntary basis, the Finnish Association of Hunters and Fishermen (Suomen metsastajaja Kalastajalitto) founded in 1946.

The Hunting Act presently in force dates from 1962. The underlying premise in Finland is that the right to hunt in any area is the property of the owner of the land. The right to hunt can be transferred to another for a specified period, 5–25 years, by means of a written rental agreement. In this way those without land are assured the possibility of hunting. The holder of the right to hunt may also surrender his right to another in the form of a permit. Often the species of game that can be hunted and the bag limits are specified in the permit along with the time period for which it is granted. Separate provision is made for hunting on state lands. There hunting takes place either by special permit or by payment of a rental fee. In addition, in the County of Lapland and in certain municipalities of Oulu County, the local population has the right to hunt in state lands in their own municipality. Every Finnish citizen has the right to hunt on the sea outside of village boundaries and in coastal waters and on islands belonging to the state. Likewise the residents of a municipality have the right to hunt on large open lakes outside of village boundaries and on islands there belonging to the state.

In Finland game management is entrusted to the hunters and is supported by the state out of funds accumulated from game fees. The national Board of Forestry participates in and promotes the work of game management, by setting aside special areas of forest as game reserves, for example, where the attempt is made to combine the different interests of game and forest management. Nowadays game management means modifying the environment so that it better serves the needs of game-by feeding in winter when the natural food supply is insufficient, by restocking for the vitalization of a declining population or establishing of a new one, and regulating hunting in such a way that the structure of the game population becomes more favorable and that unintentional overharvesting does not occur.

In 1942 the Finnish Game Foundation established an institute for the purpose of game research. This institute was taken over by the state in 1964, becoming the Finnish Game Research Institute. Today its activities are continued by the Game and Fisheries Research Institute, founded in 1971 under the Ministry of Agriculture and Forestry.'' (Ermala, 1980)

Elsewhere in the world, wildlife management is either increasing (e.g. the USSR) or is primarily relegated to the preservation of areas and species (several South American countries and India). The situation in the Soviet Union has many parallels with developing countries as illustrated by Komarov (1980). Poaching is rampant, and military and party officials have exploited game populations even on nature preserves. One would expect change to occur here and in eastern Europe as the influence of the communist party declines and ''democratization'' filters down to use of the wildlife resource. In China, the recognition of wildlife conservation as being socially, economically, and ecologically important to the country and the people is resulting in a slow increase in the training of professionals and an effort to upgrade the quality of wildlife education. For many countries, the recognition of wild animals as valuable cultural, social, and economic entities has come too late. In some, there may still be time for species like the giant panda (*Ailuropoda melanoleuca*) or the snow leopard, which may occur in sufficient numbers to ensure their continued existence, given proper management attention.

In summary, wildlife policy and management around the globe tend to be grouped into intensive, extensive, and developing categories. In Europe, where the system has evolved over a longer period than anywhere else, management is most intensive, but policy often tends to be more elitist than democratic. In North America, management is primarily extensive, whereas policy with few exceptions tends to be democratic, although this is changing. Some countries, such as the Republic of South Africa, fall somewhere in between the European and North American situations. In the underdeveloped countries, both management systems and policy are evolving. Whether human population pressures, land-use changes, and industrialization will restrict the effectiveness of improvements in wildlife conservation now in progress is a question only time will answer. It seems likely that what now is a beginning in many jurisdictions has arrived too late.

Problems to Ponder

Management systems that are implemented result from policy, and policies are reflections of economic, social and ecological complexes. What is done is more likely a reflection of what can be done, rather than what needs to be done. It is reality. To help us understand why things are as they are, we need to explore far beyond what may seem usual to the wildlife manager. We here present outlines of two examples of wildlife management complexes in under-developed areas; one deals with a country and one describes a large mammal problem. There are hundreds of similar examples in Indonesia, the Caribbean, and South America as well as Africa.

The Country: Botswana (The Complex as of 1984)

Botswana is a landlocked country of 582,000 km. Most of the country is desert. Rainfall is erratic and averages 475 mm per year, but neither the distribution nor the timing is dependable. Drought cycles are an expected phenomenon. It is the least densely populated state in the world except for Mongolia. There were 647,000 people in Botswana in 1971 and there were about 975,000 in 1984. Humans are increasing through ingress (as refugees) and through natural reproduction at a rate of 2.5 percent to 3.0 percent per year.

Cattle and Botswana are almost synonymous. Except for a few minority groups, such as the Bushman, cattle are traditional with the Batswana and have been present for thousands of years. Today, cattle represent the most important political entity of the land-based resources present. Traditionally, they are the basis of the sociological complex on tribal grazing lands. Family heads consider a specified number of animals to be important in their society (15 +), but since they expect to lose about one out of three in a prolonged drought, they must keep a third more cattle during periods between droughts. Thus an already overstocked range is taxed still further. More people and cattle are pressing farther into the Kalahari, and desertification occurs in miniature around the boreholes, which are increasing in number each year. The "Tribal Grazing Land Policy" is designed to control the distance between boreholes, as well as other aspects of traditional grazing, but it has not been 100 percent effective. Agricultural research in Botswana has clearly demonstrated that maintaining fewer cattle on grassland allows for a higher biomass production and better survival through a more efficient conversion. However, the custom of maintaining numbers through the addition of cattle in nondrought periods is strong, and it is the method "proven" over centuries. Change is not likely.

There is another side to the cattle "coin" as well. Private landholders control much land as ranches. In Botswana, there are few investment opportunities for the individual with sums of money to put to work. Cattle represent an available form of investment that has always been viewed as sound and is also allied to tradition. Thus a great many influential people have vested interests in them.

When cultural-traditional and political-economic positions are understood, the obvious concern to the wildlifer is that the one resource competing directly with cattle is wildlife.

In 1981, approximately $104 million (U.S.) were used in externally financed (bilateral and UNDP) development activities in Botswana. Of this, only about $81,000 went to the wildlife industry, which was estimated in a recent economic assessment to have a total economic value of about 20,811,000 pula or ± $18 million (U.S.). It appears that the wildlife industry, at present utilization rates, receives a disproportionately low share of aid dollars, for its value approximates 6–8 percent of the gross development product while the dollar input from external aid is considerably less than one percent.

The Department of Wildlife and National Parks does not enjoy a high positive image in Botswana. The department apparently has difficulty recruiting high-calibre graduates from the University of Botswana; they have not been able to send people for advanced training in adequate numbers, and the department has not been able to retain professional expatriates for long. They have also had difficulty in justifying higher budgets for needed expenditures and recruitment.

Botswana is a country where wildlife use, both consumptive and nonconsumptive, has been recognized since independence in 1966. In underdeveloped Africa, this country ranks next to Kenya in numbers of tourists, and its tourism is strongly wildlife based. Wild animals are clearly important, and the Department of Wildlife and National Parks has produced a draft utilization policy which articulates their value and outlines activities to help realize it. The available data base for large mammal numbers distribution is good. Air photo coverage is possible and the productivity of range areas understood.

In the face of these positive indices, development of other resources is occurring rapidly. Baselines cut across the Kalahari for diamond exploration. Cordon fences that prevent cattle from moving into wildlife areas also stop traditional wildlife movements to grasslands elsewhere. Aerial spraying in the Okavango Delta is gradually controlling the tse-tse fly (and perhaps much more), agriculture is increasing, and massive hydrological plans may eventually be implemented to alter the water regimen there. The possibility of a cross-Kalahari rail line is still present, and the ubiquitous cattle continue to increase.

Then what will happen to wildlife in Botswana? Wildlife managers have the cattle complex to solve. Is it logical to expect those in influential government positions to support an industry that might act negatively in an area where they have vested interests? After the tse-tse fly is controlled in the delta, will cattle and people increase there? What are the real effects of cordon fences on wildlife? How can a department competing with the cattle industry justify increased staff, expenditures, and training? What is the role of education and public relations in such a situation? Should the wildlife manager forget about these problems and protect what exists within park or reserve boundaries, or is the resource deserving of more than such a defeatist attitude?

Many knowledgeable wildlife people have worked in Botswana. There has been no lack of expertise. Botswana is but one example of an underdeveloped country with wildlife resource problems. If for no other reason than to assure that their approaches will be realistic, wildlifers should seek to understand as many of the concerns as possible relating to their subject in underdeveloped areas. Limited success may be possible for the realist. It is unlikely for the idealist.

The Resource: Elephants

Ivory art is almost as old as art itself. Ivory was an early medium for artisans carving for the religious and the wealthy. For centuries, ivory (primarily elephant) has been known as "white gold." Collecting was also linked to the slave trade in Africa, for what better means was there of getting it to coastal ports? Once there, the ivory and the slave could both be sold! Elephants themselves have played a major role in the tradition and ritual of indigenous people in Africa and Asia. They were domesticated early in Asia, perhaps 4,000 years ago, and are still used as beasts of burden. Elephant and man have been linked for thousands of years as man has exported and imported the animal and its parts almost worldwide. The ivory trade is now well documented. Between 1976 and 1980 it could have accounted for between 37,000 and 55,000 elephant fatalities, although as many as 20 percent may have been natural deaths.

The furor over the decline of elephants began in the early sixties, increased in volume, and reached a crescendo in the 1970s. Elephants were declared threatened, were listed in Appendix 11 of CITES, were the subject of detailed and complex regulations under legislation in the U.S. and other countries, and became a great fund raising symbol for WWF and other agencies. According to the media and their suppliers, elephants were being systematically eliminated by legal hunting, illegal hunting, and even by commercial harvesting. Conservationists, mostly nonprofessional, in the West misunderstood the problems of elephant-man-land and were largely to blame for the failure of what might have been responsible management, including cropping by some African game agencies. The momentum was toward preservation; save and don't kill.

There was also truth in the concern that elephants were declining. Slaughter was common. Poaching has been heavy in Kenya, Sudan, Zaire, Central African Republic, Zambia, and elsewhere. Sometimes it occurred when legal commercial harvesting stopped (see Chapter 8), but wherever it took place, it did so in the absence of sound policy enforcement. Social upheavals and military struggles also combined with illegal activities to decimate elephant numbers. This was true particularly in Uganda and to a lesser extent elsewhere. It is true that elephants were killed in an uncontrolled manner. They still are being killed, but in 1983 the problem lessened for a while. What preservationists did not understand was that elephants existed in many areas that were beyond the means of their range to support them. They often concentrated in protected areas and increased, destroyed their range, and sometimes died. This happened in Tsavo, where conservationist pressure had effectively prevented culling.

Guesstimates on elephant numbers were apparently low for several years. Figures given in 1968 for the Luangwa (Dodds and Patton 1968) for instance were only 20 percent of those presented by Naylor and Caughley et al. (1973) five years later after more intensive aerial surveys and statistical testing. Other estimates suggested populations of elephants much lower than actually existed. Douglas-Hamilton (1979) provided a conservative estimate of 1.3 million African elephants, including a number of low density, threatened populations particularly in west Africa, but also a number of high density, healthy populations. It is now clear and well accepted that the African elephant, although not endangered, may well be threatened. The 1989 population was estimated at only 622,000 animals. Despite this, countries like Botswana, South Africa and Zimbabwe have seen increases in their elephant populations. In 1989, CITES listed the African elephant on Appendix I, with any nation requesting a return to an Appendinx II listing required to ensure that certain management and trade control criteria would be met.

Wherever elephants and men exist near one another, man suffers. Darling (1960) wrote of the conflict in eastern Zambia. In 1967, gardens were still being destroyed. They still are today. Elephant control has been a main part of game department work in Africa since the departments were first established under early colonial regimes. Control units exist today as they have in the past, and the elephants continue to trample and eat villagers' crops, sometimes destroying a season's food in a single night. Elephants and people do not usually mix well.

Elephants are valuable. Tusks, tails, ears, and feet are commercially important, and the meat is edible and tasty. A single, average-size elephant may be valued at close to $2000 U.S. (in Zimbabwe, $1,800.00). When license fees, ivory, meat, and expenditures are considered, it suggests a conservative capital value of about $1.2 billion for the remaining elephants of Africa, although the nonconsumptive values are certainly far greater.

In most countries, less than half the elephants are located within park boundaries. Many parks are a burden on national economies, although some do provide profits. If park lands remained essentially inviolate, elephants probably could continue to exist in lower numbers and might never be really threatened as a species. But land for elephants, and other wildlife, may not always be an affordable luxury as human populations increase and more land is needed to produce food.

Elephants can be managed. When productivity is known, range carrying capacities understood, and populations and movements are also known, "excess" can be harvested from the herd(s) at a profit. This allows the range to be kept in reasonable condition, as in Kruger National Park (RSA) and in Zimbabwe. Within park or reserve boundaries, protection usually is a prime component of management. On an Africa-wide scale, the IUCN African Elephant and Rhino Specialist Group is approaching the continental elephant complex with realism and sanity. Lands for elephants will still decline; poaching will continue, political disturbances will occur again where elephants exist; and human populations will continue to increase. Management must relate closely to the spatial requirements of people first and elephants second. Where elephants exist, they should be husbanded and used for the benefit of the people.

Elephant management has to be a primary responsibility of African governments. All national and international (outside Africa) efforts, including conventions, legislation, and IUCN groups must serve to support with dollars and advise on sound internal African management and not controvert or emasculate its efforts. At the very least, the work of all nations concerned must be harmonious.

Bibliography
Ables, Ernest, D. S. Shen, and Q-Z. Xiao. 1982. Wildlife education in China. Wildl. Soc. Bull. 10(3):282–285.

Bubenik, A. B. 1976. Evolution of wildlife harvesting systems in Europe. Trans. Fed.-Prov. Wildl. Conf. 40:97–105.

Clutton-Brock, J. 1981. Domesticated animals from early times. Univ. Texas, Austin, TX. 208 pp.

Darling, F. F. 1960. Wildlife in an African territory. Oxford. London. 160 pp.

Dasmann, R. R. 1981. Wildlife biology. Second ed. John Wiley and Sons, New York, NY. 212 pp.

Dodds, D. G. 1976. Evolution of wildlife harvesting systems in Africa. Trans. Fed-Prov. Wildl. Conf. 40:100–113.

Dodds, D. G., and D. R. Patton. 1968. Wildlife and land-use survey of the Luangwa Valley. UNDP-FAO, No. TA2591, Rome, Italy, 176 pp.

Douglas-Hamilton, I. 1979. African elephant ivory trade study. Final Rep., IUCN-WWF-NYZS Elephant Survey and Conservation Program. 105 pp.

Ermala, Aslak. 1980. Hunting. Atlas of Finland. Folio 232–233. (Updated personal communication, October 1989.)

Gottschalk, John S. 1972. The German hunting system, West Germany, 1968. J. Wildl. Manage. 36(1):110–118.

Komarov, B. 1980. The destruction of nature in the Soviet Union. M. E. Sharpe Inc., White Plains, N.Y. 150 pp.

Myrberget, S. 1971. Game management in Norway. Norwegian Game Research Institute. 2. Series, nr. 35. 22 pp.

Myrberget, S. 1989. Comments on Norwegian hunting system. Personal communication, April 1989.

Myrberget, S. 1990. Wildlife management in Europe outside the USSR. NINA Utredning. Trondheim. 100 pp.

Nagy, J. and L. Beneze. 1973. Game and hunting in Hungary. Wildl. Soc. Bull. 1(3):121–127.

Naylor, J. N., G. J. Caughley et al. 1973. UNDP/FAO. FO:DP/ZAM/68/510. Working Document No. 1. 259 pp.

Newman, J. 1979. Hunting and hunter education in Czechoslovakia. Wildl. Soc. Bull. 7(3):155–161.

Parker, I. S. C. 1979. The ivory trade. U.S. Fish and Wildl. Serv. Rep. Typed.

Parker, I. S. C., and E. B. Martin. 1982. How many elephants are killed for the ivory trade? Oryx 18:235–239.

Petrides, G. A., and W. G. Swank. 1958. Management of the big game resource in Uganda, East Africa. Trans. N. Am. Wildl. Conf. 23:461–477.

Ricciuti, E. R. 1980. The ivory wars. An. Kingdom 83(1):6–58.

Riney, T. 1964. The economic use of wildlife in terms of its productivity and its development as an agricultural activity. FAO African Regional meeting on animal production and health, Addis Abada. UN-FAO, Rome. 13 pp. mimeo.

Salo, L. 1976. History of wildlife management in Finland. Wildl. Soc. Bull. 4(4):167–174.

Sinclair, A. R. E., and M. Norton-Griffiths. 1980. Serengeti: Dynamics of an ecosystem. The University of Chicago Press, Chicago, IL. 384 pp.

Swank, W. G. 1972. Wildlife management in Masailand, East Africa. Trans. N. Am. Wildl. Nat. Resour. Conf. 37:278–287.

Teer, J. G., and W. G. Swank. 1977. Status of the leopard in Africa south of the Sahara. The office of Endangered Species. U.S. Fish and Wildlife Service, Washington, DC.

Recommended Readings

Students should familiarize themselves with "Uniterra" published by UNEP; "IUCN Bulletin" published by IUCN; "UNESCI, Occasional Papers" from UNESCO (various countries) and "CERES" from FAO for general information. Specific wildlife information is available from CITES national officers and its Secretariat, the IUCN Species Survival Commission, the WWF national offices and numerous other sources.

Jones, R. F. 1990. Farewell to Africa. Audobon (September):51–104.

This Audobon magazine special report graphically illustrates the changes occurring in east Africa and its wildlife.

Lyster, S. 1985. International Wildlife Law. Gratius Publ. Limited. Cambridge, U.K. 470pp.

An excellent summary of major international wildlife laws and conventions including CITES, RAMSAR, and The Bonn and Berne Conventions. The treaties are described and analysed in detail.

Owen-Smith, R. N., ed. 1983. Management of large mammals in African conservation areas. Haum. Pretoria. S. Africa 297 pp.

Riney, T. 1982. Study and management of large mammals. John Wiley and Sons. New York, NY 552 pp.

XI WILDLIFE 1991–2000—The Profession and Management

There is no dearth of futurists who venture to predict today what our world will be like in ten, twenty, or hundred years although few would have predicted the political changes that have occurred and the rapid decline of communism in the past four years. Insightful scientists tell us what is in store for the planet and its people for decades to come based on their knowledge of research developments or from results they can predict with some certainty. The bomb must be avoided at all costs, and we can only hope that even with the current nuclear proliferation in Middle East and African countries it will be. Population growth must also be controlled if we are to realize the great wonders of the future. Humans throughout the world must understand the necessity of maintaining their numbers within their own society's abilities to feed and care for them and within the planet's abilities to absorb the environmentally hazardous wastes, and toxins beng produced.

Understanding that many dilemmas exist even as the technological revolution explodes around us, the wildlife manager must begin to chart a new path. What kind of a wildlife world will the manager be dealing with and what will be his role? How will the growing communications network affect him and his job? What massive land use and engineering developments will he have to cope with—perhaps a giant North American water scheme or an Okavango plan to moisten parched throats in the Kalahari? Such developments could make the Aswan and the Kariba in Africa, or the Itaipu development in Paraguay, seem small by comparison. Intensifying land use and productivity of the soil for food and fiber will leave fewer natural areas and will force wildlife management into competitive efficiencies barely glimpsed today. The development and management of all the industrialized world's land-based resources will become more efficient, and the underdeveloped world will soon follow.

As these massive changes occur rapidly all over the world, instant communications, rapid transit, and bewildering differences in life-styles catapult us toward Toffler's "Third Wave," with increased leisure time, population pressures and sporadic anarchy, *what is to become of wildlife*? Lasers and transplants will allow us to live longer, and we will learn more secrets of aging to permit healthier people an additional ten, or even fifty, years of life. Economic trade zones will become realities, and ideologies may be masked by the practicalities necessary to allow us to live together. With these, and other, man-induced climatic and natural changes altering the face of our earth, and perhaps even the meaning of what life is to us, *what is to be the fate of wild things*?

Changing Patterns

One of the clearest signals we have of things to come for wildlife and its managers is the increasing interest shown in animals and nature by the non-consumptive user. The manager's clientele is changing and it is increasing in size. Recent surveys in both the United States and Canada indicate that *most* people partake of wildlife oriented experiences each year and that the majority of them are nonhunters. Many encounters are essentially passive on the part of the user, but the number of persons actively engaged in a wildlife activity such as bird watching or bird feeding is growing rapidly, too. We believe this contact-with-nature phenomenon is of extreme importance in helping millions to maintain a degree of sanity in what all too often seems an insane world. Wildlife managers must feel the reality of this importance. So far, it has been under-rated by politicians, social scientists, and medical practitioners alike. Contact, even passive contact, with nature is an element that can help humanity bridge the treacherous road to the new waves of the future.

Patterns of use are also varying among the hunting fraternity in North America. Primitive weapons hunting including bow hunting, increased attention to dog handling, and the ritual attending the hunt, like in European hunting associations, tend to emphasize the *hunt* rather than the kill, although the kill remains the focus about which the prehunt ritual, the hunt itself, and the posthunt rituals are conducted. Hunting will continue, though it will be challenged, and we will carry it with us into the future, but hunters in North America will be better trained and will conduct their hunts within the confines of stricter regulations than in the past. Hunting is the primary mortality factor with most managed game species, and hunters, as well as wildlife managers, must realize this. There can, and should be, space and time for hunters and nonhunters alike. Management for both will intensify and the proportion (if not the total number) of people who hunt will decline by the year 2000. North American wildlife management will gradually move closer to some European systems, and as far as hunting is concerned, management probably will become more elitist in doing so. The changes have already begun, with shooting preserves, the harvest systems employed in Texas, and the various state acts intensifying wildlife management and control of hunter numbers on managed lands.

Internationally, the wildlife profession and the conservation movement are rapidly developing the institutions that a shrinking world must have to save wildlife and enjoy it through use. The Ramsar (wetlands) Convention (1975), the World Heritage Convention (1975), CITES (1975), and the Bonn Convention on migratory animals (1979) are all important steps even through many countries have not yet ratified the treaties. On paper, the African Convention on Conservation of Nature and Natural Resources of 1969 was an important development promulgated by the OAU. In this new decade, sustainable development has become a goal fostering real integrated forest and wildlife management, a strengthening of environmental impact procedures, an increase in the preservation of vegetation types, and worldwide movements to preserve tropical rain forests and protect our oceans.

In all underdeveloped areas of the globe, controlled wildlife use will continue as long as the resource remains competitive. But just as increased control is becoming evident in North America, so is it becoming a reality in the world's less developed regions.

All of these changing patterns are signs of things to come. The wildlife manager's role should increase in importance and his day should be a bright one in the future.

The Wildlife Profession

The public image of the professional wildlife manager has not always been good. Sportsmen have in past years held the "book-learned" biologist up to scorn, and sports columnists often gave wildlifers a hard time. The professional's image has gradually improved over the years, largely through the efforts of state publications like the *Conservationist* and nongovernment organization magazines such as *International Wildlife*. We still have a long way to go; and if the profession is to play the role open to it over the next few decades, we must work very hard at improving our management product and communicating the reasons for our work. For many years, elements of the wildlife protectionist movement have attacked wildlife managers with much emotion and few facts. Today, the attacks are using published wildlife data against accepted management procedures, and whether the arguments are valid or not, they are having considerable influence in public and political circles. Such writers as Favre and Olsen (1982) and Grandy (1983) will continue to condemn the profession as the credibility of their positions increases. We must counter this movement with more intensive management based on better data. Where our data are not adequate, our ''errors'' should benefit wildlife populations and not the using public: we should err on the conservative side, for wildlife. In spite of the difficulties inherent in ecological systems research and our inabilities to measure and control the elements we study, it is time we adhere as closely to the scientific method as our animals and habitats will allow. We can probably never attain the level of respect the medical profession has enjoyed over the past one hundred years, for medicine deals with the human animal whose life, in all of its complex philosophical, religious, and biological aspects is personal to each of us. It is logical that advances in medicine should enhance the image of physicians and medical researchers. Gains in wildlife knowledge, regardless of how important they seem to wildlife professionals, do little for our image.

How should our profession react and change? We need to consider this question carefully. Although our management and policy approaches are gradually adapting to new national and international needs, the roles of the professional and the profession are not clearly defined. It does seem clear that cohesiveness is, and will be, important. If two or three societies vie for members when the membership pool is limited, they should consolidate. Professional consolidation on a worldwide basis with branches in affiliated countries is an admirable goal. We need a single, strong voice in government circles and in public forums. We need to mend our fences where differences of opinion seem to separate us.

The profession will require more generalists in the future. Wildlifers will need basic ecological knowledge, as always, but they will also require computer, personnel, administrative, and management skills. They will have to understand the larger concepts, including the management and resource values of other competitive land uses, as managers from several professions participate in comprehensive planning, development, and policy formation. Some wildlifers will be needed as specialists, but even these people must learn to play their advocate role with broader interests in mind.

If wildlife is to benefit society as we have suggested, policies governing the use of resources must be more than ''motherhood'' statements. They must be based on sound economic and sociocultural data, without which management activities delineated in policy will not be supported by funding and so will not be adequately implemented. The first steps in articulating wildlife policy must deal with the accurate accumulation of such data as are available in these categories as well as data on the extent and distribution of the wildlife resources. If the data base is sound, accurate projections for the policy period should be possible. Policy formulation requires that generalists and specialists (particularly wildlife economists) work together if the senior administrators (generalists) are to sell their ideas to higher levels in government. Policy statements will tend to become more specific and should determine the direction management is to take, as exemplified in "A Wildlife Policy for Canada (1990)."

Wildlife professionals will play many different roles in future years. They will be planners, advisors, managers, administrators, consultants, researchers, pilots, biometricians, interpreters, writers, communicators, and programmers. Generalists and specialists will fit into each niche and will be bonded by a common interest in wildlife as reflected by their professional society.

When the door to sustainable development was opened with the Bruntland report, "Our Common Future," in 1987, the door was also opened for the wildlife profession, for there may be no other single group suited so well to help guide jurisdictions toward the maintenance of our ecosystems and habitats in perpetuity. Policies influencing our natural systems require consideration both from man seeking to advance humanity by intervening in natural processes and from man seeking good from nature itself. Professional wildlifers exhibit such a dualism perhaps better than any other group, and the challenge to the profession is to create the avenues of influence for the wildlifer's voice to be heard.

Education

In recent years a plethora of papers has been produced suggesting that the academic community is not responding quickly enough to what are perceived as needed modifications in the education of wildlife managers. Academic institutions have their bureaucracies, protocol, and politics which have existed together for decades and even centuries to form a rigid system, slow to change. It is unlikely that major alterations in course structure will become reality overnight. The movements to reform university senates and other governing bodies and the collectivization of campus faculties have not, unfortunately, made change easier. Power has shifted and become less centralized, which has often made change more difficult. Power politics has created a system whereby more, rather than fewer, impediments are placed in the path of progress in higher education.

The changes that some in the wildlife profession view as necessary deal either with practical training or with an interdisciplinary approach. In the first instance, universities do not usually take kindly to playing what many academics view as essentially a vocational or technical role. In the second instance, the interdisciplinary approach is often resisted as one that weakens first degrees in university departments. Finally, the need for broadening the basic background of wildlifers will only be possible in the larger institutions offering wildlife management. Many smaller ones do not have the required programs, schools, or departments to provide the additional courses deemed necessary. Nevertheless, it seems likely that change must and will occur once the debate has quieted and something akin to consensus has been reached.

In 1980, Cookingham, Bromley, and Beattie surveyed wildlife agencies and reported to the North American Wildlife and Natural Resources Conference that "additional courses in the areas of public relations, wildlife law, business management and administration, social sciences and the humanities were suggested as needed." They also said that agencies questioned whether *professors* had administrative, management, or field experience and stated that their new employees were not well oriented to the working world. The same researchers surveyed academic administrators and found that academics rated their own students as being inadequate in law enforcement, administration, and business. Even at graduate levels, only a third or less of the students were perceived as being well educated in administration, law enforcement, business skills, and political science. Though a majority of academic heads recognized such weaknesses, some two-thirds of them indicated changes were not planned. Among the arguments against change were: "administrative constraints," "full curricula and full loads for professors," "resistance to external suggestions," and the lack of time on the part of students. It was stated that other departments had the responsibility to produce business and law professionals, and academics "would not compromise the integrity of their programs by teaching inappropriate topics such as law enforcement and on-the job techniques." Cookingham et al. recommended that universities be accredited and that the standards for such accreditation be established by The Wildlife Society even though half of the academics surveyed in their poll believed accreditation would not strengthen wildlife programs.

The Cookingham et al. paper is similar to that of Eastmond and Kadlec (1977) in its emphasis on change and the need to broaden the wildlife manager's background before he is released into the work force. Eastmond and Kadlec noted that "the traditional emphasis upon fish and game training for sport fishing and sport hunting is no longer adequate . . . " and "in addition, being able to deal realistically with political pressures and cost considerations are crucial for tomorrow's wildlife graduate."

More recently Hein and Bates (1983) have suggested that "the best academic courses . . . appeared to be in ecology, writing, and wildlife with diverse support from other areas. Computer science, management skills and knowledge of environmental laws and impacts continue to increase in importance."

The Wildlife Society has been struggling with the academic education and training of wildlifers through its certification program for several years, and some change in course background has been reflected in that program. We believe these standardization attempts are positive and know that most academic institutions have tried to meet TWS requirements. It may be however, that establishing a minimum background is all that The Wildlife Society should do, leaving at least four courses (in a twenty course curriculum) to be filled as institutions are able, in such areas as administration, business, management, law, and political science. We believe that the wildlife manager must continue to have a sound background in ecology, resource management, plant taxonomy, vertebrate taxonomy, and general zoology and botany as well as statistics (or biometrics), computer science, chemistry, resource economics, and general land-use planning. Although many skills required of wildlifers are doubtless better learned from experience than in the classroom, some aspects of general business administration such as introductory accounting, budget procedures, personnel management and cost-benefit processes should first be dealt with in a structured classroom setting. This also applies to the basic background of Canadian and U.S. jurisprudence, environmental law, and the important aspects of international, national, state, and provincial wildlife conventions, treaties, acts and their regulations.

The enforcement of wildlife law is clearly a tool of considerable importance employed in wildlife management. A basic understanding of investigative procedures and techniques, charges and apprehension, rules of evidence, court procedures, adversary techniques, and penalties is needed. In such courses as ornithology, guided field experience is necessary before the student can obtain the "feel" and the insights of avian life histories; so field experience with the legal aspects of wildlife management is required. These experiences should prevent such occurrences as adjudication on the part of the enforcement officer before a court has heard the evidence. Considering the effort, time, and money spent on wildlife law enforcement, it is a management tool that has been too much neglected for far too long. As wildlife management intensifies in many of the world's countries, enforcement clearly must be brought into the "third wave" through an understanding of the social, cultural, economic, and psychological causes of violation behavior; through the computerization of license, violation and other data; through development of usable and acceptable techniques of investigative procedures and evidence; and through the implementation of many other practices of modern police agencies. Sigler (1972) considered wildlife law enforcement specifically in a full text, and more recently Giles (1974a, 1978) has provided important insights in several areas of the subject.

In the future, it will become increasingly important for wildlife managers in training to obtain work experience through cooperative programs between government and/or private agencies and academic institutions. Several informal and formal approaches are presently in effect, and we view these as one answer to the problem of orienting students to the working world. Students can be told in the classroom, but it means little without actually living the experience. We view tomorrow's wildlife education as a meld of the solidly academic and the practical, with field experience, work experience, and case studies playing as important a role as basic academic knowledge and theory.

It will also be necessary, over the next few years, for university and agency (public and private) employees to work more closely together through exchange programs, the formulation and use of external advisory committees for academic programs, and professional training programs beyond the terminal degrees. Shoning (1982) has recently brought some of the agency-academic conflicts and misunderstandings into sharper focus. One very important point made is the need to interface students with the "real world." As Shoning said, "Social, economic, ecological and political factors play significant roles in management decisions. Biology is always considered, but it is not always the over riding factor." Mechanisms must soon be found to get professionals on both ends of the academic-agency spectrum back together rather than have them continue to drift apart. Shoning provides a reasonable template for addressing the problem.

Management

The extensive regulatory management approach was effective in North America as long as large wildlife populations existed in adequate habitat and hunters were only able to effect minimal annual reduction in numbers of all age classes, with total populations either stable or increasing. Managers used kill statistics to give them clues to what might be happening to deer populations. They "monitored" annual grouse or rabbit harvests, trusting in the reproductive capacities of these animals to bring harvest numbers back in a year or so after declines appeared. With cervids, condition indices gradually became popular as measures of "healthy" or "unhealthy" populations, and general range surveys provided indices to the effects grazing and browsing animals were having on vegetation complexes. Even today, many hunted or trapped populations of harvested animals are managed by using a few key indices, and in many cases they still work. But they are not likely to work for long. North American management will change greatly over the next twenty years.

The factors that will force more intensive management are probably obvious to the student by now, but repetition should serve to add the emphasis we feel is required. The first is that habitat for wildlife is declining in all countries; even now in some places there is little left for many species. The use of land by man's increasing populations is the primary cause of extinction, both local and extensive. Land in North America will continue to be subject to competing uses until human populations and world economic forces stabilize. Under some administrations, the loss of wildlife lands or the loss of a wildlife agency's influence over lands inhabited by wildlife will be considerable. The increasing ubiquitous urban sprawl, the continued loss of lands to apparent needs of transportation, and the intensification of forest, range, and agricultural production and management all mean wildlife will have less habitat. Fewer of our tolerant, or plastic, species will benefit, at least until sustainable development becomes a reality.

A second factor is that more people with highly diverse interests in the resource will be using it and will demand that their interests be met. The bulk of these clients will be nonhunters and nontrappers who will show a range of attitudes toward wild things even greater than we understand today. The growing importance and recognition of conservation biology is both a reflection of this trend and an indication that at least some of the older, traditional approaches to managing wildlife must change.

A third factor is the need to justify expenditures. Solid socioeconomic and cultural data will be required to justify policy, annual expenditures, and new management programs. It will fall to the wildlife manager to extract data from his programs to inform and educate the public, planners, and policy makers so that management practices and programs can continue.

For these and many related reasons, management will become far more intensive than we now understand it. Big game hunting in North America will become similar to that in Central Europe and will be more closely related to selective harvesting and culling than at present. Specific sex and age groups will be removed from populations as husbandry is introduced and fewer trophy animals taken. For waterfowl, species management will combine with systems management from nesting and brood cover enhancement through to fall harvests. Some furbearers will be totally protected and harvest levels for others essentially predetermined. For all species, more specific harvesting, additional controls, and increased overall protection will be evident. But most important, perhaps, will be the overall change in approach toward ecosystem management as we strive to maintain an appropriate distribution of habitats and protect representative vegetation types through combinations of integrated resource management and preservation.

To accomplish these goals by the year 2000, the North American hunter will be more knowledgeable about wildlife and will be expected to assume a more responsible role in managing game species. There is no doubt in our minds that if hunting and trapping are to continue, consumptive users of the resource must also become responsible managers. This means that massive efforts must be put into the Information and Education budgets of wildlife agencies, and programs of most agencies will have to shift considerably. It also means new legislation, and whether we like it or not, more regulations with highly trained staffs to enforce them. If hunters and trappers avoid their developing obligations, their activities in North America will be sharply curtailed a few years hence.

Wildlife management will also be increasingly important in providing accurate ecological, economic and social data for land-use planning and meeting the political realities each jurisdiction must face. Among these realities is the aforementioned diverse client base which must be catered to. Management has to provide the services demanded, i.e., animals to watch, animals to film, and natural systems to enjoy passively as well as populations to be harvested under controlled conditions on designated lands. Management data in development situations must be accurate and adequate so that wildlife habitats may be enhanced wherever possible. The manager will similarly continue to provide accurate data and expert judgement in the impact assessments accompanying development.

In underdeveloped countries, the need for more intensive management will be just as great as in industrialized nations. The need for improved understanding of interspecific and intraspecific co-actions, wildlife-range-cattle complexes, and the effects of harvesting various sex and age classes will all be required as management develops, geared as much to use as to protection. The hunter's role will not change as rapidly in these countries as it will in North America, but by the year 2000 all users will begin to play a more important part in both policy formation and management programs as utilitarian influences decline.

Research

The wildlife manager must have accurate data from well-planned research if management is to become as intensive as we expect. In the next few years, we should view an intensification of management-oriented research and less research for the sake of our own curiosity. Research will employ models more consistently and will be directed toward answering specific questions for specific management situations. In this context, research will necessarily be more applied than basic, although the questions asked may indeed be basic. Management concerns will be addressed by drawing upon the work of many different kinds of researchers in addition to those involved with wildlife. Research in many areas of nutrition, population dynamics, and behavioral ecology will continue to provide results useful to the wildlife manager, even when it has not been wildlife oriented. It is only research conducted on specifically wildlife-centered problems that will necessarily become more applied. This will happen because management must quickly become more intensive and will need to justify research expenditures by applying its results. There may be less wildlife research conducted in the future, but what is done will be "better" in that the results will apply to existing problems.

Romesburg (1981) suggests a number of reasons why much wildlife research has not always been valuable in the past; research has indeed been the subject of criticism from many quarters in, and out, of the profession. Unfortunately, criticism in our profession often comes more easily than cooperation, and unconstructive criticism is very common indeed. We believe that adhering as far as possible to the scientific method, sound planning, sampling and testing, and maintaining focus on the specific problem involved will continue to be most important in wildlife research. The use of sophisticated computer models in population studies and systems research will continue to increase and the use of advanced electronic techniques will be commonplace. Subjective, observational approaches will be present only to add insight to certain co-actions in some behavior studies, and quantification will be continuously improved.

The most important step in establishing a research program is a precise definition of the problem. Until, and unless, the problem is clearly defined and completely understood, no hypothesis can be articulated and no testing undertaken. Once the problem is understood, stating the hypothesis and determining the objectives of ensuing research activities and/or experiments and observations should be carefully planned and spelled out. In most cases, combining the expertise of several people in a team approach will be beneficial. Even when research is conducted by one person alone, he is less apt to err or stray from specific objectives if he consults with peers or advisors.

Research needs of the future will continue to become evident as management needs intensify. Giles (1979) has provided us with three lists of general requirements in the categories of man, habitat, and wildlife populations. It is really the responsibility of the astute wildlife manager to determine research needs because it is he who must recommend management changes and implement them if accepted. The manager, then, should be the one to observe needs, define the problems, and ask for answers.

Communicating Management Purposes, Results, and Needs

At the time this book was first being prepared (1983–85), we were aware of threats to curtail wildlife research and management or ensuing management in several jurisdictions. Perhaps foremost in the minds of many North American wildlifers was the struggle in the United States to save cooperative wildlife research units from budget cuts. Wildlifers in Ontario were on the defensive as well, and their research station at Maple was threatened by the budget chopping block, as were programs in British Columbia and elsewhere. In 1985, the Canadian Wildlife Service was disrupted by severe budget and personnel cuts. Chapter 10 also mentioned the lack of funding in underdeveloped areas. When there is so much apparent interest, as we have noted, why are governments cutting budgets or failing to fund wildlife agencies? The answer lies in the profession's failure to market its product! We have failed to translate wildlife research findings and wildlife management practices into social and economic benefits. Only an occasional management practice has been perceived by a portion of our clientele as having some value. Wildlife is losing out at political levels during budget crunches, such as those induced by the 1990–91 recession, almost by default.

It appears that elected government officials may be misreading the interest shown in wildlife by a host of natural history, environmental, and sportsmen's organizations that have become far more vocal than they were only ten years ago. Their interest clearly does not go as far as wishing to supplement reduced government spending. Most citizens' organizations view any reductions leading to serious declines in the work of maintaining and managing the wildlife resource as an abdication of government's responsibility. It is true that these organizations represent different attitudes, and among the many clients there are great differences of opinion about how and where money should be spent. But, they are in general agreement that wildlife budgets should not be cut, although they might favor redirection.

We have been too complacent and too comfortable in believing that what we are doing is of value to the resource and to the publics we were supposed to serve. These publics are both internal (in government and the wildlife system) and external. But, we failed to let these publics in on what we were doing and how our activities benefitted each. Our attention has been too much on the side of research and management and too little on information, education, and public relations. As managers, we have been unable to articulate adequately what we were doing, and why. Our clientele also has changed and is still changing. Millions of North Americans do have an interest in wildlife. Millions hunt but many more millions do not. Most of the clientele we are supposed to serve are nonconsumptive users of the resource, and a great many of them have not been happy with our activities. The profession has been too slow in responding and so has not been able to take advantage of the great nature-oriented movement in industrialized society. Instead, increasing interest has sometimes acted negatively upon the profession, and all too often an adversarial situation has developed with the "killers" squared off against the "humaniacs." Now we must face reality. Either we serve all publics to the best of our ability and let each of them know clearly how their interest in the wildlife resource is being served, or we will fail to meet the challenges to the year 2000.

More of our budgets must go toward marketing. If the product isn't sold, the business will fail. Each time a significant event in the translocation of animals, the preservation of an area, or the setting of a special hunting season occurs, our interested clients must hear about it and see it published or on their television screen. If they do, and if they approve, they will support our activities. Their support, in turn, will be rapidly brought to the attention of politicians. Not that we, ourselves, must not use all the means at our disposal to spread the "gospel" within the system; we must, but we will fail unless the word also come from the external publics.

Managers must be the vanguard for establishing direction through conservative management approaches that appeal to the majority and benefit wildlife rather than having to react when confronted with problems expressed by one, or more, pressure groups. Managers will only succeed through leadership and the effective communication of their work in future years.

Many jurisdictions in North America do have nongame biologists (Chapter 7). All should have them, and most should have more than just one or two. All jurisdictions need modern, skillful information and education sections, as well as better trained and more effective enforcement bodies. It is the responsibility of all wildlife managers to spend a greater portion of their time informing superiors and clients about the value of their activities to the wildlife resource and subsequently to the social and/or economic improvement of the public, itself.

Back in 1971, The Wildlife Society published *Natural Resources and Public Relations*, written by Douglas Gilbert, who categorized and defined the various publics and the importance of each to the resource professions. Since then others have examined the marketing problems of (1) financing and changing public attitudes (Schick et al. 1976); and (2) the importance of the social acceptance of wildlife management (Todd 1980). Todd warned that "the rate of change in wildlife programs and policies must accelerate—if government agencies are to broaden their political and financial support." Perhaps we cannot expect change in relation to wildlife to occur any faster in public policy systems than it is at present; but once having been the target of budget cuts, it will take us even more time to bring about the needed change. If we are to meet the needs of the future adequately, we must accept and face the challenge at all levels. Wildlife management requires a cadre of skilled, dedicated spokesmen who can speak forcefully to industry, government, and the general public about what must be done for the resource. They must show its immense social, cultural, and economic value.

In coming years, wildlifers and conservation biologists will be regarded as one and the same. We will be working together toward the utilization of resources to optimize social and economic benefits while maintaining the potential for their future use. Systems approaches to integrated resource management will have to become a reality, and incentives for private landowners and public users of wildlife to cooperate must be successfully applied. The movement toward sustainable development is real and the wildlife manager's future is bright.

Bibliography

Cookingham, R. A., P. T. Bromley, and K. H. Beatie. 1980. Academic education needed by resource managers. Trans. N. Am. Wildl. Nat. Resour. Conf. 45:45–49.

Eastmond, J. N., and J. A. Kadlec. 1977. Undergraduate educational needs in wildlife science. Wildl. Soc. Bull. 5(2):61–66.

Favre, D. S., and G. Olsen. 1982. Surplus population: A fallacious basis for sport hunting. Society for Animal Rights, Inc. Clarks Summit, PA. 12 pp.

Filion, F. L., S. Parker, and E. DuWors. 1988. The importance of wildlife to Canadians: Demand for wildlife to 2001. Can. Wildl. Serv., Ottawa, Can. 29 pp.

Gavin, T. A. 1989. What's wrong with the questions we ask in wildlife research? Wildl. Soc. Bull. 17:345–350.

Gilbert, D. 1971. Natural resources and public relations. Second ed. (1975) The Wildlife Society, Washington, DC. 320 pp.

Giles, R. H., Jr. 1974a. Criteria for wildlife laws. Wildl. Soc. Bull. 2(2):68–69.

Giles, R. H., Jr. 1974b. Wildlife law enforcement research needs (1971). Pp. 557–561, *In* Readings in wildlife conservation. The Wildlife Society, Washington, DC.

Giles, R. H., Jr. 1978. Wildlife law enforcement Pp. 343–377, *In* Wildlife management. W. H. Freeman, San Francisco, CA.

Giles, R. H., Jr. 1979. Research to meet future management needs.Pp. 219–224, *In* Wildlife conservation, principles and practices. The Wildlife Society, Washington, DC.

Grandy, J. W. 1983. The North American black duck (*Anas rubripes*): a case study of 28 years of failure in American wildlife management. Int. J. Stud. An. Prob. Supplement to 4(4). 35 pp.

Hein, D., and S. F. Bates. 1983. Criteria for hiring wildlife employees. Wildl. Soc. Bull. 11(1):79–83.

Romesburg, H. C. 1981. Wildlife science: gaining reliable knowledge. J. Wildl. Manage. 45(2): 293–313.

Schick, B. A., T. A. More, R. M. DeGraaf, and D. E. Samuel. 1976. Marketing wildlife management. Wildl. Soc. Bull. 4(2):64–68.

Shoning, R. W. 1982. Reflections on an intergovernmental personnel assignment. Assoc. Univ. Fish Wildl. Progr. Administrators 9 pp. (mimeo)

Sigler, W. F. 1972. Wildlife law enforcement. Second ed. Wm. C. Brown. Dubuque, IA. 360 pp.

Todd, A. W. 1980. Public relations, public education, and wildlife management. Wildl. Soc. Bull. 8(1):55–60.

Recommended Readings

Grandy, J. W. 1983. The North American Black Duck (*Anas rubripes*): A case study of 28 years of failure in American wildlife management. Int. J. Stud. An., Prob. Supplement to 4(4):35 pp.

Recommended for a critical class exercise to study in an in-depth manner. The references used in this publication and other records available to individual instructors should all be carefully studied in reviewing this publication.

Naisbitt, J. 1982. Megatrends. Warner Brooks, Inc., New York, NY. 333 pp.

An explanation of the transformation from the industrial society to an information society in the western world. Wildlifers can benefit from an understanding of present social, economic and political trends.

Appendix
Important Canadian and United States federal legislation affecting wildlife resources and management.

United States (listed alphabetically)

Agriculture Appropriation Act of 1907
Alaska National Interest Lands Conservation Act of 1980
Anadromous Fish Conservation Act of 1965
Bald Eagle Protection Act
Classification and Multiple Use Act of 1964
Clean Air Acts of 1970, 1990
Clear Water Restoration Act of 1966
Coastal Zone Management Act
Endangered Species Act of 1973
Endangered Species Conservation Act of 1969
Endangered Species Preservation Act of 1966
Estuarine Areas Act
Federal Aid in Wildlife Restoration Act (Pittman Robertson Act)
Federal Environmental Pesticide Control Act
Federal Farm Act
Federal Insecticide, Fungicide and Rodenticide Act
Federal Land Policy and Management Act of 1976
Federal Water Pollution Control Act
Fish and Wildlife Act of 1956
Fish and Wildlife Conservation Act of 1980
Fish and Wildlife Coordination Act
Food Security Acts of 1985, 1990
Forest and Rangelands Renewable Resources Planning Act of 1974
Forest Reserve Act of 1981
Forest Reserve Transfer Act of 1905
Fur Seal Act
Insecticide Act of 1910

Knutson-Vandenburg Act
Lacey Act
Land and Water Conservation Fund Act
Marine Mammal Protection Act
Migratory Bird Act of 1913
Migratory Bird Conservation Act
Migratory Bird Hunting Stamp Act
Migratory Bird Treaty Act
Multiple Use-Sustained Yield Act
National Environmental Policy Act
National Forest Management Act of 1976
National Forests Organic Act (1897)
National Park Service Act
National Wildlife Refuge System Administration Act of 1966
North American Wetlands Act (1989)
Organic Act (1897)
Refuge Recreation Act of 1962
Refuge Revenue Sharing Act (amended 1974)
Sikes Act of 1960
Sikes Act Extension
Taylor Grazing Act
Toxic Substances Control Act of 1976
Water Bank Act of 1970
Wetlands Loan Act
Whaling Convention Act of 1949
Wild Free-Roaming Horses and Burros Act
Wilderness Act

Canada

Agriculture Rehabilitation and Development Act
Animal Contagious Disease Act
Canada Water Act
Canada Wildlife Act
Canada Wildlife Week Act
Customs Act
Environmental Contaminants Act
Export and Import Permits Act
*Export, Import and Interprovincial Transport of Wildlife Act (pending)

---

* Will replace Export and Import Permits Act and Game Export Act.

Fisheries Act
Forest Development and Research Act
Game Export Act
Indian Act
Maritime Marshland Reclamation Act
Migratory Bird Convention Act
National Parks Act
Plant Quarantine Act
Prairie Farmer Rehabilitation Act

Index